A BIOGRAPHY BY BARRY HYAMS

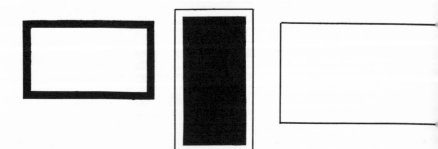

HIRSHHORN
Medici from Brooklyn

 E.P. DUTTON New York

To Midge—
who saw it begin;

and Marilyn—
who saw it to the end.

For information contact: E.P. Dutton, 2 Park Avenue, New York, N.Y. 10016

Library of Congress Cataloging in Publication Data

Hyams, Barry.
Hirshhorn, Medici from Brooklyn.

1. Hirshhorn, Joseph H. 2. Art—Collectors and collecting—
Biography. I. Title.
N5220.H575H9   1979   704'.7[B]   78-10120
ISBN: 0-525-12520-5

Published simultaneously in Canada by Clarke, Irwin & Company Limited,
Toronto and Vancouver

Designed by Ernie Haim

10 9 8 7 6 5 4 3 2 1

First Edition

Contents

Alexander said:
"If I were not Alexander I would choose to be Diogenes."

Nick told Jay:
"You're better than the whole lot of them. . . ." but did Gatsby believe him?

There was a jolly miller once
     Lived on the River Dee.
He danced and sang from morn til night,
     No lark so blithe as he.
And this the burden of his song
     Forever used to be:
I care for nobody, no, not I,
     Since nobody cares for me.
          —OLD ENGLISH BALLAD

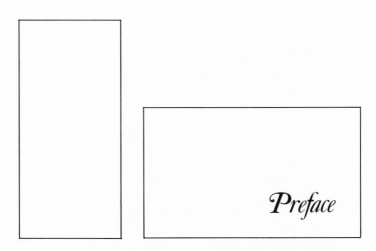

Preface

One Tuesday in August of 1974 the front page of the *New York Times* carried a picture of Bourdelle's craggy *Great Warrior of Montauban* swinging over the trees on the estate of Joseph H. Hirshhorn in Greenwich, Connecticut. And there, on page eighteen, was Hirshhorn gazing up at the helicopter which was airlifting the sculpture off the lawn onto a truck for delivery to the museum in Washington which had just been completed to house the art collection he had donated to the United States. It was so like Hirshhorn as I remembered him, always a streak of flamboyance underlying his practicality.

We hadn't met in more than twenty years. Somehow we had lost touch after his early days when I enjoyed a close friendship with him and his first family. In the fifties I had read of his phenomenal success locating and promoting uranium mines in Canada, and later of his art collecting. He'd been called a twentieth-century Medici—and a lot of other things, too.

The appellation Brooklyn Medici fit Hirshhorn, in style and fact, to the extent that he shared with the Renaissance bankers a passion for painting and sculpture; so much so that their renown as art collectors outran their reputations for accumulating wealth. As patrons, the Medicis entered the early lives of Fra Angelico, Ghiberti, Donatello, and Botticelli, and Hirshhorn had been an early supporter of numerous American artists such as Milton Avery, Philip Evergood, Chaim Gross, Arshile Gorky, and Raphael Soyer. But there the likeness ended.

Cosimo Medici inherited $4 million from his father, to whom it had passed from his great-grandfather, the gonfalonier of Florence, a century before the Renaissance. The money brought power, which the Medicis wielded with shrewdness and moderation, "tempered," as Will Durant put it, "with occasional violence." They lent large sums to their city-state, to neighboring kings, popes, and bishops. By controlling the forces of law and order, by purchasing senators, signories, and mistresses, they outstripped their eighty rival houses of banking in Florence. The money they piled up, said Durant, enabled them "to pay a Michelangelo or a Titian to transmute wealth into beauty and perfume a fortune with the breath of art."

Hirshhorn, however, was a product of Brooklyn tenements who could trace his lineage no further back than a grandfather in Latvia. Starting with nothing, by the time he was twenty-nine, he had made $4 million. In two decades he carved an empire of gold and uranium out of the Canadian wilderness. Along the way he acquired four wives, a library of 4,000 volumes containing such rare items as a Coverdale Bible and a First Folio Shakespeare, and paintings and sculptures in such profusion that his gift to his country numbered 6,000 works of art.

No product of Choate and Harvard, Hirshhorn dropped out of high school after three months. Lorenzo di Medici could quote Petrarch and compose a *terza rima*. Hirshhorn educated himself pragmatically: he gleaned knowledge in the course of his work and culture through acquiring art. No one knows the amount of his total worth, at one time rumored to be $130 million. He maintained silence on the subject and not only because he considered it confidential. When the question arose, he parried it, saying, "I'd feel vulgar if I had $130 million." How much he spent for his entire collection is also a matter of conjecture—and contention. From 1950 to 1969 alone, his expenditures for art averaged $1 million annually. Estimates of his gift to the nation ran at the time from $30 to $50 million.

Why Hirshhorn so avidly collected riches and art has puzzled the thoughtful. Psychologists who have probed the instinct to possess have concluded that it represents anything from an anal fixation to a fear of castration born of narcissism. Hirshhorn's mania for collecting was known to denude an entire studio of paintings in order to store them under his bed, in his closets, in his car trunk. Unlike Norton Simon, who paid $2.5 million for a Rembrandt, $1.5 million for a Renoir, and $15 million for the Joseph Duveen collection, Hirshhorn bought art and, to get the bottom price, haggled like a rug seller. He agreed with Jean Groult, the nineteenth-century connoisseur, who paid a large sum for a picture only to exclaim, "I'd give fifty thousand to have discovered it for a hundred francs!"

Hirshhorn often asserted he could not have achieved his wealth and position anywhere but in America. He liked to point to past collectors who, like himself, embodied the Horatio Alger myth: P.A.B. Widener, who began as a butcher; John G. Johnson, who started as a blacksmith; George A. Hearn, who ran a department store; and J. P. Morgan, whose father sold dry goods.

Hirshhorn notwithstanding, America in this respect was not singular. In England, Joseph Duveen, one of twelve children of a Dutch immigrant, rose from lard salesman to the British House of Lords by merchandising the great art of Europe to rich Americans. The difference between them was that Hirshhorn, youngest son among thirteen children from Eastern Europe, grew up to buy art, not to sell it. Duveen's strategy was to glorify the collector. Hirshhorn's patronage often brought living American artists to eminence. His reward was a museum bearing his name on the Mall of his country's capital.

Hirshhorn's is not altogether a chronicle of virtue. When President Johnson accepted the gift of his art collection to the United States, dark mutterings were heard in Congress about Hirshhorn's methods of accumulating money and art. But time may do for him what it has done for the Medicis. After five centuries the veil of munificence has obscured their exploitation of Florence. For Hirshhorn, too, the years may "perfume a fortune with the breath of art."

I phoned Hirshhorn that Tuesday and he greeted me with a shout—"I was just thinking about you!"—as if we had seen each other the day before. With rapid-fire queries he updated himself about me.

"What about you?" I asked. "Has anyone done your biography?"

"No," he replied. "Why, you want to write it?"

"Yes."

"You know," Hirshhorn warned, "I'm no angel."

"I know that."

His tone suddenly filled with suspicion. "What do you mean?" he shot back.

"Well, Joe," I said, "angels are bores; they make dull reading."

For a moment he considered this. "Come on over and let's talk. I'd like to see what you look like after all these years. Are you bald?"

We met and after two weeks he agreed to cooperate, with no strings attached.

Many people made this account possible. First, of course, was Hirshhorn who neither commissioned the work nor retained control over its content. Yet he opened his home to me, made files available, and provided introductions to key persons whose lives crossed his in many parts of the United States and Canada. To the degree of their accessibility and aid, I am deeply grateful to those members of his immediate family, relatives, friends, business, mining and art world associates, artists, gallery owners, and dealers—212 individuals who granted personal interviews and faithfully responded to correspondence. Not least was the help of Marian Skedgell, my editor.

Hirshhorn's life, as it coursed over seven decades, mingled legend with fact, at times innocently, at others not, which made necessary the kind of cross-checking practiced by detectives and investigative reporters. Here and there an accession date or price of an artwork was missing from his records and I was forced to rely on the limbo of memory. However, whether I found his activities documented in newspapers, periodicals, and books, or verifiable elsewhere, I have had a single objective: to present the private portrait behind the facade of a remarkable public personality. This narrative will confirm what some people know of him, will reveal what some never knew, and will disclose what still others may challenge. Among all three will be Hirshhorn, himself.

PART ONE

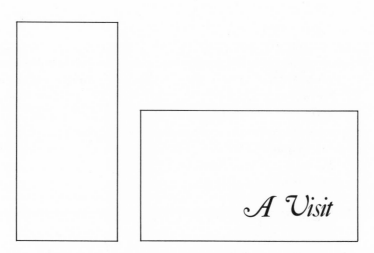

A Visit

I On Wednesday, the last day of April 1975, Hirshhorn awaited me in his New York office on the sev-
enth floor of an apartment building on Park Avenue and 75th Street.
I was to spend the next two days with him there and at his Greenwich residence. The hour was seven-fifteen A.M. Hirshhorn liked to
start his day at a sprint. After wintering in his home in Naples,
Florida, he was headed before the weekend for Virginia and Washington, and after that, Paris. His timetable permitted few wasted
moments.

His greeting, as usual, was hearty. Only a few weeks short of
seventy-five, he had the clarion-clear voice of a man of forty. By
seven-thirty we were walking to breakfast in a restaurant on nearby
Madison Avenue. Hirshhorn's pace, by temperament and habit, ignored the chest pains which had been troubling him since his heart
attack in 1967. Occasionally he popped a nitroglycerine pill. A
number of years ago he had been forewarned. It was during the
period his uranium lode in Blind River, Ontario, had shot him into
the orbit of international finance, and Rio Tinto Limited of London,
with its chairman, the Earl of Bessborough, was bidding for the
treasure. During negotiations, Her Majesty's seventy-five-year-old

uncle, grown fond of Hirshhorn but disconcerted by his kinetic intensity, cautioned him to slow down for his health's sake. "Look here, Earl," Hirshhorn, then fifty-six, assured the venerable nobleman, "I got plenty of health."

Hirshhorn then was a trim 148. Now, with 12 added pounds making his midriff a shade portly, he still did not suggest his three score and fourteen. Five-feet-four in his shoes, his gait was that of a pugilist stalking his foe, shoulders hunched forward and swinging, toes slightly pigeoned. His eyes alternated between agate frost, liquid geniality, and guile. Suddenly they hooded and darted, and a moment later turned pensive. Between smooth cheeks his nose jutted below a furrowed brow to dominate his face. He had the look of an anxious clown. Said one of his daughters, "I think of him as a cross between Spencer Tracy and Jimmy Durante."

Hirshhorn wolfed two eggs and dry rye toast with gusto. "I don't usually eat breakfast," he said. "I just have coffee." He was chafing to get to his phone.

The office-apartment had a spacious living room, comfortably furnished, which served as a reception area and outer office. The dining room accommodated a secretary and ranks of filing cabinets. A large bedroom provided a pied-à-terre whenever Hirshhorn remained in the city overnight. The walls were hung with paintings by Picasso, Monticelli, Albers, Still, and Eilshemius among others. Everywhere, sculpture littered the floors, tables, desks, windowsills, any level space; here a Houdon bust of Benjamin Franklin, there a small Moore, Daumier, Matisse, and a construct by Kenneth Snelson. Against the wall behind Hirshhorn's desk were photos of John F. Kennedy and Lyndon B. Johnson inscribed to him. Before him on the desk was a pen-stand from Richard M. Nixon.

Tucked away, in back of the kitchen, a tiny room housed the nerve center of the Hirshhorn complex. From it he directed the farflung enterprise begun in Toronto in 1933, the finding and developing of mineral deposits and petroleum in Canada for which he formed a company, Technical Mine Consultants. Gradually it expanded its explorations to Alaska, England, and the Near East. TMC passed to Rio Tinto in 1956 as part of the Blind River uranium sale, at which time Hirshhorn replaced it with International Mines Services Ltd. and installed Stephen Kay, his associate, as president. Its American counterpart, located in Darien, Connecticut, was Callahan Mining Corporation, diversified in mining, manufacturing, and natural gas. With Hirshhorn as chairman of the board, Callahan's interests ranged across six of the United States through Canada to Alaska.

From this same cubicle on Park Avenue, Hirshhorn trafficked briskly in the stock market. He operated by phone through brokers in New York, Florida, and California with such celerity as virtually to be on the floor of the New York Stock Exchange without owning a seat.

At 8 A.M. Hirshhorn was at his desk. The phone glued to his ear, he spurted conversation at me between rapid-fire calls, the first to Taft Schreiber, a trustee of the Hirshhorn Museum and Sculpture Garden.

"The concrete doughnut" on the Washington Mall was exhibiting signs of a runaway success. In the museum's first six months its display of contemporary art had attracted over a million visitors. The Hirshhorn had begun life with over 6,000 works of nineteenth- and twentieth-century art, constituting the most prodigious gift in the annals of American art. The collection had resulted from an obsession that had gripped Hirshhorn in childhood, and had hypertrophied until the paintings and sculptures overran his several homes, offices, and three floors of a Manhattan warehouse. He had had no ulterior motive to start with. Only gradually, as his acquisitions proliferated, did his purpose take shape. The first inkling surfaced in 1960, the day Hirshhorn strolled up Fifth Avenue deep in conversation with his son, Gordon. At the corner of 70th Street, Hirshhorn came to a sharp halt before a temple of white sandstone.

"Who," he asked abruptly, his eyes on the block-long shrine, "was Henry Frick?"

"Frick?" The sudden turn in the conversation made Gordon stammer. "Oh—why—he was a tycoon; mining, railroads, and—"

"I know that, and you know that," Hirshhorn cut in impatiently, "but the public, they know him for that museum—" and staring at the building, he muttered, "Someday that's what they'll know me for."

Hirshhorn dialed Washington. He caught Charles Blitzer at breakfast. The assistant secretary of the Smithsonian was one of the yeomen in the eight-year struggle to bring the Hirshhorn Museum to fruition. Hirshhorn spoke of his concern, that the National Gallery's new wing for contemporary art, then being built, might encroach on his museum. He proposed a meeting of the heads of both institutions, and hung up.

"There was a big argument about the name, you know," he confided to me. "There would've been no fuss if my name was Woolworth or O'Connor, or Smith or Jenkins."

He was referring to the storm which broke over Washington when President Johnson concluded the arrangements by which the people of the United States received from citizen Joseph H. Hirshhorn the gift of art valued at the time up to $50 million.

"I spent $500,000 on art in 1972," he said, "and in 1973 four or five pieces cost $500,000. I bought Brancusi's *Torso of a Young Man* for $67,000 and was offered fifteen times as much to sell it. That makes it worth a million or more." A half-dozen of the 6,000 works in the collection had been officially appraised at $1.9 million: sculptures by Rodin, Moore, Brancusi, and Picasso, and a painting by Thomas Eakins. "You couldn't buy the collection today for $125 million," Hirshhorn growled. His tone softened and he clucked judiciously. "Well, we're still young. We've only been open six months. You can't rush things."

The road to establishing the museum had been pitted with congressional investigations. Hirshhorn was bastinadoed in private and in the press. A scarred campaigner in corporate boardrooms, art auctions, and the Canadian bush, he was not going to be caught napping again.

"I want you to know," he said solemnly, "I'm thinking of setting up a fund. The agreement in Washington with the government is that my name is to be there in perpetuity—the Hirshhorn Museum and Sculpture Garden. If it isn't, we have the right to withdraw all the art."

He paused reflectively and shrugged. "I don't think they'd ever do it."

Without taking a breath, Hirshhorn launched into his day. In the half-hour before trading began on the exchanges, he swarmed over the several brokers who tended his accounts. Among them were his son, Gordon, and his stepson, Graham Cunningham.

"What the hell's going on with Crown? . . . How many traded? . . . Yeah; yeah. . . . Where did it close? . . . Get the size [the bid and offer]. . . . Listen, Al, I want to tell you something. I think you're one of the greatest men in America." Hirshhorn roared with laughter and sang into the phone: "Toot-Toot-Tootsie, good-bye; Toot-Toot-Tootsie, don't cry. . . ." Chuckling, he hung up.

Acting upon instinct schooled by long experience, his responses to stimuli were instantaneous. Decisions flashed. He operated the same way in both markets—stocks and art. Consulting a pad with

columns of figures, he fished a pencil from his pocket and made notations in a neat hand. The phone rang. Hirshhorn listened.

"That your story? . . . Okay. Where's Stevens? . . . And
Rowan? . . . Bid-and-ask? . . . Yeah . . . You have no orders?
. . . Okay."

The secretary buzzed on the other wire. "It's Mr. Eichel-
berger."

Appalled, Hirshhorn yelled, "You mean Igelheimer! You got
your radio going? How can you work with your radio on?" He
stabbed the phone button.

The instrument with three extensions was a far cry from the
"jitney" he had the phone company design and install in his Toronto
office in 1933, ninety-three direct lines to brokers and banks, no
bells, only lights flashing and keys to press. Handling the calls
required four men. Hirshhorn by himself manipulated it as if he
were at the console of an organ. He had served his novitiate at the
feet of Jesse L. Livermore and Frank H. Tubbs, the Wall Street
gurus of the twenties, whose phone techniques he adapted to his
own style and later introduced into the wild north territory to the
discomfiture of the "bandits" of Toronto's Bay Street.

"Yeah, Dave. . . . What were the closings? . . . That stock
won't come in. . . . I'll be talking to you."

He dialed again while rustling through sheets of stock transfers,
at the same time scanning the financial pages of the *New York Times*
and headlines of the *Wall Street Journal*. "Gee," he said into the
phone, his voice dripping regret, "I'm sorry to break our lunch date
tomorrow. I've got to get back to Greenwich. The house is up for
sale. . . . Yeah. . . . We'll set another time very soon. I'm sorry."

The secretary buzzed. "It's Mr. Igelheimer again."

Hirshhorn snatched up the phone, triumph gleaming in his
eyes. The secretary had the name right this time; or, perhaps it was
what he was hearing Igelheimer saying. "It's down, Dave, isn't it?
. . . Yeah. . . . Yeah. . . . No. . . . Okay, thanks. I'll read it."

He retrieved the *Wall Street Journal* and turned to the back page.
In a matter of seconds he absorbed a report on the upbeat attitude of
Morgan Guaranty Trust toward the behavior of the market. Suddenly he dropped the newspaper and rushed from the room only to
be summoned back immediately. Gordon had more information
about the market averages. Another buzz announced Igelheimer.

"How much down is it? . . . Where is Valley Industry? . . .
I'll hold the wire. . . . Okay; take it. . . . 6,500 at 8½. . . . Say it
back to me. . . . Right."

Interrupted by another signal, he scooped up the phone. "You'll have to wait. . . . Yeah. . . . He's working on it. . . . Yeah; call me tomorrow morning in Greenwich." He switched to another line, a call from an art dealer. "I know Zuniga's work. . . . Yeah, he's very good. . . . Well, there's only one Henry Moore. . . . To Mexico? Not now. . . . No, I can't tell you right this minute. . . ." A buzz on the intercom. "I've got another call. . . . I want to see Zuniga. . . . Yeah, talk to him. . . . Keep in touch." Transferring to the other line, he continued without transition. "Yeah, Dave; what's going on? . . . Can you sell at three-eighths? . . . Sell the balance. . . . You know how much I have left. . . . Say it back to me. . . . Right."

He replaced the phone in its cradle and fell back in his chair with satisfaction. His eyes glinted with self-mockery. "I wish I was rich," he sighed, "instead of a nice boy."

Briefly his chin sank on his chest. Leaning forward, he rested his elbows on his desk. "You know," he said wistfully, "I never had any toys when I was a kid. Once I found a pair of broken skates somebody threw away. I learned to fix the ball bearings so I could use them. When I was twelve, I was working, and I saved my allowance to buy my first basketball."

What I was hearing was a tape of prerecorded feelings, a Hirshhorn anecdote at tongue-tip command. ". . . It hurt me no end to see my mother work so hard. . . . I was seventeen when I went into the market and in ten months I made $167,000. . . ." The phrases, released automatically, sounded deceptively like nonsequiturs. Tripped by something deep within him, they were meant less to inform the listener than to reassure himself.

Hirshhorn jerked back and sat up stiffly. "I don't want a lot of possessions anymore. I don't want to spend money like I used to. I really can't afford it. I'm in a lot of things, of course, but nothing is finished until a deal is made and it's sold. Arctic Islands, for instance, part of Callahan Corporation; I'm waiting on that for twenty-six years." His voice became plaintive. "You know what I'm doing now? I really want to get out. I want to stop all this. The reason I'm maintaining the Toronto office with Steve Kay is that he's very loyal, and he's learned the game. I don't go up there; last year, I think, I went once or twice. This year I haven't been up there at all. This apartment—the office—is up for sale and I'm not going into anything new. I've got a lot of real estate all over the place. Steve can handle all the other things."

"Why don't you wind up your business and take it easy? You've earned it, haven't you?"

At my question, Hirshhorn blinked, startled. Quickly his eyes hooded. "I don't want to live in New York," he said. "It's tough; I can't stand cold weather anymore. I have to live where it's warm—if I want to live. In Washington I can rent a small apartment, a three-room co-op. That's all I need."

He had played with the prospect of spending his days in Washington, looking after his "children," the artworks in the museum. He and Olga, his wife, had house-hunted some years prior to its completion and purchased the home of the late Gen. George P. Scriver for $125,000. Its four stories with 13-foot ceilings contained five bedrooms, a 30 by 20-foot drawing room, and a dining room to seat fourteen. Within three years the cost of renovation had jumped over 70 percent. "I put it up for sale last week," Hirshhorn grumbled. "The Greenwich house, too, is a waste." That had been acquired in 1961 "to house the art," and the lawns and gardens had been converted into an al fresco gallery.

The phone resumed ringing. Hirshhorn spoke with Gordon. "Yeah? . . . Yeah. . . . Is that all? . . . Okay. How are the children? . . . Everything all right? . . . Good. What else? . . . Call me later."

As Hirshhorn plunged onward, his manner changed intangibly. He completed another call, replaced the instrument, and reclined in his chair, elbow resting on its arm, hand cupped to prop his chin. His compressed lips slanted downward; his brow knitted.

"It still hurts," he said.

Pain was apparent. He elaborated, and I was to hear this lament reiterated in identical words, a sad refrain, a playback. The feelings were rehearsed, yet somehow the effect was spontaneous, even genuine.

"The lawsuit," he muttered. "Jennie sued me. The kids— You've never been sued by your family. You have no idea what it did to me. I never got over it." The litigation, begun in 1947, two years after the divorce, dragged into 1955. Jennie, his first wife, had recruited the aid of the children. "Kids?" Hirshhorn scowled. "Robin was already twenty-four when it started; Gene was twenty-one, Gordon was eighteen, and Naomi sixteen. Robin called me a monster." He registered wonderment. "She did!"

During the strife, Hirshhorn once asked Robin whether the hostility would ever cease, and she retorted, "When you house, clothe, and feed your children as you do your art!"

"I threw myself into my work," said Hirshhorn, "nothing but work. And in order to work, I had to forget my family. The only pleasure I got out of life was to buy art. I lived in another area completely. The kids would call to ask how I was. It was only to ask for something. In the end I gave it to them but it left a sour taste."

On their part, the children had found communication jammed.

"He felt we never did anything for him," his daughter Gene observed mournfully. "Long ago I knitted him a pair of socks for his birthday. He gave them away to the postman, or maybe it was the gardener. It was a little thing but it signaled something big. Once in a while he gave me the opportunity to cook him dinners of his favorite dishes. He probably thought they were just preludes to putting the bite on him. When it didn't come, I don't know what he thought. You never built up a bank account with Daddy Joe of trust, faith, respect, or love."

Hirshhorn bore a heavy sense of failure. "Kids never get over a bustup of marriage," he said. "I don't tell anyone what to do. Even my own family—they can do or say anything they want. I should have done what the Italians and French do: stay together and have a lover on the outside." He paused briefly, then continued, more to himself than to me. "How do you repair a relationship with children? I don't think I can; but I'm going to do what I can." His thoughts turned inward, his face reflecting a debate of options, considered and rejected. "I don't know what I'll do." He drew a sharp breath and exclaimed, "I don't expect them to come to my funeral. How do you like that?" His voice, truculent and harsh, softened plaintively. "And I'm satisfied. I've already made up my mind to accept that."

Slowly reaching for his glasses, he settled them on his nose and took up the telephone. "I don't want to neglect my business," he said somberly. "That comes first."

He dialed a number. "Let me speak to Ian MacGregor, please. . . . This is Joseph Hirshhorn. . . . I'll wait. . . . Yes; Mr. MacGregor? You remember me? I'm that little bit of a man. . . . I'm semi-retired now. You're talking to a seventy-five-year-old boy. . . . I'd like to meet you, see what you look like. I haven't seen you in two hundred years. . . ."

And so it went until noon.

■ ■ □ □

We strode to Madison Avenue for lunch at a counter. At twelve-forty he repaired to Bella Fishko's Forum Gallery to see the work of a young artist she was introducing to New York. At the building entrance his eye caught an American weather vane, a sculptured horse and rider, displayed in the window of the Scott Elliott Gallery. As he entered, the manager, Martin Diamond, recognized Hirshhorn and advanced to greet him. Brushing amenities aside, Hirshhorn indicated the horse and rider in the window and inquired, "How much do you want for that?"

In a split second Diamond computed cost and gallery commission, and tacked on a margin for haggling. "Thirty-five hundred," he said.

The brief hesitation, hardly discernible, was not lost on Hirshhorn. "I'll give you twenty-five hundred," he said laconically. The dealer revised his price by $300. "No good," said Hirshhorn and moved on to a painting of a house in a New Mexico landscape. "How much for the Hartley?"

Again the fractional pause before Diamond replied, "Sixty-five hundred."

"Keep it," said Hirshhorn.

He paced through the gallery, releasing his tension and heightening the dealer's. Hirshhorn inquired about an Andrew Wyeth on the wall and without waiting for a reply crossed the room to halt at a brass figure by John Flannagan.

"What do you want for that?" he asked.

"Fifteen hundred."

"You know," said Hirshhorn, his face pained, his voice prideful, "Flannagan was the first sculptor I bought; a stone figure. I paid a hundred for it in 1930. It's in the museum now." Turning away, he spoke over his shoulder, "For the Hartley and Flannagan, sixty-five hundred."

"Can't do it," Diamond said regretfully.

"I'm a cheapskate," Hirshhorn said. His eyes swept the gallery, noting a Feininger, a Nadelman, a Lurçat, and two Epsteins. "You've got some beautiful things," he added pugnaciously. "What are you asking for the Wyeth?"

"Twenty-three," Diamond mumbled, meaning thousands.

Hirshhorn emitted a cry. "You see," he called upon the world to witness, "you see how they appreciate all I've done. Stop with those telephone numbers," he reproved Diamond, adding abruptly, "All right, ten thousand for the three—for the Hartley, Flannagan, and the weather vane. Is it a deal?" He stuck his hand out. Off balance, Diamond grasped it. "Have them delivered to my office this afternoon and you can pick up the check," said Hirshhorn, and departed for the Forum Gallery on the fifth floor.

Bella Fishko was abroad. A girl attendant guided Hirshhorn through the exhibit of paintings by Dan Gustin of New Haven to four canvases reserved for his inspection in the rear sanctum. Hirsh-horn pointed to a large one.

"How much for that one?"

"Three-fifty," said the gallery attendant.

"And the other?" asked Hirshhorn, pointing to its twin.

"The same."

"I'll take them both for six hundred," he said.

On his way out, Hirshhorn paused near the elevator before a vi-trine. His glance rested on a sculpture of Zero Mostel by Laura Ziegler.

"That's mine," he said. "Wrap it carefully in a carton and send it over to my office. I want to take it home to Greenwich. It's for my wife." He contemplated the figure for a moment. "I overpaid," he grumbled and entered the elevator.

At two, Hirshhorn was back at his office, on the phone to Steve Kay in Toronto. ". . . It's a cash deal? Take it. . . . What's the other? . . . What should we take? . . . Forget it. The property's in a growing area; forget it. . . . What about the one on Seventeen? . . . What'll we take? . . . Fifty? Okay, take it—fifty or sixty. . . . But on the other, hold out for seventy-five."

The doorbell announced Diamond and the new acquisitions. The dealer had brought along art books with illustrations of an un-usual Marsden Hartley. Hirshhorn expressed indifference, due more to the price than to the picture. Diamond gazed at the walls of the apartment, his eyes glittering at sight of the Léger, Arp, Picasso, Giacometti, Stuart Davis, Albers, and Morris Louis.

"Mr. Hirshhorn," he exclaimed, "you could go into business just with what you have in this room."

Fortunately for the dealer, Hirshhorn was already through the door and out of earshot. No one risked Hirshhorn's wrath by suggesting he profit from art, not since an agent tried to get him to buy an unknown artist's work by assuring the collector its value would increase in time. Hirshhorn had drenched him with scorn.

"Don't tell me how to make money. I don't collect art to make money. I do it because I love it."

We sped across town to West 68th Street to look in on Jerry O'Con-nor, who had once worked at the warehouse where Hirshhorn stored his art. Jerry, turned painter, had introduced himself to Hirshhorn at a Whitney Museum show and the collector had asked him where he lived.

"I got so nervous," Jerry recalled, "I couldn't remember my own address."

"Call me," Hirshhorn said peremptorily.

Jerry had phoned on the chance he was serious, and here Hirshhorn was actually on his doorstep. Breathlessly, Jerry ushered us into the single cramped room which was home and workshop. Hirshhorn's glance went at once to the wall on which hung a pen portrait of Giacometti.

"Did you do that?" he asked, and upon affirmation, said curtly, "I'll buy it. How much?"

Abashed, Jerry said, "I didn't expect you to buy anything. I just wanted your professional view of my work. I'm grateful you're here."

"Don't exaggerate my professional knowledge," Hirshhorn said gruffly. "I like the drawing, that's all."

From a pile, Jerry pulled another sketch. After a sharp look, Hirshhorn offered to buy it as well. Jerry spluttered more protestations. They sounded hollow. Lifting a mound of collages, he spread a few on a table for Hirshhorn to study. Hirshhorn returned to the first drawing and renewed his offer. Jerry demurred. He wished to keep the picture "for sentimental reasons." He presented a collage to Hirshhorn as a gift. Declining, Hirshhorn paid him a hundred dollars for it and the second pen sketch and went off with Jerry's vociferous thanks ringing in his ears.

Hirshhorn stopped next at Beth Israel Hospital, downtown on the East Side, to visit Alan Emil, a friend and investor in a Hirshhorn venture in England. Emerging from the sickroom, Hirshhorn wagged his head, puzzled.

"He was such a lively man when I saw him last," he said. "He owns a lot of AT&T; but he's very ill."

Beside the East River and nearby Chinatown, Hirshhorn alighted from a cab in front of a century-old house. Eight years ago he had visited Domenick Turturro, asked to use his phone, and while making five calls bought six of his paintings. One now hung in the museum, another in Hirshhorn's office. Spryly Hirshhorn mounted steep stone steps from the street. The door opened to frame Domenick, shirtless and unshaved.

"You're early," the artist said. "I was just about to make myself pretty for you."

"You don't have to look pretty," said Hirshhorn as he entered.

A long staircase minus a handrail led to the studio, formerly a synagogue, two stories high with a balcony on three sides. Domenick switched floodlights onto a brick wall to exhibit his work of the past ten months: ten abstract oils on canvases measuring up to 6 by 7 feet, and three mixed-media on paper. Hirshhorn shed his jacket, draped it over a chair, and prowled the studio.

"How much you asking for these pictures?" he asked. "If you give me telephone numbers, I'll walk out. I don't need more paintings; I need another like a hole in the head. I can't afford it."

Domenick quoted an average of $2,200 for the vari-sized canvases.

"I'm buying three pieces," Hirshhorn remonstrated, "but not at those prices."

Taking the artist aside, he dictated in hushed tones a deal for five oils and the three mixed-media: $6,500. Sighting two tiny canvases and an ink-on-paper, he added $400, the latter pieces for his wife's collection. "What's more," Hirshhorn crowed, "I'm going to take you to dinner. It's my treat."

Stunned, Domenick responded in an uneven voice. "We celebrate. There's a great Chinese restaurant in the neighborhood. I'll get a bottle of wine for the table."

Awaiting his return, I asked Hirshhorn what prompted him to purchase in volume.

"If I bought one or two," he replied, worry creasing his face, "I'd pay as much as for five or six. This way they're cheaper. Besides," his expression lit up, "I like them all."

The dinner, sumptuous and convivial, relaxed Hirshhorn into expansiveness. He spoke of New York and the artists who phoned relentlessly, pleading for him to view their work. He shied away until their need broke down his resistance.

"I guess," Domenick admitted sheepishly, "I must have phoned you fifteen times in the last couple of weeks."

Hirshhorn summoned the waiter. "Don't you have any dessert?" he asked.

"That's extra," said the waiter.

"I can afford it," Hirshhorn whooped.

He ordered chocolate ice cream all around. Breaking open his fortune cookie, he read: "Unlooked-for prosperity when least expected." Hirshhorn handed it to Domenick. The artist smiled.

As they left the restaurant, Hirshhorn turned to Domenick and with eyes smiling in a perfectly straight face he said, "Can I pay you the money over the next three years?"

■ ■ □ □

Early next morning, back on the phone, Hirshhorn complained to one of his brokers that his desk was piled high with junk because he had been away all the previous afternoon. Before him lay market analyses, clippings from the *New York Times* and the *Wall Street Journal*, mail to read, correspondence to sign, the ever-present pad with his fine jottings of the day's stock fluctuations and the time of each change. He kept the pads on file for three years, a procedure from his novice days when he worked the chartroom in a brokerage house. Cool, concentrated, with intermittent bursts of jollity, he fielded all calls. I clocked twenty-eight in thirty-three minutes.

With the closing of the Stock Exchange at 4 P.M., the business day ended. Hirshhorn issued rapid instructions to the secretary, stuffed a portfolio with documents, newspapers, and a couple of art journals, and made for the door, where David Tarlow, his fiscal watchdog for a half-century, intercepted him. Helping him into a light overcoat, Tarlow quizzed Hirshhorn about a missing stock certificate. On the street below, chauffeur John Williams and the limousine waited. We settled ourselves in the rear seat and the car glided uptown to the expressway.

The city slid past and soon the windows framed the greenery of Westchester. The sun, still strong, warmed the interior of the car. Doffing his coat, Hirshhorn folded it neatly and draped it over the front seat. He nestled back into the soft upholstery.

"The first million is hard," he said. "After that it's a game for power. Today," he added, "it's only a game."

"Why didn't you quit after the million?" I asked.

"It came so fast," Hirshhorn replied, almost apologetically. "Should I have stopped when things were going so right?"

He considered this. "In my life," he continued, "I witnessed two panics on Wall Street. Last year was the worst. There was no reason for stock selling for nothing. It was Watergate; it frightened an awful lot of people. They lost faith in the administration. What could be worse? It never happened before. Herbert Hoover was a nice man; people didn't lose faith then in the government. With Watergate it was clear to everyone the fellow was dishonest but nobody knew where things were going to land. I've been in Wall Street since 1916, and I never knew anything like it. Kimberly-Clark, one of the great companies in the world, sold at fifteen. Crazy! I could go through the whole list: Disney went to sixty from one hundred and forty; Steel, selling at sixty-two, went to twenty-seven!"

Hirshhorn paused. In one of his favorite books, *The Robber Barons*, Matthew Josephson quoted Andrew Carnegie saying, "The

man who has money during a panic is the wise and valuable citizen."
Spoken in the parlous days of the Gay Nineties, the words were a
constant monition to Hirshhorn.

Money, power, politics, Hirshhorn called it all a game. Yet he
did not dissociate himself from the little man. "Last year [1974] was
devastating; people went broke," he said in an aggrieved tone.
"There were more people involved in the market, more than in
1929—about forty million stockholders."

The car's engine purred. Tires beat a tattoo on the cracks in the
concrete road, a rhythm of sensuous ease. Somehow Hirshhorn's
face did not reflect the luxuriousness. Some incongruity struck him,
a recollection from childhood.

"Once, in Latvia," he recounted, "—I couldn't have been more
than four or five at the time—two big wagons were harnessed with
horses and everybody was up on the wagons. We were going—I
don't know where—because the hooligans were coming and they
were killing Jews. They were maybe only forty or fifty miles away
from where we lived in Jukst outside of Libau. My mother and my
family knew about it through the grapevine. We were all packed; but
we didn't go. That's always stood in my mind. It was frightening to
a little boy."

A moment's silence and he attacked the portfolio of documents
as the limousine rolled homeward through the lush Connecticut
hills.

In Greenwich, the limousine turned off John Street, wound up a
steep stone-paved road past a commodious garage where stood a gray
Rolls-Royce, and drew up to the Tudor manse perched on the crest
of Round Hill. The wide mullioned bays of the manor glinted in the
sunlight with friendly formality. White magnolia blossomed everywhere amid birch and pine and trim hedges; forsythia flamed yellow.
In the distance through a rift in the woods, the hills of Westchester
leaned in the sun against a hazy sky. The smooth lawns showed no
rents where Rodin's massive *Burghers of Calais* and monumental *Bal-
zac* once stood. The green expanse which at one time bristled with
144 sculptures was bare except for an Anthony Caro, iron painted
red, and Henry Moore's *Vertebrae*.

Bolts clacked as the heavy oak door swung open and Paul Nicolet, the butler, greeted us. From the direction of the garage, Pepper,
an aging Irish setter, ambled over to the flagstone terrace to wag her

welcome. She accepted Hirshhorn's exuberant affection and waddled back to her rest.

In the foyer beside the entrance, the shaft of Brancusi's *Bird in Flight* spiraled upward. The original marble, irreparably shattered in the move from Nelson Rockefeller's former apartment in the West Fifties to his Fifth Avenue triplex, was miraculously reproduced by Joseph Ternbach from a photo. The marble phoenix went to Rockefeller. Its model at Round Hill was destined for the Hirshhorn Museum.

"I just want to enjoy it a while longer at home," said Hirshhorn. "The museum has more Brancusis: *Torso, Sleeping Muse, Prometheus*— others."

Alice Nicolet, housekeeper-wife of the butler, came from the kitchen to greet Hirshhorn. Informing her that Mrs. Hirshhorn would be returning from Florida the coming weekend, he inquired if there had been any calls.

"Yes, m'sieur," said Alice, "some gentleman he call."

"What was his name?"

"Ah—I don't know, m'sieur," she apologized. "I cannot remember the name. It maybe is not important?"

"Alice," said Hirshhorn sadly, "you must write the messages down. You know," he reproved her gently, "it may not be important to you but it is to me."

He gave instructions to Nicolet for dinner and went upstairs to freshen up, leaving me to browse through the house.

The intimacy within belied the formality of its exterior. Simple forms and rich detail blended in the drawing rooms, dining room, and library. Sheraton and Queen Anne furniture, products of early Philadelphia craftsmen, rested unobtrusively on the handwoven Kerman and Ispahan rugs. On walls, floors, and window ledges, in every direction the eye fed from a cornucopia of American and French imagination—Cassatt, Avery, Pascin, Léger, Nevelson, Mondrian, Motherwell, Laurencin, Soyer, Henri. Over the fireplace, Picasso; above a sideboard, the exquisite *Mrs. T* by Bellows; casually on a table in one of the five guest rooms an eighteen-inch ceramic platter from a limited number of *Centaurs* fired for Picasso in the kilns of Madoura; and tacked to the paneling beside one archway, two tiny Dürer etchings, the works which in 1917 launched Hirshhorn on his career of collecting.

More pictures lined the upstairs corridor. One bore the legend: "On November 23, 1963—it was in the morning while I was painting these roses and fruits, the newsflash came—the assassination of John Kennedy—the painting was left at that point—never to be completed." The inscription read: "To Joseph and Olga Hirshhorn from Irving Block, a Los Angeles artist, and his wife, Jill."

When Hirshhorn first saw Block's work, he exclaimed, "You paint with your breath—or with your penis!"

The phone shrilled. Hirshhorn answered it in the upstairs study. His tone clearly expressed annoyance—with himself. "I'll look for it and call you back."

Hirshhorn hung up. A methodical search through portfolio, desk drawers, and piles of folders proved fruitless. He stood still a moment, reliving recent movements and places. Abruptly he went to a clothing cupboard and rummaged through the pockets of several suits. The search ended as he withdrew from one jacket a certificate—the missing 210,000 shares of mining stock. He phoned Tarlow.

"It's here, Dave. I mislaid it. You weren't around so I stuck it in my pocket, figuring when you came I'd give it to you. I would have done it yesterday when I came up with the six hundred shares of bank stock, but I was wearing a different suit. I knew I had it somewhere. Sure enough, there it was in one I wore weeks ago before I left for Florida. It wasn't signed and it's made out to me. Nobody could do anything with it."

In reassuring his auditor, Hirshhorn sounded worried. His lapse mirrored the time in 1954 when things got out of hand in the euphoria of his uranium bonanza and Hirshhorn could barely keep pace with his accelerated moneymaking. In his Toronto office one day a roll of bills, several hundred dollars, dropped from his pocket onto the floor. It went unnoticed nor did he miss it until one of the staff brought it to his attention. Hirshhorn's physician, recognizing the signs of exhaustion, had ordered a complete cessation of activity. And now Hirshhorn was almost twenty-one years older.

The sun was disappearing behind gray wet clouds. A chill crept into the study. Hirshhorn ignited the kindling ready laid in the fireplace and the logs leaped into a comfortable blaze. He leaned back in his chair and stared at the flames. The desk before him was laden with what he termed his collection of toys: Ashanti gold weights and figures of wood and pre-Columbian jadeite, a small Picasso bull, a contortion by Henri Laurens, a head of Georgia O'Keeffe by Mary Callery, and *Big Mamma*, an amusing grotesque by Niki de Saint-Phalle. Strewn among them were a piece of "found art"—a brass gas jet—a Mexican owl, a tiger, mule, steer, and roadrunner—and two piggybanks half full of pennies. Shelves along the walls, together with those in the library below, held nearly 2,000 volumes on art and artists. Directly facing the desk on a tall easel stood a 3-foot photo portrait of Picasso autographed: "pour mon ami—Joe Hirshhorn—7-7-67." The Chinese rug on the floor was machine-made.

"This room takes a lot of wear," Hirshhorn explained.

The phone rang and Hirshhorn pounced on the instrument.

"Yeah?" He listened intently to one of his stockbrokers. The recent ruling of the Securities and Exchange Commission against excessive brokerage fees was about to go into effect. The volume of his buying and selling, Hirshhorn felt, merited consideration. In one year that broker's commission had amounted to $886,000. That very day, "just cleaning up a couple of situations," Hirshhorn had unloaded a million dollars in stocks. He growled; he complained; he groaned; he wrangled. His parting shot: without a new arrangement, his trade would go elsewhere. He hung up. His manner changed.

"In addition to the commissions they made on me," he commented calmly, "I got them other accounts which made them another $100,000."

His coolness contrasted with the heat of his ultimatum. It bared the actor beneath the skin. Haggling seasoned his sauce. It also gave rise to legends.

Once, scanning the sculptures in the studio of an artist, Hirshhorn pointed to one and asked the price. Knowing the collector's penchant for bargaining, the artist tacked on an extra third. Without demur, Hirshhorn said, "I'll take it," and went on to a second piece. The artist rubbed his bruised conscience and quoted his normal price. Hirshhorn nodded. He pointed to still another work. Crushed by remorse, the artist reduced the price by one-third. Hirshhorn accepted and prepared to take his leave. Accompanied by a contrite sculptor, he went to the door. On the way, he halted beside a fourth work. "I bought the three pieces back there," he said. "Why don't you throw this one in for the same price?"

Once Hirshhorn met his match, in Billy Rose. The midget impresario wooed Hirshhorn, hoping he would give his collection to the Jerusalem Museum. In 1964, its disposition had not yet been determined though Hirshhorn was inclined toward the United States. Blandishment and persuasion availed Rose nothing. At lunch he played his trump card.

"Come to Israel," he urged.

"I will," said Hirshhorn.

"I bet you won't," Rose challenged.

"I'll take that bet."

"All right," said Rose. "How much?"

"Ten thousand," Hirshhorn whipped back.

They shook hands on it and set a deadline. When word of the wager reached Wall Street, smart money booked odds Rose would welch.

Hirshhorn married Olga in May, honeymooned at the Venice Biennale in June, and at the end of the month, just under the wire, arrived in Jerusalem. News of his arrival was cabled to Rose, who enplaned to Israel and handed him a check for $10,000. Hirshhorn endorsed it over to the Jerusalem Museum. Subsequently, after Rose presented his own sculpture to Israel, Hirshhorn learned that his contribution was channeled into a fund for the museum's Billy Rose Sculpture Garden.

■ ■ □ □

Hirshhorn ate dinner with relish and uncharacteristic slowness, a discipline forced upon him long ago by a fifteen-year bout with diverticulosis. He returned once more to childhood memories of poverty.

"I envied the boys who had papas and mamas," he said. "Benny Green—he rode a bicycle to school and brought lunch in a paper bag filled with snacks and chocolate. I never saw chocolate before I came to America." The lines around Hirshhorn's mouth drooped sharply. "On Humboldt Street, Number Seventeen, where we lived in Williamsburg, my older brother, Herman, slept on a couch in the living room. There was only one brass bed; I think the girls used it. I always slept on a folding cot."

When fire destroyed Number Seventeen, neighbors gave the children refuge. Little Joe lodged with the family of a prosperous dry-goods-store proprietor. "There I slept in a real bed," said Hirshhorn.

Weighing the difference between those days and his present circumstances, he adjudged it pragmatically. "I live better now," he said simply. "I'm at ease, no anxiety about my bills. I've taken care of a lot of people and it gives me a great deal of comfort."

"Do you need to be so active now?" I asked.

"It's a game," Hirshhorn chuckled. "I enjoy it."

"With that kind of money it must be more than a game."

"No," he explained. "I back my judgment and I'm having fun. That's all." After a moment he continued. "I bought something last

week—about five thousand shares—I don't remember how much."
He looked up. "I don't need it, is that what you're thinking?"

"Yes. You dealt in about a million—"

"I sold!" Hirshhorn snapped. "I didn't deal."

"All right, you sold—"

"That's what I said," his injured tone driving the point home.
"Dealt is different."

"Sorry. You sold a million dollars' worth of stock. Is a million a
game?"

"Everything is relative," said Hirshhorn. "If a guy has $50,000,
and he's on a salary, that's a great deal of money. A guy like J. Paul
Getty, to him five million doesn't mean anything; he's got two billion. It depends on how much you have and what your thinking is. I
saw a market way down in the basement. The stocks were cheap.
Prices at the end of last year reminded me of 1932. That's forty
years ago. I backed my judgment. I happened to be right."

"In other words," I said, "this is not your livelihood; it's really
your life."

"I don't put it that way." Hirshhorn smiled. He tilted his head
sideways and knitted his brow. "I'm not a philosopher and I'm never
going to be one."

"You prefer action."

"I also do a lot of thinking," Hirshhorn laughed. "My life con-
sists of a lot of things."

"Then why do you want to make more?"

"It's not a question of making more," said Hirshhorn. "I don't
want to become a mumble-stumbler and stay home all day and read
the paper—"

"And buy art?"

"I bought art," he countered swiftly. "And I'm still buying. If I
was in the art business, that would use up my energies and my
thinking. I've been considering opening an art gallery. The only
reason I'm not doing it now is that I might hurt the museum. I'm not
afraid of buying young artists. When I see a boy or a girl who's
talented, I buy 'em. I don't buy one but two, five, maybe ten. See? I
buy them because I want to back my own point of view."

"The same as with stocks?"

"I know a great deal about both," said Hirshhorn emphati-
cally. "It's not just a hop, skip, and a jump. When I buy a Francis
Bacon for $750 [in the mid-fifties] and go to England—I went on
business [in 1961] and took Sam Harris, my attorney, with me. He
thought I was crazy. We had a Rio Tinto board meeting at nine in

the morning. I called the girl at the art gallery to be open and we showed up at eight. In fifteen minutes I bought four Bacons. [In 1967] I took a credit of $65,000 for the one I had [for $750] and bought a triptych for $150,000. You couldn't get it today for three-quarters of a million. The point is, it's part of my life, not because I wanted to make money in pictures."

"Would you equate that with power?"

Hirshhorn shook his head. "Power is another story. I'm not looking for it. If I did, would I turn over the art to the government? I have nothing to do with the museum. I can only suggest. I attend meetings by invitation. Does that mean I want power? If I did, it would be another story."

His gaze upon the distance, Hirshhorn appeared enthralled by a dream he was unable to interpret, a mysterious force which hurtled him onward. His thoughts, however, were not remote. He was not like the man Disraeli described who "carried on long after he lost his purpose."

"What kind of power have I got?" Hirshhorn sighed. "I don't run an investment advisory service. They have power. I only talk to some friends. Last December, at a dinner party, a woman told me her brokers were recommending her to sell. I said to her: Don't sell a damn share! A lot of important people were there that night. One was an officer of Standard Oil's European market, and I said it openly—loud. I told her I bought $3 million worth. I did; and I was right. Out here in Greenwich some guy—probably making $125 a week—went on the radio to tell everybody to sell their stocks, that the market was dropping. I tried to get him on the phone the next day but he wasn't there, to say what right does he have to get on the air and talk like that, to frighten people. That's why we had this kind of uncertain market."

Hirshhorn took it as a personal injury. In his mind the scene had rolled back four decades. He was reliving the early thirties when he dropped a million bucking the market.

"I told you," he said. "I'm liquidating a big position from back in December. Stocks may go higher, and I think they will, but I'm picking up my chips and I'm walking away from the game."

Gravely, Hirshhorn voiced a portent. "Write this down. Before the year's out we're going to have days with a volume of thirty to forty million shares. The Stock Exchange will have to sell additional memberships to handle the business."

"And you'll resume the game?" I asked.

Hirshhorn pushed back from the table and rose. His face was the more solemn for the wily glint in his eyes.

"I don't know," he said. "I can't tell you. Only God can, and He doesn't talk."

It was time to turn in for the night. We mounted the curving staircase to the landing, which broadened into a grand foyer with doors at both ends leading to the sleeping quarters. Paintings hung everywhere.

"Are all these going to the museum?" I asked.

"Maybe, eventually," Hirshhorn replied. "I think I have left over as much as I gave away—here and in the warehouse. And I'm buying more; not as much as I used to, but all the time." High on one wall hung two large portraits of Hirshhorn and his wife by James Fosburgh. "You like that of me?" Hirshhorn inquired.

"Impressive—for a bank president," I said.

"You like the expression?"

"It captures a certain look in the eyes."

Many had tried in painting and sculpture to capture Hirshhorn's elusive quality, among them Raphael Soyer, Pablo Serrano, Abel Chretien, and Laura Ziegler. All achieved only partial success. The Hirshhorn physiognomy was relatively immobile, the expression in his eyes evanescent. Arrested, they appeared frigid, even sinister. Larry Rivers, painting Hirshhorn's portrait, merely sketched in the head and prow of a nose and focused everything in the eyes. To one critic it pictured "an immensely intelligent face." Abram Lerner, who became curator of the Hirshhorn collection and later director of the museum, felt it made him "look like a mobster."

Paul Nicolet appeared. "We should instruct the guest about the alarm system," he said. "If not, in the middle of the night—"

The butler broke off with a gesture auguring an apocalypse. He led the way to the guest rooms along a corridor which connected the two wings of the manor. At the far end of the passage, he shut the door and returned to the one off the grand foyer. Upon closing this one, he advised, the system would be activated. Thereafter all movement would be restricted to inside the bedrooms.

Nicolet entered the hall outside Hirshhorn's chamber. On the wall a cluster of switches and lights, one flashing white, indicated the far half of the house was already hooked into the alarm system. With the shutting of the second door, the other light would go on and the entire house would be secured. Should an intruder get past the outer relay, his movement anywhere within the house would trip the alarm.

The system had been installed subsequent to the theft of six paintings valued at nearly a half-million dollars. Early in March 1974, with the Hirshhorns in Florida, three burglars broke into Round Hill through the pantry and made off with an Edward Hopper, two each by Winslow Homer and Monticelli, and a rare self-portrait by Thomas Eakins. Three months later, thanks to Ronald Timm and David Hughes of the Greenwich Police Department, the paintings were located. After some plea bargaining, they were delivered to the U.S. Attorney at a rendezvous in the Federal Court Building in Bridgeport at 6 A.M. on June 7. Wrapped in plastic bags and coming from "someplace in New York," the canvases were intact, only two minor chips in the frames. Promptly, Hirshhorn ordered the security system.

■ ■ □ □

At six, Hirshhorn took his coffee propped in bed listening to the early news. At seven-thirty, breakfast awaited us in the dining room below. Sitting at the head of the large table, Hirshhorn brought to mind the Little King of Otto Soglow. Beneath his imperiousness lurked a small boy filled with wonder at his surroundings, constantly on the alert against their sudden disappearance. A lifetime of achievement separated Hirshhorn from the uncertainties of his childhood. Still, the master of the mart and exploiter of the earth's recesses distrusted what the next moment might bring.

As the butler filled his coffee cup from a silver service, Hirshhorn spoke of racing home from grammar school, scrambling up four flights to gulp the lunch his mother set on the kitchen table each morning before she went off to work.

"My mother worked hard," said Hirshhorn, wrinkling his brow. "It hurt me to see her work so hard." He emptied his cup and set it on the saucer. Nicolet entered from the kitchen to refill it from the silver carafe. "I came out of a hellhole, and I was lucky. Those kids were my neighbors; some were friends. Two wound up in the electric chair. A third was crushed between the cars of a train when he skipped the El to save a nickel. One," he shook his head in disappointment, "became a cab driver." His face brightened. "One became a stockbroker. He did very well. When we lived on Lewis Avenue, a kid neighbor was Nathaniel L. Goldstein. He became Attorney General of New York State."

Hirshhorn took a final gulp of coffee. Wiping his lips, he creased his napkin on its folds.

"When I was a little boy, a lot of things bothered me. We had three bedrooms, two for the five girls, one for us three boys. When my brother Herman came from South Africa, he used the living room. My mother slept in the kitchen. She got up at six o'clock to make our breakfast and put things up to cook so we could eat at night. Then she went to work and came home late. My little sister, Dora, and I set the large table in the kitchen for the evening meal. It was the only one the family took together."

His mother worked in the neighborhood so as not to spend money on carfare. She earned $12 a week making pocketbooks. All the girls but Dora labored at ladies' shirtwaists and neckwear. One brother had a job after school in a candy factory. Another, sickly, joined him when his health permitted. The family's collective earnings went for rent and food, and to pay the installments on their ship's passage from Latvia.

"On Saturday nights," Hirshhorn continued, "my mother was a cook, for weddings and parties. She'd bring back big bags of food—chickens and leftovers. She worked like hell. It bothered me no end. I used to walk a mile to the nearest Bohack's for two cans of condensed milk—two for fifteen cents—to save a nickel. To this day I hate drinking milk."

He dropped the folded napkin on the table. Staring at it, he leaned back in his chair. "Poverty has a bitter taste," he said. "I swore I'd never know it again." He turned to the butler. "No lunch today, Paul. I've got some phoning to do and then we're going over to Darien to the Callahan office. We'll eat there. Tell John to have the car ready at eleven."

The early morning downpour had washed the landscape until it shone. The limousine hissed on the wet road as it headed for Darien and the headquarters of Callahan Mining.

A relatively small mining company, Callahan extracted new resources from old fields. It owned the largest silver mine in Idaho. The corporation was thirty years old in 1954 when Hirshhorn acquired control through the purchase of 770,000 shares. He brought with him the rights to a million and a half acres in the Canadian Arctic Islands east of Alaska which extended the company's mining and manufacturing operations into natural gas and oil. Hirshhorn was voted chairman of the board. In five years revenue had more than tripled and dividends showed an increase of almost 500 percent.

In the center of Darien we alighted from the limousine at the bank building in which Callahan occupied an entire floor. On the way to the elevator, passing a stock brokerage, Hirshhorn dropped in to check the market. The young broker in attendance obliged with computerized data.

Thanking him, Hirshhorn inquired, "How's business?"

"Fallen off," was the dispirited reply.

"It'll hit bottom in June," Hirshhorn prophesied. "By September it'll be better. What the hell! They manufactured this recession. They put the money rate up to twelve percent and held it there for three months."

In the Callahan offices, the board chairman's quarters looked sterile, with only a desk and a phone. "I hardly ever come here," said Hirshhorn, dialing Florida. "Hello; this is Joe Hirshhorn. . . . Yeah; any action? . . . Okay; sell six thousand at seven/eighths. . . . Yeah; say it back to me. . . . Yeah; keep in touch." He replaced the phone. "In 1951," he said to no one in particular, "I bought sixty-seven properties in three weeks in Regina, Canada."

He made his way to the office of Charles Snead, Jr. "You're looking tired, Charlie," Hirshhorn observed. "What's the matter, you working too hard?"

The president of Callahan shook his head wearily. He wasn't getting much sleep. His corporate duties were complicated by having to drive 20 miles each morning to get his son to school. Hirshhorn listened. The lines in his face creased in sympathy, but his eyes remained cold. He switched the subject to Callahan. Reviewing the scope of the company's operations, his questions, seemingly casual, probed Snead's management of the various divisions under his direction. Hirshhorn conducted the appraisal informally, briefly, without sentiment.

The annual board meeting was scheduled for mid-June in Fredericksburg, Virginia, where Callahan had holdings of zinc, copper, and silver. Hirshhorn suggested that Snead include with notices for the meeting an invitation to all members and their wives to be Hirshhorn's guests at the museum. None of them had seen it as yet, and the two-hour drive to Washington from Fredericksburg made it convenient. Hirshhorn proposed a luncheon in the museum's board room, followed by a tour of the building and the exhibit.

On the way out, Snead detoured his board chairman through the corporate premises. Remarking on the walls, shiny and nude, Hirshhorn muttered, "All that empty space! We should hang paintings—make the place look warm and homey."

Snead nodded. From the stockroom he fetched a copy of an annual report. The cover illustration reflected Hirshhorn's influence. Its caption read: "A native bird by Lucy, an Eskimo artist of the Canadian Arctic where Callahan has interests of growing importance."

"I got the art myself for that cover," said Snead with quiet pride.

Leading the way to the parking lot, he drove his chairman and guest to lunch.

Throughout the ride back to Round Hill, Hirshhorn sat silent and pensive. The lunch had been pleasant; the president had reported continued good health for Callahan. The clouds had been blown away and left the sky a sparkling blue. Almost home, Hirshhorn finally spoke.

"When I was a kid," he said, "I made up my mind I wanted to make a million dollars—very badly. To me it was one of the great accomplishments in the world."

Since he had never known his father, Hirshhorn believed his ambition was born of his mother's hardships. His sister Anna, ten years older than Hirshhorn, had known their parent well.

"He was a lovely man," she told me. "He was honorable and he made a good living. Mama was tall; Papa was short. Joey was her favorite; but he looks like Papa. Papa used to say: Fear God; beware of men. Joey takes after him."

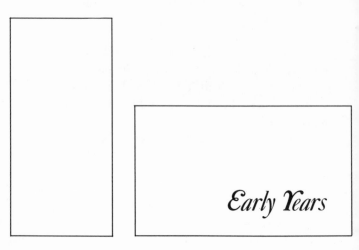

Early Years

II His youngest son was one year old when Lazar Hirshhorn died of heart disease at the age of forty-four. He had fathered a dozen children, and at the time of his death in 1901, his wife, Amelia née Friedlander, was pregnant with their thirteenth. Joseph Choneh Hirshhorn, their twelfth, had arrived on August 11, 1900.

The village of Jukst took little note of the event. In general, Latvia paid scant attention to Jews except when ingrained anti-Semitism periodically erupted in pogroms. Riga, the capital, was a center of Jewish culture, and Vilna, in neighboring Lithuania, was for centuries a seat of scholarship and the breeding ground for writers and musicians. Nothing of this remained after the Nazis overran the Baltic states in 1941. Into oblivion went all the Hirshhorns and Friedlanders who had not emigrated before the Holocaust.

In 1900, of Latvia's 90,000 Jews, four families, including the Hirshhorns, lived in Jukst, roughly 100 miles southwest of Riga and almost the same distance from Libau, the Baltic port to the north. Latvian law prohibited Jews from owning land. Jukst being a backwater town, the market for the farmers of the area, Lazar served the region as grain broker and ran a thriving general store which sold everything from herring and housewares to horseshoes and axle grease.

Of his grandparents, Hirshhorn knew little. His paternal grand-father died while Hirshhorn was an infant, and Grandma, a kindly little lady, lived with her other son in Tukums, too far from Jukst for frequent visits. Amelia's parents resided even farther away, in Mej-heik. Hirshhorn remembered them as a haughty, forbidding woman and a gray-bearded man dwelling together in an elegant house whose living room had a balcony on two sides.

Amelia had a sister in Mitau, and another married to a Jacobson in a town forty minutes by cart from their brother, Peretz, who lived near Libau. Amelia's other brother, Hessl, had left his wife and son and gone off to Johannesburg, South Africa.

Three of Lazar's offspring died in childhood. By the time Hirshhorn was born, Herman, fourteen and the eldest, was assisting their father in the store, and the others beyond the age of seven were attending district school. Rahla, twelve, the eldest of the daugh-ters, had gone on to the gymnasium in Mitau.

Lazar strove mightily for his family. Their stuccoed frame house stood on a half-acre rented from the local baron. A brick stove heated the dormitories for the four boys and six girls. Lazar and Amelia slept in a curtained-off section of the spacious living-dining room which doubled on Sabbaths as a synagogue, complete with Ark and Torah scroll. A door in the kitchen gave access to the store. A mark of distinction in the house was its inside toilet, with places for three.

Lazar, the son of poor parents, was determined that Amelia should never regret leaving her girlhood home. While he lived, he employed a wet nurse for his inveterately pregnant wife. He sup-plied Amelia with a cook and a housemaid, and a farmhand tilled the truck garden and husbanded two cows, a team of horses, four sheep, and innumerable chickens. Sundays in summer the Hirshhorns pic-nicked at the lakeside and went boating. On occasion they hitched up the team and went off to celebrate the wedding of a relative.

At Lazar's death, Amelia was forty, her hair as black as her large eyes. Until the end of her days at eighty-three, her head re-mained innocent of gray and her eyes flickered with intimations of passion. Her grandchildren nicknamed her "the black witch." In 1962, nineteen years after she died, Hirshhorn spent almost a quarter-million dollars for a collection of paintings by Thomas Eakins which included a portrait of the artist's wife. It reminded Hirshhorn of his mother. "Every time I looked at it," he said, "I could bust out crying."

Amelia sent Herman to Mitau with a thousand rubles to restock the supply of flax. He went instead to Libau and thence to London, where he stopped to cable his mother not to worry and proceeded to his uncle in South Africa. Amelia hired two townsmen as store clerks. Business at the general store declined.

Two years after her husband's death, Jews were massacred in Kishinev. Fear of further pogroms increased in February of 1904 when Russia declared war on Japan, and the insurrection in 1905 sent waves of rioting over the land. In Libau a protest against the departure of reservists to the front was met by army rifle fire. Charging cavalry sabered the crowd and left the streets strewn with ten dead and fifty wounded. Amelia prepared for flight.

In 1906 she appointed Rahla, who had married, caretaker of the store. Like a sergeant billeting troops, Amelia deployed the children: four of the youngest—Abe, Irving, Fanny, and Dora—were assigned to Rahla; Anna was put to work in nearby Dovlin; and Ella and Frieda accompanied their mother to America. Hirshhorn was entrusted to her brother, Peretz Friedlander, and his wife, Zetta.

Uncle Peretz, a lumber merchant and a toper, had a jolly red moustache. He and his childless wife doted on their diminutive nephew, denied him nothing in the way of dainties to eat, clothes to wear, and a comfortable bed all to himself. Daily Hirshhorn trundled forty minutes by cart to school where he joined his cousins, the Jacobsons, in their study of Latvian, German, Russian, Hebrew, and arithmetic. From this instruction he retained a smattering of German and Hebrew, and the memory of a whipping from his teacher. Uncle Peretz relieved the tedium of the boy's schooling and private tutoring with outings and fishing trips for which he fitted his nephew with a specially crafted life vest of cork because, said Uncle Peretz, "A man should live if only to satisfy his curiosity."

A year passed. Throughout the separation, Amelia corresponded with Anna for news of her children, particularly her youngest son. When Uncle Peretz announced his desire to adopt the boy, Amelia became frantic. "You must not leave Joe behind," she wrote her daughter. "You must bring him with you to America."

She could have put her anxiety to rest. Hirshhorn had no wish to remain with Aunt Zetta. "She feeds me well," he told his sister, "and she dresses me nicely. But one thing—she's crazy. All the time she bathes me. She gets up at three o'clock in the morning to give me a bath."

Later, this childhood aversion, reversed, became a Hirshhorn maxim: "If it's clean, it can't be bad." After using a tub or wash-basin, he rinsed it, even when lodging in the best hotels.

Hirshhorn's qualms about Aunt Zetta were evidently shared by Uncle Peretz, who was fond of reiterating, "Your health comes first; but you can always hang yourself." One day he slipped off and went to live with his brother in South Africa.

When Amelia sent six ship's tickets from America, Anna rounded up her siblings and made for Libau. Uncle Peretz and Aunt Zetta accompanied them to the port to say farewell and to present their little nephew with a portmanteau filled with clothing. Three weeks later in Liverpool, Anna herded her charges into steerage aboard the SS *Cedric*, which sailed for America on September 26, 1907. The voyage took nine days.

Each morning Anna dressed Hirshhorn in crisp garments pro-vided by Uncle Peretz. No sooner was he clothed than he made for the hatch to clamber on deck. A man leaning against the first-class rail smiled down at the boy and suddenly threw a golden sphere toward Hirshhorn. Deftly the boy caught it. It was an orange, the first he had seen. He looked up. The man, still smiling, gestured an invitation. Without an instant's hesitation, Hirshhorn scampered up the gangway. During the entire crossing he was the guest of the gods of the upper decks, beguiling them with his charm. "Joey," said Anna, "always wanted to be in first class."

On October 5, 1907, the *Cedric* entered New York harbor. Amelia waited on the dock. Delayed in clearing immigration, the Hirshhorn children had their first meal in America as dinner guests of the United States Government on Ellis Island. At nightfall they trudged ashore. Amelia embraced them and shepherded them across the Williamsburg Bridge to the Brooklyn tenement at 32 Morell Street.

The very next day Hirshhorn began his American education. Descending to the street, he came upon some boys huddled back of the stairs around a pair of rolling dice. Ignorant of the sport, speak-ing no English, Hirshhorn had three pennies, incentive enough for the others to induct the greenhorn into the mysteries of the spotted cubes. The easy mark won 18 cents and broke up the play. In con-sternation, his tutors set upon him, raided his pockets, and left him on the hallway floor dazed but wiser in the mores of the gutter.

In Williamsburg, the Hirshhorns changed addresses seven times in fifteen years. By taking advantage of the fierce competition between landlords who offered tenants leases with two to three months free rent, Amelia managed with each move to upgrade slightly her family's living condition. But conditions changed little for Hirshhorn. In school, when his class lined up according to height, he was unfailingly in first place. He suffered gibes. "Ask your ma to bury you in the sand in Coney Island; that'll make you grow." Amelia comforted him. "You don't have to be tall to be great," she said.

Hirshhorn did not attain his full height of 64 inches until his early twenties. At sixteen he still had not broken the 5-foot barrier. His future sister-in-law, Ruth, graduating from Eastern District High School, sent him an invitation to her commencement exercises. At the auditorium entrance the doorman refused Hirshhorn admittance because he could not be persuaded that the boy was sixteen.

At P. S. 145, his teacher, Tim Jordan, once reprimanded him for creating disorder. "You little shrimp!" Mr. Jordan called out from the regal height of 6 feet. "You just stop that."

Hirshhorn retorted, "If I'm a little shrimp, you're a big shrimp."

Mr. Jordan said no more, but later, playing down the block, Hirshhorn spied his teacher coming out of his tenement doorway. When he got home, Hirshhorn's mother, shocked by his disrespect for a teacher, struck him across the mouth. Hirshhorn felt the injustice of the blow, not the pain.

Choice did not always decide the Hirshhorns' moves. On May 3, 1908, the family was asleep in their second-floor flat at 17 Humboldt Street. A cry pierced the night followed by a battering on the street entrance below. Herman went to investigate. The hallway was an inferno, the stairs enveloped in flames. He slammed the door, roused his mother and the children, and herded them into the front room. Fire engines careened into Humboldt Street to disgorge men, hoses, and life nets. Herman leaned out the window and waved to the firemen. They spread a net. Herman grabbed Hirshhorn and tossed him into the net, where he bounced to his feet. One by one, Herman jettisoned Irving, Dora, and Abe. He coaxed the five older girls onto the sill to make the jump. Next he assisted his mother, but something went wrong. She overshot the net and landed on the pavement where she lay inert, unconscious. An ambulance took her to St. Catherine's, where she was hospitalized for internal injuries.

The fire, starting in the basement, had gutted the four-story building. Despite several spectacular rescues, the nine engines and three truck companies responding to the triple alarm could not save six from death, including an entire family trapped on the top floor.

The hairline separating Amelia and her family from disaster thinned further. Six days a week from eight to five, Ella and Frieda were employed at the Triangle Shirtwaist factory, sewing bodices in the style set by Charles Dana Gibson. On a Saturday in March the girls requested leave to quit an hour early to prepare for a masquerade party that night. Permission was denied with a warning from the forelady not to return if they disobeyed. Nonetheless, Ella and Frieda took off, departing from the eighth floor a few minutes to four. At 4:10 a conflagration swept through the building's top three stories. One hundred and forty-six Triangle workers burned or plunged to death.

To seal off her terror, Amelia purchased insurance policies for her family. Every Saturday evening a knock at the door heralded the agent of Prudential Life on his round of collections. Amelia paid him a dollar premium to assure the cost of burial to each of her ten children. At Christmas, the insurance agent left behind his firm's greetings, an illustrated calendar. Legend has it that this token of good business engendered the $50 million art treasure which sixty-five years later came to reside on the Washington Mall.

In the drabness of the Brooklyn tenement, the calendars introduced the excitement of color. Each month as Hirshhorn tore off a calendar leaf, before his child's eyes passed the world of the French Salon artists: panoramas of battle, animals, religious scenes, all the staples of the nineteenth-century academicians—of Adolphe-William Bouguereau, who could depict oversized nymphs dallying with a satyr on a 6 by 8-foot canvas without a hint of sensuality, or Sir Edwin Landseer, whose dogs had a mawkish appeal. Hirshhorn's bedroom walls were painted the green of a police night court and he covered up the ghastly expanse with the illustrations cut from the calendars. Nightly, before sleep overcame him, the last things he saw were those pictures, and mornings he woke to them.

A vision formed in young Hirshhorn's mind the day his fifth grade class set out for a field meet on Staten Island. Marching with his track teammates across the Williamsburg Bridge, Hirshhorn had his first view of Manhattan. In the foreground loomed the steel skeleton of the Woolworth Building. To the south rose the skyscrapers of the financial district. The way to Battery Park and the ferry wound down Nassau to Broad Street, where the Curb Market in those days literally conducted its stock transactions on the street between Beaver Street and Exchange Place. The spectacle Hirshhorn beheld stopped him dead in his tracks.

The scene could have been painted by Breughel. Men darted

about in a swirl of color, hatted in red, pink, green, some in shirts with special collars. Out of the tangle of bodies rose arms wigwagging signals to the windows of the buildings on both sides of the street whence came semaphores in code to confederates on the pavement below. From all sides rose shouts of offers, bids, and buys. The din was paralyzing.

Little Hirshhorn stood rooted, oblivious to everything but the fascination before him. While the rest of P. S. 145 tramped onward to Bowling Green and disappeared across the bay, Hirshhorn remained where he was until the Curb closed. He never ran the relay against Staten Island.

At the age of ten, Hirshhorn became a newsboy. He took his stand on one of the five corners converging at Broadway and Flushing to hawk the *New York Sun* and the *Evening Journal*, or boarded the trolleys to vend his papers to workers homeward bound. The newsies waited on one corner, across from Batterman's Department Store, for the trucks to dump the bundles of dailies and, whiling away the time, they entertained one another with song and dance. There Hirshhorn learned the "buck-and-wing" which he delighted in performing all his life.

Hirshhorn handed his earnings over to Amelia and received a weekly allowance of a quarter. Four-fifths of this went for admission to B. F. Keith's Gates Theater, the Fox Follies, or the neighborhood burlesque house. A nickel bought a small pie—"We never had them at home; Mama baked only strudel"—which Hirshhorn munched during the shows with the same relish he derived from the antics of Joe Laurie, Jr., George Burns, Jack Benny, and Gypsy Rose Lee. He became a devotee of Jack London from film versions of *Burning Daylight* and *Call of the Wild* and others starring Hobart Bosworth as the hero of the frozen north. On a Saturday night Herman treated his young brothers to the Turkish baths on Segal Street and Manhattan Avenue, were they luxuriated overnight and breakfasted on bagels and lox.

At twelve, Hirshhorn worked in an optometry and jewelry store owned by S. Lesnick and Sons of Bay Ridge, cousins of Myron and David Selznick of Hollywood. During the day he ran errands—"I was fast; I'd be back before I started"—and evenings at closing he helped transfer the trays of gems to the safe. One morning, sweeping up before opening, he found a ring with a fair-sized diamond in a corner by the window, ostensibly dropped the night before as the trays were stored. Hirshhorn took the jewel to the proprietor, who received it gratefully, pleased at the boy's honesty. As a reward for passing the test, Lesnick permitted him to dress the windows and to utilize his free moments winding the clocks.

Running errands for the jeweler took Hirshhorn across the East River to Maiden Lane, where he soon became familiar with Manhattan's financial district, and beyond, a short distance to the north, with the streets of the Lower East Side. On one trip, Anna entrusted him with a delivery of ties she sewed nights at home.

Trotting along Allen Street near Delancey, Hirshhorn was accosted by a stranger. "Hey, kid, you want to make an easy quarter?" Hirshhorn halted, seeing visions of an extra show and apple pie at the Fox Follies. "See that house?" the man indicated. "Take this message up to the fourth floor. Here, I'll hold the packages for you."

Depositing them in the man's arms, Hirshhorn bounded up the steps and returned swiftly, flushed and expectant. The man was gone. So were the ties. When he reported the loss to Anna she did not scold him. She didn't have to. He berated himself mercilessly.

One day Jennie Berman came home to tell her sister, Ruth, "I met the cutest little fellow at school today." It was Hirshhorn. When Ruth saw him, she was impressed by his modesty and manners, the pleasant directness of his personality. Soon Hirshhorn was walking Jennie to school every day and carrying her books. They adored one another.

Jennie was thirteen, tinier than Hirshhorn and eighteen months older. Her father, a tailor, had died when Jennie was nine. She went from grammar school to Manhattan Trade to become a seamstress skilled enough to work in the alterations department of Bergdorf Goodman. When her mother moved their home to the Bronx, Hirshhorn frequently visited the steam-heated flat, particularly in winter when it offered relief from his Brooklyn tenement which was so cold that knives and forks were difficult to handle at mealtime.

At thirteen, Hirshhorn became a Bar Mitzvah in a synagogue on Moore Street, the one his mother attended. To please her, he dutifully continued his religious observances until he graduated from elementary school. The Sabbath candles Amelia lit on Friday evenings, the mezuzzah on the doorpost of their flat, her attendance at synagogue, all connected her with her spiritual past, slender pickets in a fence of tradition by which she separated herself from her alien, often hostile, surroundings. But Hirshhorn wanted one thing only: to eradicate the stench of penury. He had no father to wash it away with immigrant sweat, to give his child a leg up to a better life.

Forced into the dual role of son and provider, he departed from the ways of his mother. He went on to Bushwick High School and to jobs in the afternoons and on Saturdays.

But classrooms slowed his progress toward riches. After a couple of months he dropped out of Bushwick High and enrolled in evening sessions at Eastern District which allowed him to return to full-time employment in the jewelry store at $20 a week.

Every time errands took him to Maiden Lane, shopkeepers enticed him to come to work for them. The bait did not tempt him. He was irked by the dullness of work in the shop, by the daily trip to Bay Ridge which required transfers to two Els and a trolley, and by late homecomings. Above all, the prospect was unattractive. Not quite fifteen, Hirshhorn quit his job and his school. His mother was appalled at his disregard for the family's wants and her anxiety turned to anger. She slapped him. But Hirshhorn was undeterred. He had taken his first gamble—on himself.

■ ■ □ □

Hirshhorn arrived on Wall and Broad streets in the summer heat of 1915. The First World War cloaked the stock market in a pall. The Curb and New York exchanges suspended operation. Trading stood still. Instead of the frenetic scene of his fancy, Hirshhorn found men lounging on the steps of the Treasury Building listlessly playing cards. Gone were the variegated hats, the unusual shirts and collars, the bustle, the roar. So poor were conditions that the straw-kelly of summer was nowhere in evidence; everyone sweated under his winter derby.

Hirshhorn walked up to one group to inquire about a job. The men laughed. "Hell, sonny, we're looking for work ourselves." Hirshhorn gazed from them to the cards, turned away, and walked west to the new Equitable Building at 120 Broadway.

He took the elevator and, starting on the thirty-fifth floor, worked his way down three levels, applying at American Smelting, Nevada Copper, and about fifteen other offices. In each, the same man appeared to interview the boy, which confused Hirshhorn and irritated the man. He informed the lad that Guggenheim Brothers occupied all the offices on the three floors and there was no opening in any of them. On the twenty-eighth story, Hirshhorn knocked and opened the door to the Emerson Phonograph Company. The manager, Billy Colen, regarded the little fellow in knee-pants.

"Can you work a switchboard?" he asked.

Hirshhorn looked him in the eye and said, "No, but I can learn."

"Come back Saturday," said Colen.

Down to the street went Hirshhorn and up Broadway to the New York Telephone Company. From a sympathetic receptionist he obtained permission to study the switchboard. By the week's end, he could handle the plugs, lights, and toggles with an ease he drew upon in later days as a trader.

On Saturday he presented himself to Colen and was hired as office boy and switchboard operator. Hirshhorn had a foothold in the environs of the market, if not in its affairs. His salary, $6, fell $14 short of his weekly pay at the jeweler's. To make up the difference, he scouted for additional work, something closer to his goal. He hit upon the Western Union service at Fulton and Broadway, only a stone's throw from the Stock Exchange, where the night shift hummed with cabled reports of the European market. An hour after the day ended at Emerson found him dashing about the block-square building bearing messages for transmission to traders on the bourse abroad. Like Nathan Rothschild scooping the news of Waterloo, he perused cables before delivering them, receiving in the process an education in market procedures and confirming his guess that, buyer or seller, profit or loss, the gain was always the broker's, and the more transactions the merrier.

From 6 P.M. to 2 A.M., for $12 a week, Hirshhorn ran rounds which frequently took him to Cyrus J. Lawrence and Company, brokers since 1830. Its senior partner, the son-in-law of Harry Lawrence, was W. J. Hutchinson, who taught Hirshhorn the meaning of the squiggles on the market graphs as they registered the rise and fall of the stocks.

Hirshhorn also encountered Richard De Mille Wyckoff, "the tough crazy genius" who owned the *Magazine of Wall Street* which published a financial trend letter on the floor below Emerson Phonograph. As a subscriber to the letter, Billy Colen, the Emerson manager, took advantage of the ticker in the publication office, and when the Stock Exchanges resumed activity, he monitored the market for Wyckoff. On the slightest pretext, Hirshhorn slipped down from the Emerson office to listen to the siren clack of the tape.

With the approach of Labor Day, Colen called for a volunteer among the four office boys at Emerson to work the holiday at the trend letter as a favor to Wyckoff. To the relief of the other three, Hirshhorn stepped forward. The day arrived and Hirshhorn knocked on the door of the publisher's private office.

"Mr. Wyckoff," he said, "I don't like being just an office boy. I want to learn to be a stockbroker. I don't know anyone; but you do business with Schuyler, Chadwick and Burnham. Please, Mr. Wyckoff, would you give me a chance and—"

"Joe," said Wyckoff, his voice striking terror, "you know I was a stockbroker. It's a terrible business. You don't want to be in it."

"Mr. Wyckoff," said the boy, "I love it."

The publisher seemed upset and Hirshhorn said no more. A week later Billy Colen approached him. "Joe," he said, "how would you like the job of watching the market down on the twenty-seventh floor?"

Hirshhorn left his job with Emerson for employment at the *Magazine of Wall Street*. He received a salary raise to $8 which, with his night work at Western Union, restored his weekly earnings to $20.

"I worked like a dog," he recalled. "In those days the market was wild. Stocks like Mexican Petroleum and Pan-American Petroleum hopped like frogs, and I had to note each dollar move, up and down, and the averages. It was great!"

In keeping with his station in the financial world, Amelia raised his allowance to 50 cents a day, which Hirshhorn budgeted rigidly: a dime for fare, another for lunch, and 15 cents for dinner. The rest he hoarded. To celebrate his new dignity, he took to himself a middle initial. Only 4-feet-11, he felt "it would add to my height," as in his eyes it did to that of Richard D. Wyckoff. For a time he used the "C" of his second Yiddish name, Choneh, which he translated sonorously into Joseph Conrad Hirshhorn, until he came upon his paradigm, Jesse L. Livermore. The double "L" had a distinguished look. Adopting the name of his eldest brother, Herman, he began to sign himself "Joseph H. Hirshhorn." And so it remained. The "H" might just as easily have stood for Horatio, of Alger fame.

Hirshhorn loved Wall Street. In the Equitable Building a few floors below where he worked, he discovered B. C. Forbes, founder of *Forbes Magazine*, whose sketches of the nation's fifty moguls he had read in *Leslie's Weekly*. Advertisements said the series was to be issued shortly in book form.

On a lunch hour Hirshhorn bustled down to the Forbes office. The girl behind the barrier heard the door open and shut but saw no one enter. Leaning over the bar, she beheld the serious face of a boy in green knee-pants. She inquired the purpose of his visit and was met by a torrential apostrophe to the fifty *Men Who Made America*, which ended with a declaration of his intention to buy the forthcoming volume.

The girl said, "It costs ten dollars."

"Okay," said Hirshhorn, "I'll take it."

Wide-eyed, she fetched Forbes to listen to the boy's discourse. "No volume," Hirshhorn declaimed to the publisher, "existed to enable the ambitious young man to make the intimate acquaintance of so many of the nation's foremost men of affairs, and learn from their own lips the most useful wisdom their eventful experiences have taught them."

Hearing his own rhetoric quoted from his advertisement, Forbes bowed to the flattery. The publisher autographed an advance copy and presented it to Hirshhorn for half-price. The boy pored over the sixteen cardinal qualities of those "certain men endowed by nature." Virtues "within the reach of all" ranged from "essential patience, perseverance and unflagging courage" to "superior judgment, personal magnetism and common sense." Thirstily Hirshhorn drank the mixture of idealism, platitude, and self-interest. He searched the lives of these fifty tycoons to discover what he had in common with them. Like himself, few had had formal schooling; a good number were short in stature; and many had lost their fathers in boyhood. Hirshhorn determined to be the fifty-first in that fraternity—with one difference. They had risen to their rank at an average age of sixty-one. Hirshhorn, in a hurry, did not intend to take that long.

After months of moonlighting as a messenger, Hirshhorn's feet were blistered. Again he gambled. He resigned from Western Union without even bothering to collect his final two weeks' pay. Years later at a businessmen's lunch he met the president of Western Union. "You owe me twenty-four dollars," Hirshhorn said. The following day a check arrived—by mail.

At the *Magazine of Wall Street* Hirshhorn toiled beside Thomas L. Sexsmith, who wrote the trend letter which had shocked the skeptics by predicting that U.S. Steel would go from 40 to 90. It did. From him Hirshhorn learned to read the ticker, to chart stocks, and to interpret the track on the graph. Hirshhorn decided to test his acuity as a trader. He put his hoard of nickels and dimes on the line.

"I was fifteen years old," Hirshhorn laughed, "and I always fascinated older men. One guy, a darling little fat man named Cevasco, made these tiny buys for me. He'd say to me, Joe, why do you throw your money around? You can't win in this game. He didn't tell me he was running a bucket shop, and I guess I wouldn't have known what it was if he did. I didn't learn until later that they don't buy the stock; they put it on the cuff. When the price dropped, the buyer was wiped out and they pocketed the money. But it was great experience, a great education."

Wyckoff moved his trend letter midtown to the Marbridge Building and took Hirshhorn along, raising his salary in stages to $50. The boy gulped Automat lunches and raced to the Waldorf Hotel, nearby on Fifth Avenue and 34th Street, to study the trading board and to hang around the ticker tape with one of the regulars, Jacob Fields, an old and respected member of the Stock Exchange, and shorter even than Hirshhorn in stature. Together, the septuagenarian and the teenager scrutinized the market, discussed its action, and swapped opinions, in the course of which Hirshhorn imparted his ambition to his new friend. Observing his young companion over several months and liking what he saw, old Jake Fields said one day, "Hey, Joe, why the hell don't you go down to the Curb? Go on over and tell my son Eddie that I'll guarantee your account."

Hirshhorn hustled back to the office and cornered the publisher. "Mr. Wyckoff," he said, "I can't learn anything more working here. I want to quit."

"Why?" Wyckoff asked.

"Because," the boy replied, "I want to start trading. I don't have any money but I've got—"

"I'll stake you," Wyckoff cut in, "two hundred and fifty dollars, on condition you stay on here at the magazine."

Hirshhorn sensed his employer's need to keep him. For the time being the arrangement suited them both. When Hirshhorn eventually struck out on his own, his replacements were a man and two girls at an aggregate salary of $150.

Down to 50 Broad Street went Hirshhorn to set up an account with Leonard J. Fields and Company, run by old Jake's sons, Leonard and Edward. At the end of several months, Hirshhorn was able to repay Wyckoff and show a reserve of an equal amount plus $5. He also resigned. With Papa Fields's warranty, he departed for the Curb.

Each morning at eight, an hour before appearing on the Street, and again after the closing bell, Hirshhorn charted stocks for W. J. Hutchinson, who paid him $25 a week. Another client was Walter Case of Case-Pomeroy, investment bankers, whose Curb business Hirshhorn acquired. In the winter of 1916, age sixteen, he took his place in the crowd of traders on Broad Street. He stationed a broker in a fourth-floor window to whom he wigwagged signals which he changed periodically. Once a code was cracked, the trader was at the mercy of specialists in the crowd who by anticipating orders to buy and sell could raise or lower prices accordingly. Some brokers maintained phones in adjacent basements and protected themselves with couriers who dashed out to the street to place and pick up orders.

Still in short pants, the feisty little trader met hostility from several competitors, particularly the Gallagher Brothers, who were specialists in the stocks Hirshhorn traded and, until then, had monopolized the field. Their malice went so far as to stuff chunks of ice down the lad's collar.

"They were two husky guys," Hirshhorn remembered with a chuckle. "The one with a moustache was bright, the other one wasn't. Until I busted into the crowd, they were making money like they had a cash register. I made up my mind they'd have to kill me to get me out. The only way I knew to win was to take it out of their pocketbooks."

The method he devised he later used with success in Canada. Holding a large order for a stock selling at $12, Hirshhorn sent a broker into the crowd to shout "buys" at the lowest bid—"You could hear him in Brooklyn"—and Hirshhorn would offer the buy at 10. Pretty soon the Gallaghers had to match the price, whereupon Hirshhorn bought from them. After a while the decoy faded from the crowd; the price returned to 12 and Hirshhorn earned not only his broker's commission but the gratitude of his customer. He turned over a steady rate of $20,000 in weekly trading, and ten months after his seventeenth birthday had earned $167,000, multiplying his original stake almost 660 times.

Wyckoff took Hirshhorn to lunch at Fraunces Tavern. "Joe," his former employer said, "I need your advice."

"What kind of advice can I give you?" Hirshhorn asked in astonishment.

Wyckoff explained. His magazine needed to do what Forbes had done with *Men Who Made America*. Hirshhorn suggested that he write a book on the technique of buying and selling, print a limited edition, and price it at $500. Wyckoff autographed the first copy for Hirshhorn. The entire edition sold out.

Hirshhorn made his mother quit her job and moved her to a house in St. Albans, Long Island. Subsequently he transferred her to nearby Laurelton, where she remained until her death in 1943. Throughout the vicissitudes of his career, Hirshhorn sent her a monthly remittance. "She never spent it all," Hirshhorn told me. "I'd ask her: 'Mama, what do you do with the money?' and she'd turn away saying, 'Don't ask me, Joe, I spend it.' I guess she gave it to my brothers and sisters." And pausing a moment, Hirshhorn added, "That's one good thing I did."

He also graduated to his first suit of long pants. It cost $7. By the end of a year, the trousers had to be patched. His shoes rarely fit since his mother bought them sizes too large so they would last longer on a growing boy. He owned three shirts, which his sisters laundered and ironed.

To Brooklyn's young blades, Weber and Heilbroner dictated the fashion, and thither Hirshhorn repaired to deck himself cap-à-pie in keeping with his new fortune: two suits, a supply of shirts and neckties (replaced in 1950 by clip bowties), cuff links, tie clips, gloves, and a Dobbs hat. With his feet shod in French, Shriner and Urner shoes, he felt himself properly outfitted.

"I became a gentleman," said Hirshhorn.

That season, too, the first sign of the collector appeared. Browsing in the second-hand bookshops along Fourth Avenue looking for biographies of tycoons, Hirshhorn came upon the Phaidon series of art books imported from England. He picked them up at $2 each and in one of them discovered Albrecht Dürer. Near Exchange Place, in the financial district, Hirshhorn chanced upon Assenheim and Son at 37 New Street, seller of "Paintings and Art since 1870." The window displayed the work of the sixteenth-century German engraver. Hirshhorn purchased two engravings, paying $75 each. He never parted with them.

World War I drew to a close. Hirshhorn continued charting stocks for W. J. Hutchinson. Evenings, he lingered with the older men of the "back room set," enjoying their camaraderie and a good deal of horseplay. Often he did a spirited buck-and-wing with George Courtney, an ex-vaudevillian. Theirs grew into a lasting friendship. In the twenties, Hirshhorn employed Courtney for a short time, and continuously for twenty-four years beginning in 1945.

One evening, Weiss, the cashier, took the youth aside. "Listen, kid," he said, "you know who Bodman is?"

"Sure," said Hirshhorn. "George M. Bodman. He's senior partner here."

"Right," said Weiss, lowering his voice. "He's buying Lackawanna Steel."

"What about it?" asked Hirshhorn.

"Don't you know?" Weiss asked in surprise. "He's married to the daughter of the company's president."

It was a rare bit of inside information. If the president's son-in-law was buying Lackawanna Steel, that's what Hirshhorn ought to do—the chance of a payoff for months of drudgery. He began to pick up the stock at 62, then at 55, more and more as the price dropped. It occurred to him that if he was buying, someone was selling; however, the unimpeachable tip stilled his doubts.

"What did I know at eighteen?" Hirshhorn commented. "I was a kid. It was inside information, so I kept buying the goddamn stock. A week before the war ended, the false armistice busted the market wide open and I was knocked out of the box, sold out of my position. It taught me a lesson I've never forgotten: never buy a stock on a scale-down unless you're an insider. Wyckoff wrote that in his book and I read it; yet I did it! How stupid could I be?"

■ ■ □ □

Chastened, Hirshhorn started over. He studied the Forbes book and learned the iron rule: deal in money not in goods or services. He read Matthew Josephson and saw how the Robber Barons acted out the tenets of the Street—J. P. Morgan and the steel monopoly; John D. Rockefeller and the oil monopoly; Samuel Insull and his "natural monopoly" of utilities. Wall Street continued to admire Jay Cooke, who had paid newspaper editors to boost the sale of $2.5 billion worth of Civil War bonds as sound patriotic investments from which he realized $100 million in commissions. Commodore Vanderbilt turned the "short" tables on an adversary in the Erie Railroad manipulation, then quipped, "He that sells what isn't his'n/Must buy it back or go to pris'n."

Hirshhorn's ideal was Jesse L. Livermore. Not only had he patterned his initials after the Boy Plunger, but Hirshhorn was struck by similarities in their beginnings. Livermore had started at $6 a week posting stock quotations, had parlayed $12 into $2,500 in "bucket shops," and had sold Union Pacific short for a profit of a quarter of a million. The year Hirshhorn landed in America, Livermore, then thirty, had manipulated the market up and down for Anaconda Copper to clear $3 million. First, Hirshhorn adopted Livermore's trading techniques. Later, he also imitated a few facets of his private life.

With the $4,000 remaining to him after the Lackawanna fiasco, Hirshhorn resumed his climb uphill. Despite an unfavorable market and unstable conditions, slowly his $4,000 grew to $8,000 and then to $10,000. In 1921 he established a partnership with Thomas Sexsmith, his former associate at the *Magazine of Wall Street*, who was then counselor to Patrick Cusick. Hirshhorn engaged J. Victor Galley as office manager, and George Courtney, returned from a hitch in the merchant marine, came aboard as cashier and bookkeeper. Sexsmith and Company was financed by Hirshhorn for $20,000, with $40,000 more supplied by Cusick, whom Courtney described as "a Scranton brewer during Prohibition and a mortician who had a contract to bury all members of the mob run over by the Lackawanna Railroad." In addition to his place on the Curb, Hirshhorn purchased a seat on the Consolidated Exchange.

From Monday to Friday, Hirshhorn disposed of lunch while manning the phones. Saturday was another matter. After the market closed at noon, he and Courtney repaired to the Epicure, a pseudo-Hungarian house at Broad and Beaver, to dine on goulash, spaetzle, and chicken paprikash. Saturday night they double-dated, attending a Broadway show or the Metropolitan. Hirshhorn favored *La Bohème* and hated German opera. He walked out on *Die Walküre* because it was "cruel and raw." That summer he and Courtney shared a bungalow in Brighton Beach and went to the movies with their girls.

Early the following year, Hirshhorn married Jennie. While they were on their honeymoon, his office manager, Galley, traded the company "into the cellar." For a year Hirshhorn labored to rescue it, but the company went broke. The partnership dissolved and Patrick Cusick picked up the debts.

Late in 1925, Hirshhorn formed a partnership under the name of McCann and Company composed of John McQuade and Michael J. McCann, a young trader whose prime recommendation was his $1,300 in cash. With McQuade as cashier, Hirshhorn conducted the business from a modest office on the third floor of 50 Broad Street, scrounging for customers, and lunching at the phones to maintain the flow of trade. By the middle of 1926, the company showed a net of $50,000 and was escalating its monthly action to $200,000. Hirshhorn terminated the partnership, paying $18,000 to McCann, who departed, and $12,000 to McQuade, who stayed on as cashier. Hirshhorn's share was $20,000, with which he established Joseph H. Hirshhorn and Company in larger quarters on the fifth floor. Unencumbered with partners, he increased his staff by three bookkeepers, two men at the trading table, a switchboard operator, and an auditor. This last was David Tarlow, who continued with Hirshhorn for over a half-century. The others remained in his employ variously from five to twenty years.

Racing toward his goal, Hirshhorn felt the pressures mount. One safety valve was office hijinks. Catching someone unawares behind a newspaper, he would steal up and set fire to the journal. Anyone who entered his office wearing a straw hat had it snatched from his head and a fist rammed through the crown, and watched as it sailed out the window onto Broad Street. Hirshhorn compensated his victims with the price of a new boater.

By 1927, Hirshhorn presented the very model of a Wall Street broker. In his cluttered office, behind a battery of phones, he sat beside a glass-domed ticker, teeth clenched on a Corona Belvedere cigar, one hand holding the tape, the other held by a manicurist. A barber trimmed his hair, a waiter from the Savarin Restaurant served lunch, and all the while Hirshhorn shouted orders and advices to two associates at the phones. Bells rang incessantly. As a trader, he was on his way to paying the highest phone bills and the most in commissions to brokers, more than any other individual in the stock market.

■ ∎ □ □

Hirshhorn attracted women. Despite his lack of height, even in middle age, his dynamism, according to one young woman, "exuded a primal force which was sexy." He, however, preferred to convey the impression that he never made his way with women, rather that they always made their way with him.

"I've been afraid of them," Hirshhorn once declared. "I've always kept them at arm's length."

Ironically, his one episode of known misogyny resulted in his betrothal to Jennie Berman.

Frequently, in the course of his business with the brokerage firm of Rodney-Powers, Hirshhorn met its cashier, a young woman older than himself. One evening in November of 1921, she invited him to dine at her home in Brooklyn, near where Hirshhorn lived and a good deal closer than Jennie's place in the Bronx. He accepted. Dinner, a cozy affair, produced in the young lady an ungovernable desire for Hirshhorn. Unnerved, he excused himself and fled.

On his next trip to the Bronx, he recounted his experience to Jennie. She meditated deeply on his words.

"Joe, " she said at last, "why don't we get married?"

On January 12, 1922, at a catered affair on 110th Street and Lexington Avenue, with Hirshhorn's niece as flower girl, he and Jennie were wed by Cantor Joseph Rosenblatt. For $30 a month they rented a five-room apartment in the Bronx, on Walton Avenue and

181st Street, which Hirshhorn invited his mother- and sister-in-law to share. The newlyweds took off on a trip through the United States.

What he saw made Hirshhorn realize that the Stock Exchange was almost parochial as a means to wealth. A world beckoned beyond Manhattan. California particularly entranced Hirshhorn. Carried away, he bought a 250-acre chicken farm in Santa Rosa. He made a down payment of $500 and steeped himself in the literature of white Leghorns. A month passed in this feathery idyll. At its end, Hirshhorn forfeited the deposit and hurried back to New York with his bride.

In September of 1923, his first daughter, Robin, was born and Hirshhorn, because of his business reverses, had to borrow money to pay the bills at Polyclinic Hospital. With the new arrival crowding the Walton Avenue apartment, Hirshhorn sold his seat on the Consolidated Exchange and early in 1924 purchased a house for his family on Sutphin Boulevard in Queens. Jennie turned two of the rooms into the Rose Lantern Dress Shop, named for her mother, who tended to sales. Sister Ruth kept the books and Jennie did the buying. Her enterprise thrived during the next two years.

Plump, pink, shorter than her husband, Jennie Hirshhorn looked at the world through wide-set hazel eyes which readily filled with tears. She was hardly ever at a loss for words, but she was also a good listener. Friends and strangers knew her generosity which, like her kindness, flowed freely though with an odd detachment as if the better to exercise her judgment. Beneath the pink and plumpness hid a layer of steel.

In 1926, three years after Robin, a second daughter, Gene, was born to the Hirshhorns. Jennie loved her children fiercely. Her passion was the unity of the family.

"Jennie," said Hirshhorn, "was a better mother than I was a father."

That same year, Hirshhorn purchased a house in Great Neck, Long Island, in Gatsby country not far from Jesse Livermore's many-splendored estate. Jennie created a home that was Edwardian in spirit and decor, staffed with a butler, a cook, upstairs-downstairs maids, and a chauffeur for the three cars in the garage. Hirshhorn's phobia against poverty dictated that everything be brand-new—the thick-piled carpeting, the English-style furniture, china, and silver. But soon thereafter Hirshhorn became aware that old did not necessarily mean poor. He discovered that with antiques age increased their value. The reproduction furniture and wall-to-wall carpeting were replaced with antiques and Oriental rugs.

Horrified at how much a brand-new Cadillac depreciated the moment it left the showroom, Hirshhorn opted for vintage cars, but not until 1957 did he treat himself to a Rolls-Royce. However, because of his aversion to leather the car's elegant kid upholstery was replaced with cloth.

Weekends, the Hirshhorn home hummed with relatives, friends, and business associates. Hirshhorn delighted Jennie with his high spirits and anecdotes, doing his buck-and-wing, kissing and fondling her openly in front of their guests.

In 1927 Hirshhorn sailed with Jennie and his mother for Latvia, where his sister, Rahla, still ran the general store in Jukst. Later, widowed in 1935, Rahla and her five children were brought to Laurelton, Long Island, to live in a house across from where Amelia dwelt with Anna, her husband, and two daughters. Reunited after three decades, forty Hirshhorns would gather round Amelia's table on holidays.

■ ■ □ □

Hirshhorn's firm drew to it Lewis B. Hughes, a junior partner in J. K. Rice and Company. Hughes was said to have exchanged the military for Wall Street, where his family connections and golf companions produced enough income to indulge his taste for expensive tailors and restaurants, and a weakness for the racetrack. A better judge of the market than of horseflesh, Hughes earned large sums, all of which vanished down the home stretch. He played two roles in Hirshhorn's life: a minor one in introducing him to H. Preston (Chic) Coursen, who became Hirshhorn's attorney, and a major one in alerting him to the approaching disaster of 1929.

Corporate earnings were climbing, dividends increasing. The boom of business echoed in the title of the musical *Whoopee!*, starring Eddie Cantor at the New Amsterdam. New Yorkers crowded the city's 32,000 speakeasies. Lionel Barrymore arrived from Los Angeles in forty-eight hours by air and rail. And Jennie was pregnant for the third time.

Hirshhorn worried. Loans to speculators from Wall Street brokers exceeded $6 billion by mid-year. The public bought not stocks but quotations. The big bulls ran the market up and steadied the prices at new fever highs of buying. When it reached the point "where doctors and dentists quit their jobs to speculate," Hirshhorn's uneasiness turned to fear. Heeding Hughes' warning, early in August he disposed of all his holdings for $4 million.

On September 1, 1929, twenty-nine utilities were up by $5.8 billion, and trading during the previous month topped 95.7 million shares. Four days later, nature imitated the market and sent the mercury up to a record 94 degrees. At 2 P.M. "out of a clear sky," said the *Times*, "a storm of selling broke." In one hour the sale of 2 million shares wiped out thousands of small speculators. Aghast at his close brush with ruin, Hirshhorn watched Jesse Livermore and W. C. Durant go down for the count. The New York Stock Exchange closed to reopen with a shortened day. To stem the rout, the federal government promised to cut income taxes. The *New York Times* headlined, MARKET SUCCESSFULLY MEETS TESTS OF STRENGTH, and on an inside page reported the suicide of W. Paul Baron, a Philadelphia broker.

Shaken, Hirshhorn embarked for Europe aboard the SS *Leviathan*. In mid-Atlantic a steward handed him a batch of cables. In dismay he read that he had just purchased several thousand shares of stock. Phone communications at sea were then nonexistent, and it took several wireless exchanges for him to learn that Jennie, thinking to aid her husband in a market momentarily leveled, had interpreted the immense volume of sales as a time for smart buying. Frantically Hirshhorn cabled orders to sell and dispatched to Jennie entreaties to desist from trading and concentrate on her imminent childbirth.

Among his transoceanic shipmates was Lily Damita, a diminutive actress of firebrand repute. Tales soon circulated of Hirshhorn's passionate pursuit of Miss Damita above and below deck and across much of the Continent. Truth or myth, it was the first of several peccadilloes to disquiet Jennie.

Confronted with the story, Hirshhorn grunted a blunt, somewhat ungallant disclaimer. "Lily Damita? Never knew her from a bale of hay."

Hirshhorn landed back in New York in time to greet the arrival of his only son, Gordon, on September 20. On October 29 the market collapsed. At the National Academy of Design the annual winter exhibit included a painting, *The Fossil Hunters*, by Edwin M. Dickinson. When the photographer documenting the show could not determine what the work represented, it was found to be hanging on its side. The canvas had been displayed the same way the year before at the Carnegie International in Pittsburgh and the error had gone undetected for the duration of the exhibition. To Hirshhorn it typified, in the Bard's words, the "time out of joint."

The market was sluggish and Hirshhorn became restless. Normally, he steered clear of commercial ventures, but now he searched them out. "If a fellow down the block said he could grow fish," George Courtney recalled, "Joe would be interested in forming a company for a piece of the action."

Hirshhorn joined up with Jake Newmark. Erstwhile advertising director for W. C. Durant and General Motors, Jake touted papaya and its enzymes as a health drink. Hirshhorn backed it to the extent of employing a chemist and leasing a bottling plant but the laboratory could not eliminate the fruit's odor. The undertaking was sold to General Foods, which marketed it successfully. Another, a carbon monoxide eliminator devised by a scientist at Johns Hopkins, was financed by Hirshhorn and wound up with the Mine Safety Appliance Company in Pittsburgh.

Twice burned, Hirshhorn looked askance at the stranger who entered his office one day to show him a small cardboard cylinder with which he intended to revolutionize feminine hygiene. Five thousand dollars would buy Hirshhorn 2,500 shares. The scheme sounded "kooky" and the man smelled of whiskey. Hirshhorn sent him packing. A Canadian family put up the money and realized $15 million from the product that came to be known as Tampax.

The stock market continued to behave erratically. Hirshhorn's charts made no sense. The times called for prophets—or gamblers. Hirshhorn, who had scorned speculators, plunged in several stocks on the advice of his old master W. J. Hutchinson, most heavily in International Nickel, of which he bought 20,000 shares. The market burped and dribbled and after a year sank to the bottom. Hirshhorn persisted. Not until the fall of 1931 did he swallow his pride and sell. A few months later General Motors dived to $8, Chrysler to $3. The Samuel Insull empire collapsed and lost $2 billion for its investors. A bull in a bear market, Hirshhorn dropped $1.1 million. The loss being enough of a punishment, he kept his own counsel. His silence misled even close associates.

"Joe," said George Courtney, "came out thin like everyone else. He didn't stand up like the Statue of Liberty and escape the holocaust. He ate his lunch in the B/G sandwich joint. Everybody was going around in twenty-eight-dollar suits. Joe had no bankroll. He went up to Canada on a shoestring."

Hirshhorn said nothing to correct the impression.

When Hirshhorn made his killing in the 1929 market, Jennie had begun pressing him to quit and attend to their inner lives. To him that was equivalent to going out for a coffee break and never coming back. Jennie prodded. She felt her lack of education. Her need for self-improvement made her night table groan under books by Havelock Ellis, Freud, Adler, Jung, and Horney. Hirshhorn preferred the daily newspaper, and gorged on biographies of America's Bourbons and artists, world history, and rare-book catalogs.

"She read to support her attitudes," their son, Gordon, recollected. "He read to learn."

Jennie wounded Hirshhorn by disparaging his achievements. She wanted her husband home at regular hours. She was impatient with his uncontrollable drives—his obsession with the stock market and the endless phone calls into the night; with his compulsive collecting.

During slow spells in business, Hirshhorn would retrench by reducing the staff at home. Cheerfully Jennie and her mother would assume the household chores, but Jennie seethed with resentment upon learning Hirshhorn had spent thousands for a Shakespeare First Folio and a fifteenth-century edition of Cicero's *De Rhetorica* designed in vellum by Nicolaus Jenson. Jennie faulted her husband's manners, attacked his character—"You think everyone is out only for himself; you never trust anyone"—which precipitated interminable discussions. Finally, Hirshhorn softened to the extent of entertaining the idea of study at Cornell University. In 1930 they visited Ithaca.

"I didn't know anybody up there," Hirshhorn said, "and I kept thinking, What am I doing here? I was ambitious. You can't succeed—I don't care who you are—unless you give it a lot of energy, a lot of time, and a lot of thought. There's no short way—no shortcuts."

In June 1931, a third daughter, Naomi, was born to the Hirshhorns. The summer of the following year, Hirshhorn turned "very bullish on gold" and his old acquaintances William Hutchinson and Robert Stanley recommended that he investigate the mining scene in Canada. A three-week exploratory trip excited him. Returning, he learned Jennie was pregnant again. She was determined to abort. Vigorously, he opposed her. Hirshhorn volunteered to have a vasectomy, a radical procedure in those days. Jennie assented but she had the abortion nonetheless.

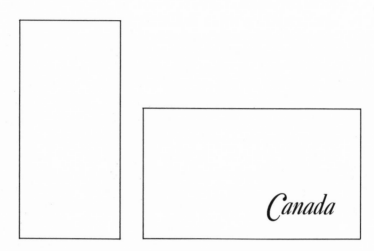

Canada

III Hirshhorn returned to Canada early in 1933. Almost a century after America began to move westward, 90 percent of Canada's population still huddled along the Dominion's southern border. Many Americans were drifting into virgin territory to explore its mineral riches.

By now Hirshhorn had thoroughly assimilated the precepts of his models, Andrew Carnegie, John D. Rockefeller, Collis P. Huntington, and Leland Stanford, who like himself had been in their twenties and early thirties when they set out in the 1860s to make their fortunes.

"Even when they drifted to the frontier," wrote Matthew Josephson in *The Robber Barons*, "they remained cool-headed and continent. . . . not to drink, to forego the gaming tables and red-lit bordellos, to be calculating, forever silently, furtively poring over books and accounts, scheming projects all night while others drank, laughed, danced and brawled—and died—this was the method and principle of the young men who were to conquer the wild frontier."

With slight emendations, Josephson could have been describing Hirshhorn standing on the threshold of Canada's wilderness.

On the day Franklin D. Roosevelt declared the "bank holiday" in March 1933, Hirshhorn entered the Canadian Imperial Bank, asked for the manager, Harry Suighet, and opened an account, depositing $60,000 in the name of Joseph H. Hirshhorn Limited of 302 Bay Street. He found the Toronto Stock Exchange devoted mostly to penny issues, the industrial market negligible, the New York Stock Exchange foreign, and Canadians hostile to Americans. Signs on the city's park benches read: "No Dogs and Jews Allowed." Forty-three years were to pass before every province, from Quebec to British Columbia, numbered Jews in their legislatures, and some in their cabinets as well. The main activity on the Toronto Exchange was gambling in mining stocks.

In his Bay Street office, Hirshhorn installed his specially designed console of phones with ninety-three direct lines to banks and brokers. He issued weekly "blue sheets" with 500 listings from New York and Toronto which he brokered like a one-man exchange. He used Wall Street houses accustomed to his trade and provided unprecedented volume to several Toronto firms, chiefly Tom and Barnt, and Lattimer and Company. He brought Jake Newmark to Toronto, and the former Speaker of the Michigan State Legislature became the "old gold commentator" of Canadian radio, broadcasting news and tips on the market supplied mainly by Hirshhorn's office.

"Toronto's society and its conservative fraternity," wrote Emmet Hughes, "did not celebrate his intrusion. Joe worked like a robot, chattered like a Brooklyn peddler and let his high spirits explode in such phrases as 'I feel felonious!' "

One afternoon, Hirshhorn bought fifteen bonds of Abitibi Paper. Confirmation of the sale failed to arrive routinely and Hirshhorn dispatched a messenger the next morning to pick up the certificates. No record was found of the transaction. Hirshhorn phoned the broker.

"What happened?" he inquired. "You sold me fifteen Abitibi at eleven."

"Listen, you goddamn New York Jew bastard," came the broker's response, "I did nothing of the kind. . . ." and he slammed down the receiver.

Across Hirshhorn's memory flashed the Gallagher Brothers on the New York Curb and how they had been brought to their knees. Similar reprisal was indicated here. The opportunity came when Thayer Lindsley, one of the elders of the mining community trading through Hirshhorn, turned the Beatty Gold Mine promotion over to him. Hirshhorn sent an undercover agent to bid on 15,000 shares. The offending broker offered 5,000 at 90 cents. Hirshhorn offered

92 and before long had whipped up a flurry to run the price up to $1.10. At that point, forced to respond to the market, the broker bought in at 20 cents above his original offer, and with his lost commissions his arrogance vanished. By the end of his first year in Toronto, Hirshhorn netted $300,000.

Throughout, Hirshhorn kept his eye glued to the big target: mining. On his office wall hung a sampler reading: "Imagination is the first law of creation." He had moved gradually up the scale from speculator to investor to trader. He turned his brokerage over to two employees, Kirkham and Scanlon, and cast himself in his ultimate role: creative promoter.

"You're a whore when you're a stockbroker," he declared. "I know what it's all about. You're a scavenger. Stockbrokers don't produce a goddamn thing. Neither does a banker."

On November 16, 1933, the *Northern Miner* carried a full-page advertisement conceived by Hirshhorn and executed by Jake Newmark. In part it read:

MY NAME IS OPPORTUNITY AND I AM PAGING CANADA

Canada, your day has come. The world is at your feet begging you to release your riches cramped in Mother Earth. . . . Carry on until the pick strikes the hard, firm, yellow metal, until the cry of "Gold!" resounds through the virgin forest. . . . As for us, we believe in the future of this great country to the extent that we have made investments in gold mining and other industries in the Dominion and shall continue to do so. . . .

In the words of Emmet Hughes, the announcement was "a mating call." Hirshhorn put it another way.

"Blue chips and dividends are all right for grandma," he said. "I've always wanted the proposition that cost a dime and paid ten dollars. You don't make money trading in and out of the market—not big money. You use your head and your ass—one to make up your mind, the other to sit on and wait. You have to have patience."

The prescription, in slightly different terms, was among the virtues B. C. Forbes had listed in his manual for moguls. Applying the second half of his formula, Hirshhorn sat back. As soon as prospectors and promoters got wind of him, they would beat a path to his door.

■ ■ □ □

Hirshhorn's knowledge of mining was scant, an ignorance he shared with most of Bay Street. Geology was a mystery to the majority of miners and prospectors who issued from the Canadian bush. As did their predecessors in the California gold rush, they came bearing shining tales in the hope of grubstakes. Mark Twain, a young reporter for the *Territorial Enterprise* in the days of the Comstock Lode, defined a mine as "a hole in the ground with a liar at the bottom."

Hirshhorn quickly discerned that a miner with a grubstake was a baited hook which the promoter cast into a sea of gudgeon. Circulating reports of drilling, most promoters ran their operation to make a killing on the sale of stock, walking off with profit on an undug hole. The public which frowned on roulette and dice tables smiled on these penny stocks. It took only an occasional promotion backed by a legitimate ore strike to keep appetites whetted. In this sea of offerings, stockbrokers swarmed like sharks, nosing about the market to detect a promoter's weakness, whereupon they struck, swiftly, surely, selling his stock short and sending their victim to the bottom.

"It wasn't a genteel operation," said Fred Wehran, a contemporary of Hirshhorn who witnessed the combat. "At times the whole goddamn tribe of brokers would get together to knock you down, using every trick in the trade from the moment the bell rang. The competition was ruthless and you had to be on the ball every day if you were in it."

No sooner did Hirshhorn's advertisement appear than two gold mine propositions turned up: Longlac, a straight investment; and Tashota, a "creative situation." The first proved profitable; the second exposed his ignorance. Tashota, because of incompetent engineering, resulted in "a little bit of a mine; a veal cutlet," a dish which cost Hirshhorn all he realized on Longlac. He had conducted himself like an ordinary sucker, again violating Wyckoff's dictum to be an insider, to deal the cards not to draw them. Hirshhorn's vision cleared. The "creative promoter" required not only guts but knowledge.

Hirshhorn scanned the minescape. Two men towered over all others. Thayer Lindsley, a geologist without equal in financing mines, had acquired the Falconbridge in Ontario after it had been abandoned by Thomas A. Edison when the inventor was a mere 20 feet from one of the biggest nickel deposits on the continent. And there was Gilbert LaBine, already a legend. Stranded in the white wilderness with a snowblind companion, he had scouted along Great Bear Lake, where his knowledge of geology located pitchblende. By 1933 his Eldorado Mines had produced the radium, and later uranium, which broke the world monopoly of the Belgian Congo.

Lindsley having granted him his first opportunity, the Beatty Gold Mine promotion, Hirshhorn's new man had to be Gilbert La-

Bine. With his brother, Charles, LaBine was about to launch the Gunnar Gold Mine at Beresford Lake in the river country of eastern Manitoba. To develop it, they would need a sharp-witted market man.

LaBine and Hirshhorn lived at the Royal York Hotel. They met and agreed that the brothers would put up $40,000 for 80,000 shares of treasury stock, and Hirshhorn would provide $90,000 for 600,000 vendor shares of which the LaBines held 742,000. The low price to Hirshhorn was to compensate him for his services as underwriter.

Early, Hirshhorn had realized that manipulation was the nature of the Toronto Stock Exchange, a game in which he had few peers. He started the Gunnar promotion at the end of January 1934. From March through May he advertised the stock at 55 cents and the Bay Street sharks, smelling blood, attacked, bearing down short. Hirshhorn, however, supported the price. The sales alone earned him $25,000 in commissions.

Hirshhorn spent the month of June in London nosing about the English financial scene. Returning, he stirred up the market so that in July the Gunnar stock zoomed to its high of $2.50. The fluctuations caused consternation and confusion in the Bay Street crowd. In October the action intensified. On the last day of the month, Gunnar opened in the morning at $1.43. Two hours later it plummeted to 94 cents. When the frenzy subsided, the Bay Street brokers were binding their wounds with canceled invoices and Hirshhorn had netted $1.1 million. Gunnar was financed.

Bay Street howled that the "public" had suffered grievous loss and called for an investigation of Hirshhorn and Gunnar. Coolly, Gilbert LaBine joined in the demand. The Ontario Securities Commission obliged and four months later, in February 1935, Commissioner J. M. Godfrey delivered his report.

"The debacle," said the Commissioner, "was caused by bear raiders. It was also attributed to short selling. Insiders had suddenly thrown on the market a large quantity of vendor shares." Then, as if biting his tongue, Godfrey reversed himself. "The drop in the stock," he said, "was not the result of an organized bear raid nor of short selling, or throwing on the market on October 31st of a large quantity of vendor shares." His analysis of that day disclosed "the curious fact that the sudden drop caused in the initial stages was by buying not selling."

"The day before," he stated, "there had been a recession of about seven cents. The floor traders thought on the 31st there would be support which would send shares up a few points. Many began to buy at the opening. They soon discovered, however, that while shares were being offered for sale, no one was bidding for the stock. To save themselves, they began to sell and notified their offices that Gunnar was not being supported. Officers called clients who, to protect their margins, had to sell. By noon, before the panic was over, the stock had reached a low of ninety-four cents. In the afternoon Mr. LaBine entered with his purchase of fifteen thousand shares and caused an upward movement."

The Commissioner likened the market proceedings that day to the game children played. "Somebody," he said, "would throw a brick in the air and shout, 'Whatever goes up is bound to come down; if you don't look out, you'll be hit in the crown.' Certainly a good many people were crowned by the sudden drop of Gunnar."

The crucial question was whether Hirshhorn was liable to prosecution. "He has not committed any criminal act," was the Commissioner's verdict. "Manipulation per se is not a crime. It is the conspiring with one or more persons to manipulate which is punishable." Manipulation, he went on to say, could be accomplished in a legal way. The manipulator sat in the center of his operation surrounded by telephones and bought and sold stocks without brokers knowing a manipulation was in progress. One broker might know that a certain party was buying; another would know only a certain party was selling. A skillful manipulator covered his tracks so the brokers he used in the transactions never had guilty knowledge of his operations. "And," said the Commissioner, "without guilty knowledge there can be no unlawful conspiracy."

Godfrey also gave Gilbert LaBine a clean bill. LaBine's support of the market had brought him almost 500,000 Gunnar shares. Neither brother had offered any of the 80,000 treasury issue for sale.

"If the company turns out to be a profitable undertaking, they will make a substantial fortune," the Commissioner concluded. "Mr. Hirshhorn had a different view. He was not prepared to wait to make his profit out of the mine."

The Gunnar Gold Mine produced bullion for seven years and yielded $4 million. Hirshhorn had learned his fundamental lesson in mine financing: know your ground before you make your stand. His rivals on Bay Street had not yet learned theirs.

Several days after the Gunnar decision, Hirshhorn received a notice of deportation from Ottawa. His "non-immigrant" status did not permit more than "casual business and pleasure," and the scale of his activities was deemed hardly casual. Hirshhorn appealed. Two uncertain months passed before the reversal of the decree and his reclassification to "landed immigrant making his home in Canada." The new category permitted him to conduct his business.

He began to spend Mondays through Thursdays in Toronto. Weekends he made for New York to divide the hours between his family in Great Neck and the art galleries and studios in Manhattan. Jennie's discontent deepened.

■ ■ □ □

Hirshhorn moved from the Royal York Hotel to a rented house on Old Forrest Hill Road. He stocked it with books on geology and mining, installed a housekeeping couple, and nightly entertained the best brains then scouring the bush and poking about the substrata of Canada. One in particular he regarded as "the most brilliant geologist in the country."

Douglas G. H. Wright reminded Hirshhorn of Uncle Peretz facially and in the regularity with which he hit the bottle. Wright's uncle was a member of the Supreme Court; his brother, Ward, was an attorney. Their mother was a leader of the temperance movement in Canada. Habitual drinking did not deter Doug Wright from regular attendance at church. Neither did it becloud his geology. From him Hirshhorn learned all about the Pre-Cambrian Shield.

Eight hundred million to 5 billion years ago it had been formed in the 30-mile-deep crust of the earth by molten masses periodically belched up from the core of the planet. Having piled up mountains and fissured canyons, the upheavals settled into comparative calm to make way for the Paleolithic era. Locked in the Shield were the world's richest mother lodes. In irregular formations, often blanketed by younger deposits, the Shield's stratification, at times vertical, at others horizontal, was known as "the basement complex" to the geologist who could read in it clues to the presence of precious minerals, thus saving untold effort, time, and money in their discovery. The Shield extended for 1,825,000 square miles under Canada, from the Arctic to Ontario, Quebec, northern Manitoba, Alberta, Saskatchewan, and outlying parts of British Columbia.

Armed with this information, Hirshhorn mapped his forays into British Columbia. His first mine, the Rex-Bar, was a loser. He went on to Labrador and its Mesabi Iron, and to Quebec's Noranda, where he found the Anglo-Rouyn mine. When its gold was exhausted, Hirshhorn converted it to copper, which the mine produces to this day. He was among the first to venture into the East Porcupine area below Hudson Bay, where he acquired the Armistice, Aquarius, and Calder-Bousquet mines which he developed over a fourteen-year period starting in 1933. In a comparatively short time, the astute stock trader was described by *The Northern Miner* as "the daring mine maker." He synthesized his experience with Lindsley and LaBine. His "secret" method, which combined geology with market adroitness, was to invest in sighting claims and in drilling. "You have to spend money in the ground," he explained. "That's the only way to make mines."

His procedures went counter to local practice. Bay Street mistrusted him. "They said I was a hit-and-run man, a fast-buck guy. Also," he added grimly, "I was a little Hebe from New York. I took a lot of abuse." But not from prospectors, promoters, and engineers. They came to know him, his attentive ear, his swift decisions, and the surety of his word. Sifting their propositions, Hirshhorn made his selections and acted promptly. Wasted time irked him.

In a typical transaction for a client mine promoter, Hirshhorn outlined a deal to an investor, concluding, "And I'll put up a quarter of the money myself." When the prospect hesitated, Hirshhorn snapped, "Let me give you some advice. Stay away from the mining business; it's not for you. Where would I be if I fortzed around like you?" And dangling his final offer, he asked, "Do you want it, or don't you?"

"I—I think"—the man wobbled—"you ought to put up—a third."

"It's a deal!" Hirshhorn grabbed the man's hand. "Send up your fifty thousand right away. I'll have my twenty-five in the bank tomorrow." As he escorted his visitor to the door, he said, "I'll show you how money is made."

Phoning his client, Hirshhorn said, "I've got you $75,000. . . . What? . . . What do you mean fast work? I spent an hour with the guy."

Hirshhorn could also show forbearance. He employed a secretary, a quiet middle-aged woman who took indifferent dictation. For five years she served with noticeable incompetence. Calling her one day, Hirshhorn received no response.

"What's the matter," he yelled in exasperation, "you deaf?"

She turned her head to him. "Yes."

Hirshhorn did not dismiss her.

■ ■ □ □

Early in 1936 Doug Wright proposed to Hirshhorn that he finance drilling in the vicinity of the long abandoned Preston East Dome in the Porcupine, one of Canada's early bonanza areas. The geologist, his credibility dissolved in whiskey, had been offering the deal around and Hirshhorn knew it. He was also aware of Preston's history.

Back in 1907 the mine had been opened by Harry Preston. Although situated in the neighborhood of the Hollinger, "the crown jewel of gold mines," the ore had petered out, a fire had destroyed the installations, and the Preston had been relegated to the graveyard of extinct mines. But Doug Wright, one-time geologist for Harry Preston, was convinced that more gold waited in the ground. He had urged Gordon Taylor of A. E. Osler Company, Preston's original promoter and present owner, to purchase the land contiguous to the depleted mine, but had failed to convince Taylor or anyone else of the presence of paydirt. The mine's outstanding stock could be found at poker tables being used as nickel chips.

Listening to Wright's tale, Hirshhorn as usual asked, "How much will it take?"

"Twenty thousand," said Wright.

"Let's make it twenty-five," Hirshhorn rejoined.

"When?" Wright asked.

"First chance we get," Hirshhorn assured him.

Several days later, on a routine trip to New York, Hirshhorn was invited to dine with Wright in the geologist's suite on the thirty-fourth floor of the New Yorker Hotel at Eighth Avenue and 34th Street. Upon arriving, Hirshhorn could see Wright was already well into his tippling, which he continued through dinner. The meal over, Wright addressed Hirshhorn.

"Joe, you made me a promise to finance Preston."

"I did," said Hirshhorn.

Wright regarded him foggily, and suddenly his voice rang out menacingly. "Listen, you little son-of-a-bitch! You keep your word because if you don't I'm going to throw you out this window."

One hard look at Wright and Hirshhorn realized two things: the husky geologist was capable of carrying out his threat; and they were on the thirty-fourth floor.

"All right, Doug," he said. "You've got a deal."

"No!" Wright yelled. "I want it right away—today. I'm not going to let you out of here."

Nothing would appease him except that Hirshhorn phone Chic Coursen and direct him to communicate with Ward Wright and arrange a meeting in the morning with a cashier's check in hand. Not until his brother called back to confirm the appointment was Wright mollified.

Doug Wright died in 1949. "There wasn't a nicer man—when he wasn't drinking," said Hirshhorn.

In due time Hirshhorn acquired Preston East Dome from Gordon Taylor and reorganized the company. He retained William H. Bouck, of Bouck, Hetherington and Fallis, as legal representative and president of the new enterprise. Hirshhorn purchased 500,000 shares of the new treasury stock for $125,000 and Wright began exploratory drilling. When Bay Street got wind of "Hirshhorn's Folly," the brokers primed their muskets, itching for revenge. The moment Hirshhorn advertised his promotion, the offensive began. Offered at 25 cents, Preston stock was driven down by a flood of old shares which Hirshhorn bought up as fast as they hit the market. Before long, with most of the company's original issue in his possession, he was Preston's principal shareholder.

Beneath Hirshhorn's superabundant vigor lurked tensions. In addition to his work strain, there were mounting pressures from Jennie; and the inquiry of the Exchange Commission followed by the deportation proceedings had threatened to topple the towering structure he was erecting. Until then his only illness had been a teenage tussle with tonsils and adenoids. Now at thirty-five, his body rebelled in giant shingles, a virulent skin disease. Silk shirts did not help. His days were torments; his nights excruciating.

During the Preston East Dome operation, exhaustion forced him on doctor's orders into inactivity. He bought a house in Miami Beach to which he removed with his family. "It was awful," Hirshhorn moaned. "I couldn't just retire to a park bench and become a philosopher. I'd have gone nuts." Instead, lolling in the sun, he "played at investing," paid $6,500 for a piece of real estate and realized $84,000. It braced him more than the sea air and sunshine. He returned to Toronto.

Wright's drilling encountered excellent ore intersections, which he followed up underground, verifying the earlier evidence of high-grade ore by charting a substantial amount of tonnage. But the Bay Street "bears" ignored rumors of his find. They regarded the spirited buying and selling of Preston stock as a "jiggle" of the exchange by Hirshhorn. Yet, despite their efforts to depress the stock it rose steadily. Hirshhorn parted with enough at $2 to leave him with 500,000 shares at virtually no cost. Preston went to $2.50 and stayed there.

With $30 million in charted ore, Hirshhorn held the equivalent of a royal flush. Without revealing his hand, he had to get $600,000 to build a processing mill. In a move unprecedented in mining history, he floated a bond issue, guaranteeing its redemption in five years at 6 percent interest with a bonus share of common stock to each bondholder. No one had ever heard of a gold-mine operator indemnifying investors against loss. Hirshhorn turned the underwriting over to Harry Knight of Draper, Dobie and Company, and the first-mortgage bond issue of $700,000, after commissions, netted $612,000. Within three years, Preston was in production. On January 1, 1940, Hirshhorn redeemed the bonds, and two weeks later the common stock paid its first dividend. Harry Knight received a bonus of 225,000 shares valued shortly afterward at nearly $1 million.

What came to light later was that Doug Wright had sunk the new Preston Mine shaft a mere 25 yards from the old one. One large pocket in the dome yielded $5 million. The abandoned mine which Gordon Taylor unloaded on Hirshhorn produced gold into 1968 amounting to $57 million. As one of Canada's "blue chip" mines, Preston East Dome also figured prominently in 1953 in the billion-dollar uranium strike which Hirshhorn engineered in the Algoma district of Ontario.

■ ■ □ □

Meanwhile his marriage was crumbling. Hirshhorn tried to shore it up, but whatever he did went bad. In 1936 he took his family to a Pocono Mountains resort. The hotel discriminated against Jews and they were turned away. Hirshhorn phoned a real estate agent and purchased 470 acres on a mountaintop near Angel, Pennsylvania. He named it Huckleberry Hill and built a turreted French Provincial manor, which in medieval style dominated the surrounding farmlands. Ready the following summer, complete with Guernsey cattle, it provided a handball court, a swimming hole, and guest rooms and dormitories for sixteen. Hirshhorn tramped over his acres accompanied by one of his mining engineers. The hills echoed with his renditions of "You made me love you, I didn't wanna do it. . ." as he executed a buck-and-wing, uncannily avoiding the platters of cow droppings in the pasture.

Each evening, as family and guests drew up to the dinner board, Jennie and Hirshhorn took their places at opposite ends of the table. Beneath the flow of hospitality, the rift between them was widening, as Jennie's disquiet multiplied with each tale of Hirshhorn's indiscretions.

In 1937, Hirshhorn experienced the first in a series of mental lapses which oddly resembled that of Jesse L. Livermore. A short time before, Hirshhorn's hero of his youth, who had been entangled in an extramarital scandal, had vanished only to turn up twenty-six hours later unable to account for his absence. He had awakened in a room of the Pennsylvania Hotel registered in the name of J. L. Lord. The initials coincided with Livermore's. A physician called by Mrs. Livermore diagnosed the case as amnesia.

One spring day, after a similar overnight disappearance, Hirshhorn, on his way to Canada, found himself inexplicably hanging onto a lamppost at 23rd Street and Seventh Avenue in Manhattan. His blistered feet testified that he had walked the three miles from his office downtown on Pine Street. A phone call brought Jennie on the double to drive him home to Great Neck. Shortly afterward, following dinner at Huckleberry Hill, Hirshhorn disappeared again. Hours later, a neighbor discovered him wandering about in an apparent daze and bundled him off to the manor. Hirshhorn was put to bed under observation as an amnesia case. Sitting beside him during the night, Jennie heard him muttering as in a delirium. Bending close, she listened to him reiterating, "Friends, Romans, countrymen, lend me your ears. . ." until all at once the refrain altered. "Friends, Romans, countrymen," Hirshhorn mumbled, "I want to pee in your ears. . . ." Jennie was not amused. The masquerade, she suspected, hid her husband's transgressions, in this case an alleged rendezvous at a hotel in the neighborhood. Hirshhorn stoutly denied it.

Of his five years of analysis with Dr. Paul Freedman, Hirshhorn said, "Amnesia was the subject of the sessions; so was Jennie. Dr. Freedman said I wanted to forget the whole past. Where the irritation came from, I can't say."

Even if the natives of Angel, Pennsylvania, didn't take to "the only Jew in captivity, the only one around for twenty-five miles," to Hirshhorn, Huckleberry Hill was "a place from the heart."

"I tried everything," he said. "I gave Guernsey calves to the agriculture clubs; I gave paintings to all the churches. But I couldn't reach them."

Their only acknowledgment of his presence came when he woke one morning to find two trees in the driveway cut down during the night by persons unknown. Hirshhorn sold Huckleberry Hill in 1947 to Rush Kress, brother of Samuel H. Kress, the dime-store merchant. It went for $130,000, one-third of its cost.

■   ■   □   □

As a father, Hirshhorn gave of himself after a fashion. He paved a rear lawn of the Great Neck house for a roller-skating rink, converting it one winter into an ice rink. All the children learned to play the piano; in addition, each girl chose a string instrument, and Gordon the trumpet. Hirshhorn cherished the fantasy of a family music ensemble. His own mother had paid $5 a month to Jacob Brothers at Broadway and Myrtle Avenue for a piano, and 50 cents for his weekly lesson, and at one time Hirshhorn could give a fair account of a Chopin waltz. He spent time with his children, but not quite like Cosimo Medici, who let an embassy cool its heels while he whittled a whistle for his grandson. Hirshhorn would excuse himself from a board meeting and slip out to an art gallery to purchase paintings, but he could not surrender himself to his family. "Somewhere along the line," said his daughter Gene, "he stopped being a father."

By 1941 Hirshhorn was living apart from the family and within a year he and Jennie were legally separated. Her determination to divorce him left Hirshhorn unstrung. He begged her to reconsider. When she set out for Reno in 1945 he was beside himself.

In June of that year he found himself in Toronto's Malton Airport being hustled into a private waiting room by Corporal Ed McElhone of the Royal Canadian Mounted Police who requested him to empty his pockets. Out came an airline ticket to New York and two bundles of Canadian currency, one of a hundred and another of fifty one-hundred-dollar bills. Hirshhorn could give no credible explanation to the constable. He was charged with attempting to export $15,000 without a foreign exchange license. The money in his pocket, said Hirshhorn, was intended for repayment of a debt in Toronto. Unable to dispose of it before departure, he had meant to hand the money over upon his return from New York. The magistrate, too, found difficulty believing Hirshhorn's story. He dropped the charge against the financier of trying to deceive a customs officer and fined him $3,500. Hirshhorn called the whole affair a "stupid mistake."

Three weeks later, the *Toronto Star* of July 12 reported him charged with six violations of Foreign Exchange Control Board regulations. According to the allegations, he had without a license sold securities in three periods between March 1943 and February 1944 totaling $137,228.71. Under questioning, the Board's inspector admitted he did not know of the "permits issued to the vendor" during that same year. He insisted, however, they "were not in connection with the figure under consideration."

The magistrate, concerned only with breaches of the regulations, ruled that the "difficulties may have arisen in a manner in which the accounts with the various brokerages were kept." Reportedly, Hirshhorn paid fines in the sum of $5,000. Years later, and in response to an inquiry for the Securities and Exchange Commission in Washington, a search was made of the files of the Foreign Exchange Control Board, the Ontario Police, the Royal Canadian Mounted Police, and the Special Crown Prosecutor which failed to turn up any record relating to the matter. Salter A. Hayden, a senior member of the Canadian Senate, who represented Hirshhorn, could not recall what he conjectured "must have been technical in nature." Criminal intent, he said, had not been a factor in the proceedings. Under Control Board rules, according to the Senator, "mere inadvertence" could have given rise to the charges of violation.

Recollecting the incident, Hirshhorn attributed it to another attempt at skewering him. "There were always guys around," he commented, "wishing I'd break a leg—or drop dead."

This brush with the Control Board, the investigation ten years earlier of the Gunnar manipulation, followed by the deportation proceedings, all were to haunt Hirshhorn during congressional committee hearings in Washington in 1970.

■ ■ ☐ ☐

In August 1945, after twenty-three years, Hirshhorn's marriage to Jennie terminated. The divorce ushered in twenty-one years of acrimony and litigation. Jennie accused Hirshhorn of nonsupport, of absenting himself unduly, of neglecting his family. She enlisted the children in dunning their father. Their own experiences with Hirshhorn alternated between intense love, uncertainty, and fear—"I don't understand Daddy; please explain him to me," Robin said to her sisters. She was twenty-two at the time, recently married to a young theoretical physicist. Gene, nineteen, was a student at DePauw University; Gordon, sixteen, was attending Great Neck High School with Naomi, fourteen. Both lived at home with their mother.

Jennie received alimony and child support, the Great Neck and Florida houses and their contents, including Hirshhorn's library of rare books. In November 1946 she auctioned the volumes, letters, and manuscripts. Under the Parke-Bernet hammer went first, second, and fourth folios of Shakespeare, the *De Rhetorica* of Cicero, first editions of Keats, Sterne, Swift, and Poe, that of Milton's *Paradise Lost* bringing $875, his *Paradise Regained* a mere $20. *A Vindication of the Rights of Woman* by Mary Wollstonecraft, published in 1792, fetched $5. Two hundred and six items yielded $33,618.

Early in 1947 a severe attack of diverticulosis ruptured Hirshhorn's intestine causing peritonitis. He went into emergency surgery. Immediately after the operation, Gordon and Naomi visited their father. They tiptoed into his darkened room in New York's Flower and Fifth Avenue Hospital to stand fearfully at the door, smelling the air heavy with ether and staring at him, his arms pinioned in a tangle of intravenous tubes. Suddenly out of the stillness, Hirshhorn yelled: "Get these goddamn things out of my arm. I've got to make a phone call!" The sound reassured his children.

Repaired, and relieved of his appendix as well, Hirshhorn recovered swiftly.

Soon afterward Hirshhorn was haled into court by Jennie. That same year he wed Lily Harmon, whom he had met soon after his separation from Jennie. He had moved out of the house in Great Neck and into two rooms at Number One Fifth Avenue in Manhattan. Painting and sculpture cluttered the closets, were piled on chests and under the bed, leaving almost no living space. What made it bearable was the fact that nearby, in the back room of Herman Baron's ACA Gallery, he could shake off his loneliness in the company of artists. On one occasion, Hirshhorn bought a drawing by Lily Harmon. Baron made sure the painter was present the next time Hirshhorn showed up.

Lily Harmon, fifteen years his junior, had dark hair, olive skin smooth over high cheekbones, enormous black eyes, and wide lips which mixed tenderness with cynicism. Her drawling tremolo hid dark wild moods.

Hirshhorn acquired her work and commissioned the struggling Greenwich Village artist to find him an apartment. Not long afterward he entertained her in his new lodgings near Washington Square. By the time she became the second Mrs. Hirshhorn in 1947, he owned thirty-five Harmons.

"It was cheaper to marry her," he confided, "than to buy her paintings."

Jennie had instituted suit in the names of the children against Hirshhorn for his mismanagement of a corporation he had formed as a family nest egg. He controlled it by retaining half of the stock and assigning 10 percent each to the four children and to Jennie's mother. Jennie charged that he was using the trust not in the family's interest but for personal gain. To Hirshhorn, the action represented malice on her part and disloyalty on the part of the children.

He fought the claim and in their eyes his opposition typified his callousness.

"The kids didn't talk to me; I didn't talk to them," said Hirshhorn. "They treated me as if I was dead. But why," he cried twenty years later, "did it have to last so long?"—and answering himself, continued, "I reminded Robin of the letter she wrote me—'You called me a monster, remember?'—and she said, 'You still hold that against me?'—'Yes, I do,' I said. 'Was I a monster? Do you know me that way?'—and she had nothing to say."

The chasm widened. In 1951, Hirshhorn launched his nephew, Leo Gold, on the American Stock Exchange. He urged Gordon, then twenty-two, to join the firm. Jennie intervened.

"I don't want you to do anything your father is involved in," she said.

For eight years the litigation dragged on until, early in 1955, the children, then grown, withdrew from the suit. Hirshhorn settled $125,000 on each child and purchased all the outstanding stock in the disputed corporation. Relatively unscathed, Gene was the first to attain objectivity.

"Daddy was too much," she said. "He had a life-force which was irresistible. It magnetized my mother—and us. She tried to resist it but couldn't. They were locked in a collision course, and in the end she was run over."

Much time passed before Gordon was able to view the struggle calmly. "My father's ambition drove him to be something, not a nothing. Passive ones, he felt, got nowhere; aggressive ones wound up dead. So, it was wise to pursue selective aggression. Punishment did not come with aggression. It was even okay to get caught.

"My mother, on the other hand, was like an evangelist: everything was either black or white. A bad person deserved punishment and became nothing.

"The morality conflict between them was on this point; but they went to war—and she declared it—on the issue of his philandering. Neither wished the relationship to end. He might have endured—given some latitude. She constitutionally could not abide its continuation."

In 1963 Jennie discovered she had cancer. Death came three years later on April 2. She was buried in the family plot on Staten Island. Hirshhorn, living in La Quinta, California, did not attend the funeral. The children did not expect it of him.

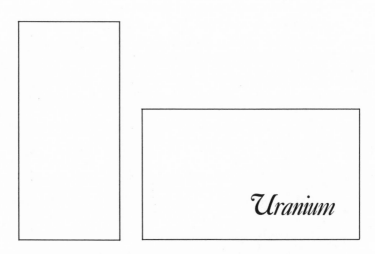

Uranium

IV Joseph Hirshhorn, ex-courier for Western Union, left New York for Toronto in the middle of the Depression. Thirteen years later, in 1946, geologist Francis Renault Joubin, a former baker's helper, arrived from British Columbia. In March of that year, Winston Churchill had visited Harry Truman in Fulton, Missouri. Facing an audience in the great hall of Westminster College, England's wartime Prime Minister uttered the baleful words: "From Stettin in the Baltic to Trieste in the Adriatic an iron curtain has descended across the Continent."

The curtain clanged shut and the Cold War began. Inside Hirshhorn's head the sound set his imagination clicking like a Geiger counter. He had successfully developed gold, zinc, and iron mines. Uranium represented the mineral of the future; it was needed to safeguard the western world and to propel it into the space age. Could it be found in great quantity—and in Canada? Daily, prospectors besieged Hirshhorn's Technical Mine Consultants. If their tales were anything but fantasy, he was ready to provide the "yakahoola for those bums I loved," aware that the odds, five hundred, even a thousand, to one, were against him.

Hirshhorn funded "six or seven items" which failed to pan out, and he dropped a goodly portion of his year's gains from the Toronto Stock Exchange. Meanwhile, he had organized a syndicate composed of former Secretary of State Edward R. Stettinius, William Rosenwald, and Barney Balaban of Paramount Pictures to explore the Mindanao region of the Philippines and to mine its gold and copper. Local Philippine officials "leaned" on Hirshhorn with "polite requests" for participation in his Philippine-American Exploration Company. "You understand, of course, Mr. Hirshhorn," he was informed, "we get this interest—twenty percent—for nothing. This is the way we operate here."

Hirshhorn dissolved the company and returned to Canada, where the climate was less genial but the brand of brigandage was democratic.

Time would pass before the baker's assistant crossed the path of the erstwhile messenger boy. When finally Joubin presented himself with no more than a theory about an indeterminate "Location X," Hirshhorn listened with an ear schooled by Canada's leading geologists and engineers whose brains he had picked clean during those nights in the house on Old Forrest Road. From them and his omnivorous reading, Hirshhorn knew what few mine promoters bothered to learn, that the subterranean Pre-Cambrian Shield stretching beneath most of Canada was the bed in which slept some of the richest minerals in the earth. Also, that uranium generally, and in Canada particularly, had a long and elusive history.

For more than a hundred years men had stood, scratched, and dug in the neighborhood, often on the very spot, where 50 to 500 yards underfoot lay a rajah's ransom in uranium. Time and again they turned away, mystified by the caprices of geology. Only two men were not deflected: Franc Joubin, who relentlessly dogged the mystery for seven years; and Hirshhorn, who pondered and waited—and gambled.

Canada's romance with uranium centered in the region of Sault Ste. Marie at the junction of Lakes Huron and Superior. It began in 1846 with Dr. John L. LeConte, physician and entomologist, who went to the Great Lakes to hunt a genus of beetle and returned to Philadelphia with rock specimens to publish a report, "On Coracite, A New Ore of Uranium," in the May 1847 issue of the *American Journal of Science and Art.* A half-century later Marie Curie isolated two elements she named "polonium" and "radium" which she extracted from pitchblende—another host mineral to uranium—obtained in

Czechoslovakia. Pitchblende was discovered in the Belgian Congo, and the price of radium at the time was $75,000 per gram.

In 1914, cut off from Europe by World War I, the governments of Ontario and of British Columbia passed the Radium Act, which offered $25,000 to anyone locating pitchblende or "any substance containing radium in sufficient quantity for commercial extraction." To spur results, the Department of Mines ordered a geological survey under the direction of W. H. Collins. Published in 1925, it attracted little attention and was soon out of print and forgotten. Collins died and his assistant, Dr. George W. Bain, joined the faculty of Amherst College in Massachusetts.

High in the Northwest Territory, Gilbert LaBine's Eldorado Mine on Great Bear Lake was able to compete for a few years in the world pitchblende market despite its location in the Arctic wilderness, 4,500 miles by water, truck, and rail from the nearest refinery. But when the Nazis gobbled up Czechoslovakia, a price war between the Belgian Congo and South Africa drove radium down to $20,000 per gram, and Eldorado, having produced $7.6 million in pitchblende, deemed further operation uneconomical. It closed down in 1940.

"Maud," the Roosevelt-Churchill code name for the Manhattan Project to make the atom bomb, needed a plentiful diet of uranium from which to derive the principal ingredients in nuclear fission: U-235 and PU-239. Dr. Bain, summoned from Amherst as consultant, reported on his tests for radioactivity made ten years earlier on gold specimens at South Africa's Rand Mines. He was sent there accompanied by Dr. Charles F. Davidson, and learned that once the ore at Rand had yielded up its gold, the tailings were piled up in a man-made mountain which constituted the largest low-grade uranium range in the world. But "Maud's" diet of uranium was cut off when the United States entered the war and her shipping became the prime target of German U-boats patrolling the sea lanes. Uranium had to be located west of the Atlantic.

Canada's Minister of the Interior phoned LaBine, who quickly reactivated operations at Great Bear Lake. Subsequently purchasing the mine from LaBine, the government reserved to itself possession and sale of all uranium within Canadian borders, and produced the vital element exclusively "for an unidentified customer" at a reasonable price. Eldorado Mining and Refining Ltd. became the agent and major source of uranium for the bomb.

On August 6, 1945, the 4½-ton missile, equivalent to 20,000

tons of TNT, annihilated most of Hiroshima and 100,000 of its inhabitants. The United States had won the bomb race.

On September 23, 1949, President Truman announced that the Soviet Union had set off an atomic explosion. The search for uranium in Canada rose to fever pitch.

Gilbert LaBine reached out to the west end of Lake Athabasca into the gold-fields district of northern Alberta and staked a concession identified as GG. Hot on his trail came W. Norbert Millar to grab six contiguous concessions held by wall-eyed "Wild Bill" Richardson. Together they brought their AA-FF concessions to Hirshhorn, who took all six in exchange for cash and a block of stock in what later became Rix-Athabasca. With Doug Wright dead, Hirshhorn went in search of "the best geology brains." The old and respected firm of James and Buffam recommended Franc Joubin, "steady and smart."

Hirshhorn recalled meeting Joubin three years earlier in the men's room of the Concourse Building on Adelaide and Bay streets where Hirshhorn and Joubin occupied offices on separate floors. In that tiled retreat the lean, taciturn geologist had been subjected to the standard Hirshhorn catechism: Who are you? Are you married? How many children do you have? What do you do? His reticence razed by the good-natured Hirshhorn hurricane, Joubin introduced himself and imparted the names of his wife, Mary, and his four-year-old daughter, Marian, who later knew the financier as Uncle Joe. Apprised also of Joubin's professional interest in uranium, Hirshhorn suggested they "get together sometime." But they never had.

Now, in 1949, Hirshhorn employed Joubin to make recommendations for sectioning the ore on the 470 square miles of the AA-FF concessions. To finance the project, Hirshhorn formed the American-Canadian Uranium Company Ltd. Its president was Paul V. McNutt, former Governor of Indiana, chairman of the War Manpower Commission, ex-Ambassador to the Philippines, and presidential aspirant in 1948. The company's vice-president was Josiah Marvel, Jr., former Ambassador to Denmark. Preparatory to promoting the stock offering in the United States, Hirshhorn registered with the Securities and Exchange Commission in Washington.

News arrived that LaBine's GG concession was "an elephant," its mammoth vein of pitchblende running along land's end of the peninsula which jutted into Lake Athabasca to form Black Bay adjoining Hirshhorn's AA-FF property. "Kicking himself" for not having acquired the seventh concession, Hirshhorn cranked up the development of Rix-Athabasca by advertising the stock of American-Canadian Uranium in the Manhattan newspapers.

Barely in first gear, the promotion ground to a screeching halt. The front page of the *New York Times* on November 27, 1950, reported that the company and its officers were under investigation by New York Attorney General Nathaniel L. Goldstein. Hirshhorn's childhood neighbor alleged that almost two-thirds of the shares of American-Canadian Uranium were owned by another company, one of whose major stockholders "has a record of convictions and jail sentence in Canada for fraud and conspiracy in connection with stock manipulation." Goldstein referred to another, Hirshhorn, as having "a record of two convictions for violating Foreign Exchange laws of Canada." The account said the company's officers and attorneys had ignored the Attorney General's notification and had advertised the stock issue. "In view of this," Goldstein stated, "I decided prospective purchasers were entitled at the very least to know as many of the facts as possible."

Josiah Marvel, questioned at his home in Wilmington, Delaware, expressed surprise. Goldstein, he said, had not asked him for information, and a registration statement had been filed with the Securities and Exchange Commission. From Philadelphia, Paul V. McNutt declared, "The prospectus by which an offering of stock is made to the public states the facts. The unquestioned character of the officers and directors is the guarantee that the funds of the company will be expended properly."

The next day, Goldstein asked 105 brokers to furnish reports of any sales of American-Canadian Uranium stock. No sale was ever made. His action scuttled the company. No further word appeared of his "investigation"; nor did Goldstein ever issue a public retraction of his allegations. The case records were filed, sealed by statute from "public scrutiny." Subsequently, Goldstein was reelected.

Hirshhorn had still to obtain a $5 million development fund for Rix-Athabasca. He cast his eye toward British finance. He appointed Franc Joubin general manager of Technical Mine Consultants and sent him up to Athabasca to prepare a geologic report for submission to a London brokerage firm, Erland d'Abo.

Joubin, meanwhile, had been dropping in on Aimé Breton, owner of the Algoma Hotel in Sault Ste. Marie, to pick up the latest rumors from the bush. Proudly, Breton exhibited his new acquisition, a Geiger counter, with which he had visited the local Mining Recorder's office to run it randomly over some ore specimens. One rock, registered as found at "Location X" in "Long" or "Lang," had excited his instrument. Breton reckoned the locus was "Long," the township east of Sault.

Joubin searched the records. Dr. A. H. Lang had reported "Location X—Long Township" in the *Journal of Geological Survey of Canada*, a find attributed to an employee of a highway construction outfit, a young German immigrant who had brought the uranium-bearing specimens to the Mines Branch in Ottawa. The young man had vanished, and was said to have drowned. "Location X" wrapped itself in mystery.

Toward the end of May, Breton and Karl Gunterman, a prospector, set out for Long Township. About 75 miles east of Sault they located old pits of unknown ownership which animated Breton's Geiger. Preparing to set stakes, he and Gunterman discovered Alex Fisher and René Audette had preceded them by a week. Norbert Millar also had recorded claims on the west. Breton registered eight claims to the north and communicated his news to Joubin. The geologist sent an associate to investigate. He returned with negative news. Not satisfied, Gunterman and Breton conducted Joubin himself to the site.

The pits puzzled Joubin. They showed a formation of a quartz-pebble conglomerate common to the host rock of South Africa's gold but not of pitchblende in Canada. Sampling eight pits, Joubin took an option on all claims, including those of Fisher and Audette, and sent his specimens to the assay office. A few days later word came back: "Uranium—traces only."

Undefeated, Joubin besieged several leading mining companies. He prevailed on Anaconda, American Smelting, Falconbridge, Newmont, and Noranda to send their geologists to test the sites. Unanimously they reported that the Geiger reaction was due to "thorium—a so-called rare-earth mineral, not itself rare, used in tungsten filament to prolong the life of electric bulbs and in the making of mantles for gas lamps." Thorium was to uranium what pyrite was to gold—a delusion. Joubin informed Breton of their blighted expectation. He dropped his options, and in the ensuing three years, Breton, Fisher, Audette, and Millar permitted their claims to lapse.

Working on the Athabasca report for Hirshhorn, Joubin puzzled over the mystery of Long Township. Tucked in its southwest corner sat the community of Algoma Mills, 18 miles from Spragge on the east and 14 from the lumber town of Blind River on the west, beyond which was Sault Ste. Marie. Along the region's southern edge the Central Pacific Railroad and Highway 17 traversed the 200 miles from Sudbury to Sault. Immediately to the north of railroad and highway the trackless bush, dense with spruce, maple, and jack-pine, stood amid muskeg and scores of little lakes, a sportsman's paradise which hunters and anglers from the States and Provinces, and an occasional surveyor, penetrated mainly by air.

For a century hordes of prospectors had strayed along the borders of this terrain, chipped at outcroppings, pitted its surface, and nothing had come of it. What if after a billion years uranium actually slept in the bed below? What if it could be located at 100 feet? Or would it take a half-mile to reach? Hirshhorn listened to Joubin and liked what he heard, fascinated by the possibility of finding the precious element at Ontario's back door rather than 1,500 miles away at Lake Athabasca or in the wild Northwest Territory.

Early in 1952 Hirshhorn rushed his geologist off to Erland d'Abo in England with the Rix-Athabasca data, and to pose his conundrum—thorium or uranium—to the chief geologist of Britain's nuclear energy division in London, the same Dr. Charles F. Davidson who had toured South Africa with Dr. Bain to reconnoiter for uranium in the Rand Gold Mines. From him Joubin learned that the radioactive surface of those mountain-high tailings at Rand reflected a uranium conglomerate 50 to 60 feet below. A mining journal, discussing pyrite ores, spoke of "the ready solubility of certain uranium materials by surface agencies when pyrite iron sulphate was present in the ore." In plain terms it meant that ages of rain and melted snow formed a solution of sulfuric acid which "leached" the uranium from the surface. It all fit Joubin's hypothesis.

Joubin's report to d'Abo produced no financing for Rix-Athabasca, but the geologist sped back to Toronto to apprise Hirshhorn of the new support for his hunch that "Location X" in Long Township hid uranium not thorium. Joubin resubmitted his samples for a thorium assay. Little enough showed up in the test to convince Hirshhorn that the radioactivity which kicked the Geiger had to have come from uranium; and if it had shown "traces only," it was due to "leaching." Only drilling would prove Joubin right or wrong.

"How much will it take?" Hirshhorn asked.

"Twenty-five thousand dollars," replied Joubin.

"You've got thirty," said Hirshhorn.

He sent Joubin and a crew into the Algoma district of Long Township where they staked thirty-six claims. The area they covered included and extended beyond the ground Joubin had optioned three years ago from Aimé Breton and the others. On May 18, 1952,

Hirshhorn recorded the claims. Months passed in study, charting, recruitment of personnel, and the other myriad preparations for drilling. In January 1953, *Industrial Review*, a journal from South Africa, arrived at Hirshhorn's Technical Mine Consultants. Hearts leaped. "On exposure to the atmosphere," the *Review* stated, "the uranium minerals oxidize to a uraniferous ochre when pure, possessing a bright canary yellow colour. An interesting fact is that on the surface the uranium has been completely leached out with the result that practically no trace of uranium can be detected on the outcrop of even the richest uranium-bearing conglomerates."

Joubin's theory was confirmed.

To direct the crucial drilling, Hirshhorn engaged Donald E. Smith, who years later became specialist in natural resources to the Royal Bank of Canada. Smith joined Technical Mine Consultants and Paul E. Young, its chief engineer, and the two men pitched their headquarters in a tent near Andrews Farm in Algoma Mills about 90 miles east of Sault Ste. Marie. For want of power lines, oil lamps furnished light, and steel bunks sufficed for comfort. Phone communication with Hirshhorn in Toronto was maintained from the single paybooth outside the trading post beside Highway 17. The drilling contract went to Wilfred Brazeau's Canadian Longyear Limited whose initial unit rumbled out of North Bay over the unpaved highway at the end of March.

On April 1, Smith marked the first spot for drilling, a location between Algoma Mills and Spragge, barely 300 yards from the railroad track and only 17 miles from the United States border. Five days later, the diamond bit the rock of Peach #1. In two days it reamed 175 feet to a pebble conglomerate. Smith cut the mineralized core in two 5-foot sections, ran his Geiger over them, and the counter chattered crazily. Satisfied, he applied his centillometer, a more sophisticated instrument, to check the reaction. He stared at the calibration. The gauge registered zero. In panic, Smith raced to Algoma Mills to phone Hirshhorn and Joubin. He was instructed to stand by while Joubin put through a call to the instrument's manufacturer in Winnipeg. Smith meanwhile paced beside the highway. An hour later the phone rang. The maker of the centillometer, just as mystified as Smith, could only suggest that the sodium oxide in its capsule had deteriorated from disuse. He would ship a replacement by air express. Joubin consulted Hirshhorn, who ordered drilling to proceed without a pause.

Plagued by uncertainty, Smith logged cores daily and taxied to

Sault to dispatch them by air to Frank Forward at the University of British Columbia in Vancouver, home of Canada's first fluorometric laboratory. Each time he inquired whether a package had arrived from Winnipeg. Finally, on April 15, going to the express office to ship samples of Peach #6, Smith found the parcel awaiting him. Upon returning to camp and the drilling of Peach #7, he was greeted by Joubin who had arrived from Toronto. With the centillometer in working order, the general manager scrutinized the record of shipments and with Smith tested the new cores.

"My goodness, Don," Joubin exclaimed, "this stuff is ore!"

By April 28 Smith had conveyed fifty-six cores to Vancouver, yet not a word of their assay was forthcoming. Joubin swallowed his anxiety until, patience exhausted, he phoned Frank Forward. What he heard made Joubin's heart sink. A fire had destroyed the laboratory. However, Forward said, the ore specimens had been rescued and were undamaged. As soon as possible, work would resume and a report be made.

Four days later, on May 2, Joubin received the verdict. His claim had been vindicated. He phoned Hirshhorn. Fifty of the fifty-six specimens showed 0.11 percent uranium oxide. The strike was without precedent.

"That lucky Joe!" said Joubin.

■ ■ □ □

Not yet aware of the full extent of the find, Hirshhorn sensed the situation called for extraordinary measures and additional resources. Above all, it demanded secrecy to head off a rush of prospectors. Within the week, Hirshhorn called in Harry F. Buckles, one-year member of TMC, from managing Rix-Athabasca. From Preston East Dome, in Ontario's Porcupine country, he summoned its chief geologist, Robert C. Hart, its general manager, William A. Hutchison, and Roy Putney, its assistant geologist. Buckles and Lyle Gatenby, another TMC staffer, he sent to reinforce Smith. The two squads extended the Peach claims across Long Township and eastward through Spragge, Lewis, and Shedden townships, often in plain view of the highway and railroad. Where the men encountered prior patents, Hirshhorn empowered them to purchase the rights. With the assessments completed on the claims in conformance with government regulation, Smith and Buckles entrained for Sault and the Recording Office. On board, Joe Metivier accosted them. The veteran conductor on the Sudbury-Sault run had observed the bustle along the road and wondered if it affected the copper claim held by his elder brother, Charles, near Lake Nordic to the north. Buckles was noncommittal. Weeks later, in the bush, he chanced upon the Metivier stakes and notified Hirshhorn. Authorization came to acquire the claim for $25,000, which old Metivier accepted gratefully. Eventually Hirshhorn named it the Buckles Mine.

Hirshhorn held council with Joubin and William Bouck. The Preston mine was idled by a strike and its treasury was full. Its men and money could be used if what Hirshhorn suspected were corroborated by the scouting of the entire Algoma territory, a district covering twenty-four townships. The 600 square miles sat directly above Lake Huron, bounded roughly on the west by the Mississagi River and on the east by the Serpent flowing south out of Whiskey Lake and emptying into the Huron's North Channel. From the lakeshore, the land stretched northward past Lauzon Lake to Nordic and Elliot lakes in its center, and 30 miles to Quirke and Ten-Mile lakes at its limit.

To make a swift pass over the area, Smith, Buckles, and Hart hired a bush pilot from Carl Mattaini's Lau-Goma Flying Base at Algoma Mills. From the air they could see, peeking out of the muskeg, outcroppings of greenish yellow. Landing on one of the myriad little lakes, they found quartz-pebble conglomerate in the same formation as the Peach cores. At Elliot Lake the yellow ore-rock showed up as well. Bob Hart was the first to grasp the dizzying import. His report back to Hirshhorn and Joubin stirred memories of W. H. Collins and his 1925 geological survey, now out of print. Hart by serendipity found one map in Timmins and almost at the same time Buckles dug one out of a secondhand bookshop in Toronto. There, on the "Blind River sheet," without specific reference to uranium, a "Z" snaked 90 miles through the central twelve townships in the Serpent River basin. Before them, at last, lay revealed the secret of "Location X."

In his King Edward Hotel suite, Hirshhorn convened a strategy session with Joubin, Bouck, and Hart. The agenda consisted of two items: maintenance of tight security, and the logistics of claiming the entire site. That night, May 23, they conceived the giant staking bee.

Hirshhorn spread out the map and Bouck, grabbing a pencil, drew a line east to west across the center of the Algoma territory. Approximately 15 miles separated the top bar of the "Z" from the middle, which was equidistant from the bottom bar. Preston East Dome incorporated the upper half; the southern half went to Peach. Hirshhorn deployed the Preston personnel to the north with Bob

Hart and Bill Hutchison in charge, and assigned Don Smith and Buckles to command a TMC force in the south.

Two hundred and fifty miles away, in the Porcupine region, the Preston contingent assembled fifty tents, seventy sleeping bags, tons of food, axes, and Geiger counters. Hirshhorn ordered out a squadron to purchase sixty mining licenses, each costing $5, at the Department of Mines in Toronto and at recording offices in widely separated districts of the province. On May 28, eighty men prepared to hit the bush and the drive was on. Airborne from the Porcupine in platoons of six, crews and supplies took off on northerly flights. Imperceptibly, the planes veered southwest to Elliot Lake and the waters surrounding the middle bar of the "Z." By the time the planes set down, the men had no idea of their whereabouts. Camps were established and in the heat of early summer which swarmed with ravenous flies the parties went to work.

Exacting rules governed the staking of claims. Each license entitled the holder to nine claims—since increased to eighteen. Each claim measured up to 40 acres marked off by stakes at the four corners of a square. According to specification, the markers could be a "blazed" tree, a monumental rock, or a picket no less than 4 feet high, squared at least 12 inches from the top. Number One, pegged at the northeast corner, was inscribed with the name of the claimer, his license serial number, the date and hour of the staking; the remaining three pickets bore the same data minus the date and hour. Stake Number Two stood at the southeast corner, Number Three on the southwest, and Number Four on the northwest. Validation of a claim required registration within thirty days of staking. Wherever land bridged two townships, a license was good for nine claims in each district. As soon as teams filled their lawful quotas in one township, Hart shuttled them to another under Buckles and vice versa.

As the time limit crept closer, additional staking hands were needed. Everyone was pressed into service—the drilling crew, Ruth Buckles and Muriel Smith, wives of the field directors, Lorraine Cook and Verna Konwalchuk, wives of two crew members, and Mary Kumamoto, Joubin's secretary. To meet further exigencies of time and stealth, four young attorneys were flown into the bush. At the end of each day, they logged the stakes and drafted the transfers of claims from license holder to Peach Uranium and Metal Company Ltd. To avoid news leaks, prospectors and lawyers remained in the bush until the entire operation was concluded.

Daily Hart and Hutchison reported progress to Hirshhorn, who exhorted them to "keep staking!" On the middle bar, where the "Z" curved northward, the yellow trail ended abruptly and Joubin was ready to call it a day. Informed of this, Hirshhorn demanded, "Where does it go from there? It just doesn't stop, does it?" To which Joubin responded with a laugh, "Who knows? Somewhere over the hill to the north, I guess." Hirshhorn barked, "Then stake over the hill"—and the crews forged onward. On the topmost bar of the "Z," the Quirke Lake mines were to sink their shafts.

The "bee" culminated and two days later, on Saturday morning, July 11, 1953, all paperwork completed, solicitors and engineers emerged from the bush and entered recording registries in Sudbury, Toronto, Timmins, Sault Ste. Marie, and other points in the province. Simultaneously they registered 1,400 claims on 56,000 acres, an area about equal to Manhattan Island. The news raced like prairie fire across the land. In the next several weeks a stampede thundered into Mine Department offices to file 8,000 claims. In the uproar and confusion, Hirshhorn's spectacular feat was caught in the crossfire of Bay Street chagrin and the mining crowd's failed opportunity. Skepticism eddied around him. "The ore is low-grade. . . . More thorium than uranium. . . . Great metallurgical difficulties. . . ." But the bonanza was real and unparalleled. Estimated conservatively, the Algoma deposits exceeded the total uranium deposits of 625 mines in the United States, including the newly discovered Pick in Utah and the Steen in Texas.

Long before any inkling of the boom circulated, Joubin, sitting on his assayed uranium cores, let a few deserving friends in on the inside. He told Mary, his wife, to phone Mrs. Tyrell, a woman in poor circumstances, and in strictest confidence instruct her to buy 300 shares of Peach Uranium at $1.50. Later, in the TMC office, Joubin heard Hirshhorn on the phone with Al White. The distraught underwriter was describing to Hirshhorn a strange little woman who had wandered into his brokerage to request Peach Uranium. She knew nothing about the stock or why she wanted to buy it except that the name appealed to her. Reluctant to quote the lowest price, White inquired how many shares she had in mind. Mrs. Tyrell had handed him $1,000, her entire savings, and asked what that would buy.

"It's crazy," White cried to Hirshhorn. "What do you want me to do?"

"Sell her seven hundred shares," said Hirshhorn and hung up.

Mrs. Tyrell acquired the stock. Later it went to $145 per share.

■ ▪ □ ▫

Hirshhorn's objective was a contract from Canada's Eldorado Company, sole agent for its only customer, the U.S. Atomic Energy Commission. When on August 20, 1953, Moscow announced it had exploded a hydrogen bomb, he had little doubt it would be forthcoming. His confidence proved well founded as rivalry between the Big Powers ensued.

In a letter of intent, the Canadian government handed Hirshhorn an order for uranium oxide which would total $206,910,000 conditional, first, upon delivery beginning January 1, 1956, and, second, on his guarantee of fulfillment of the contract by April 1962. This meant that Hirshhorn had less than two years to sink mine shafts, build mills and a refinery, provide housing for the professional staff and underground "muckers," bring in power, and construct roads—and raise approximately $120 million. He had formed Pronto Uranium Mines Ltd. and floated a stock issue to develop the southern arm of the "Z." In gratitude for granting him the Beatty Gold promotion twenty years earlier, Hirshhorn invited Thayer Lindsley to join the company, which he did by purchasing a large block of stock. Algom Uranium Mines Ltd. was organized to promote the middle and upper bars of the "Z" on which were located Algom Nordic and Algom Quirke respectively. But financing had a long way to go. New York investment bankers were keeping their distance. Toronto's Bay Street was sitting back and watching Hirshhorn squirm.

Because it was most accessible from the highway and closest to the railroad station at Spragge, Hirshhorn decided on Pronto to spearhead the development. When the Ontario Highway Department dragged its feet, he allocated $150,000 which, with some aid from the Department of Mines, allowed Bob Hart to track a temporary road out of Spragge. This road ultimately forged a 30-mile link between Highway 17 and Algom's Nordic and Quirke mines. Even before it was paved, all manner of heavy equipment was skittering over muskeg and mire to its destination.

To meet the deadline for delivery, Hirshhorn dipped into the Peach treasury and funds from Preston East Dome and commenced digging Pronto's No. 1 shaft. As the steel headframe rose against the sky, construction of the mills began. Once producing, its 1,500 tons of ore daily would be "the free world's biggest uranium mine," until Algom, which alone would require $90 million to activate, came in with 6,000 tons from Quirke and Nordic. Ore reserves were figured at 100 million tons, twenty times that of Anaconda's Jackpile Mine in New Mexico, the largest in the United States.

Less than ideal conditions prevailed in the camps. Tents, trailers, and shacks sheltered the men and their families until Hirshhorn raised a row of accommodations on the shore of the Huron. Don Smith, his wife, and three children lived in an old leaky cabin near Algoma Mills, baked by summer heat, "a little cool" in winter's subzero temperatures. Mornings they woke to bears staring in at the windows. Muriel Smith cut her own wood for cooking and heat, and drew water from a well 100 yards from the house. In winter the water barrel, trucked to the kitchen, froze over with a quarter-inch of ice.

The scale and speed of development required massive financing. To raise it, Hirshhorn was said to be simultaneously in New York and Toronto stirring up monied interest, and in Blind River trying to wake the 2,500 inhabitants of the declining lumber town from torpor. Everywhere he brought with him infectious high spirits. The weekends he was not at home in New York he spent watching Pronto's No. 1 shaft drive 1,000 feet into the earth. Descending, he saw the uranium-bearing rock, the pebbles ranging in diameter from one-quarter of an inch to three inches, and boulders at deeper levels up to two feet. Irrepressibly he burst into song—"Momma loves Mambo. . . ."—and exclaimed to Stan Holmes, his young geological guide, "Get those pebbles! That's sexy! Every one's worth a buck!"

Holmes, age twenty-eight, had joined TMC to assist Paul Young in putting Pronto into production. "I hear," Hirshhorn said to him, "you're going to have a kid. Your first? How long you been with us?"

"Three months," Holmes replied.

Hirshhorn gave him 3,000 shares in the Buckles Mine at cost, then 24 cents. The stock went to $1.50 and more than defrayed the expense of the arrival of John Holmes on Christmas Day of 1954, the first baby to be born in the Algoma tents.

Hirshhorn's capacity for work was endless. He never went to bed before attending to the day's last detail and preparing himself for the next.

"You never know," he explained to an aide, "when someone's going to take a pee behind the pyramid."

At seven in the morning he burst into his office on the nineteenth floor of the Bank of Nova Scotia building at the intersection of King and Bay streets. Alone, he spent the next three hours calling London, Paris, Rome, and other cities, on business or on transactions with art dealers. By ten the office filled with geologists, prospectors, brokers, artists, all jostling each other on the antique furniture midst a litter of modern paintings and sculpture. With the first of the day's thirty cigars clenched in his teeth, Hirshhorn embroiled himself in the minutiae of fifty-seven companies he controlled in all parts of Canada, except Newfoundland, Nova Scotia, and Prince Edward Island. Like a juggler of innumerable balls, his eye never left them.

"Mention one of the outfits," said his statistician, Bruce Attenborough, "and he could tell you how much it spent last year on erasers."

As the morning wore on, Hirshhorn removed his jacket and shoes. With a hand towel to mop his brow and neck, he attacked two phones at once, his right ear concerned with a $90 million loan, his left connected to a Montreal stockbroker. According to his mood, often released in a jig, he announced himself as "The Rabbi," or sang out, "When Irish eyes are smiling. . . ." As in his younger days, lunching at his desk on crackers and soup, he ran his business marathon without pause, compressing fifteen meetings into four hours until the time came to quit at five-thirty.

Joubin once remarked that he would have guessed Hirshhorn was high on dope but for the fact that he always behaved that way. "If I didn't," Hirshhorn shot back, "I'd have ulcers like the rest of Bay Street."

In his three-room suite in the King Edward Hotel, Hirshhorn downed two scotches neat for an aperitif and dined luxuriously as a prelude to further conferences. At midnight he bedded down with stock quotations and market averages prepared for him by his statistician, and on their fluctuations wafted off to sleep at 2 A.M. By then he had spoken with his attorney, Senator Salter Hayden, and with Dean Acheson, then representing Phelps-Dodge, one of the firms bidding on unsatisfactory terms for the Hirshhorn uranium dynasty.

Hirshhorn made a practice of consulting, never commanding, experts, even those in his own employ. Dean Acheson, former Secretary of State, who later became his Washington attorney, seeing Hirshhorn in action, was reminded of President Truman in his early days in the White House. "Mr. Truman," said Acheson, "thought it Napoleonic to make fast decisions, and he drove us nearly crazy until we were able to convince him there might be some merit in the considered opinion."

The loss of the richest section of the Quirke region nettled Hirshhorn. During the secret Algom staking, Arthur Stollery, formerly employed by Joubin, showed up on the north limb of the "Z" and sank posts into eighty-eight claims. He may have been tipped off by a phone call from Mary Joubin; or he may have learned the location from George Smith, who had piloted Hirshhorn's field directors to Quirke Lake in 1953. During the "staking bee," Smith landed Stollery there.

One day Stollery appeared in Hirshhorn's Toronto office and offered his claims for sale. His price was the presidency of the company and an annual salary of $50,000. Hirshhorn kicked him out. Stollery went across the street to Stephen Roman of Consolidated Denison and set the same deal before him.

"The company," Roman explained, "has a president—me."

"All right," said Stollery, "I'll be vice-president," and with the title received $30,000 plus 500,000 shares.

When he learned of this, Hirshhorn optioned 2 million shares of Denison at $1.25 each. As the option neared expiration, he offered to buy at $1. Roman rejected the bid.

"You're a horse's ass!" Hirshhorn told him angrily.

"I'm a farmer," Roman smiled, "and that's a compliment."

Another version has it that Hirshhorn worked out a deal with Stollery and apprised Joubin. Swamped with deadlines for nine mines, the geologist groaned, "If you take on another one, I'm quitting." Hirshhorn dropped the matter.

Some time later, Stollery mailed Joubin a certificate for 20,000 shares of Denison, with a note. "I feel," Stollery wrote, "I owe this to you and Joe."

The geologist showed the certificate to Hirshhorn, who exploded. "That double-crossing son-of-a-bitch! Send it back!"

Joubin complied. Twenty years later the certificate was worth $800,000.

"I think," Joubin chuckled softly, "Joe would do the same thing today."

■ ■ □ □

Hirshhorn's fifty-seven companies mobilized 72 engineers and close to 12,000 employees in TMC's research, exploration, drilling, mining, and milling. One former worker, broke and with a wife ill and about to have a baby, appealed to Hirshhorn for help. Hirshhorn lent him $2,000. Three years passed before the man turned up again at TMC's office full of regrets and apologies for his unpaid debt. He was "doing a lot of flying" for oil's Big-Six in the Arctic Islands and wanted to show his gratitude by passing on a piece of information which might be useful. "There are some interesting things up there," he confided. "I recommend you look into it."

On this flimsy tip and on a hunch as to the man's sincerity, Hirshhorn, in his one-man operational style, moved quickly. He didn't have to filter the information through a series of engineers who would channel it to a company president for presentation a year later to a board of directors. Hirshhorn picked up a phone, ordered an aerial survey, and obtained government permits to prospect on the islands of Banks, Melville, Lougheed, King Christian, and Devon, between Baffin Bay and Beaufort Sea.

"We spent about a million and a half," said Hirshhorn, "but I knew it was no phoney. It came from the heart; he was a fine man."

In the Arctic Islands he leased 2,400 square miles of natural gas and oil lands which in 1954 he brought to Callahan Mining Corporation. That same year, as a means of raising the funds needed for Algom, Hirshhorn applied to the Securities and Exchange Commission in Washington for approval of a Callahan stock issue to expand the corporation's activity into the field of uranium.

But the deadlines were shortening. London's Rio Tinto, a component of the Rothschild financial complex, had not yet shown more than bystander interest in Algom. The two representatives, Earl B. Gillanders, formerly a geologist with Eldorado, and his associate, Duncan R. Derry, were expected to scout fresh opportunities for the Britons, whose largest base-metals mines in Spain had been nationalized three years previously by Francisco Franco. Hirshhorn regularly advised Gillanders and Derry of progress in the Algoma mines but they stood pat in their conservative wait-and-see game.

Meanwhile, Blind River had erupted into a boomtown. Invaded by armies of engineers, drillers, pilots, and miners, the sleepy old lumber town was bursting its seams. Every train dumped more job seekers, claim speculators, and prospectors into the town's four "beverage rooms." They crammed the Harmonic Hotel, bedding down in bathtubs and corridors. With Pronto expecting to lift ore by September of the coming year, and Algom the same time the year following, up to 10,000 men, women, and children soon would be crowding into the town. The new city of Elliot Lake was on the drawing board. Dormitories for bachelors were rising on the lakeshore, later to be converted into apartments for families. "If uranium proves to be a long-range proposition," one planner prophesied, "we see no reason why that town shouldn't grow to twenty thousand."

Blind River, however, devoted itself to "more immediate" business, said *Time* magazine. A tax to pay for public improvements was rejected by the town council. Instead, two of the hotels intended to build more rooms and "Menard's department store whose basement

[was] given over to the only undertaking establishment prospered enough to plan a separate funeral parlor." Law enforcement commandeered the cellar of the Masonic Hall as an adjunct jail to handle the Saturday night drunks. As yet, Police Chief Leo Trudeau had to cope only with mobile prostitutes.

"A couple of weeks back," he reported in August, "two good-looking women drove into town in a big Cadillac. They had one price for the motel and one for the use of the Cadillac, but they stayed on just long enough to do a fast business and moved on before we got to them."

A branch of Jack Purcell's Toronto brokerage was doing a land-office business. Cabbies, clerks, even high school students were trading in penny stocks. One speculator, Joe Hagger, sold his restaurant to devote full time to the market. He shortly built himself a new home for $30,000 and was planning to open a new concern—Blind River's first pawnshop. "I know it'll be lucrative," he said.

■ ■ □ □

At home in New York, things were not good. His new wife, Lily, baffled Hirshhorn. Their styles conflicted. Lily slept late in a separate bed canopied with netting, and worked at her easel in her studio when Hirshhorn looked for her in the kitchen or bedroom. The year they wed, Hirshhorn and Lily had adopted a daughter, Amy, and three years later Joanne. With the children he had tried to restore the constellation of a family but it eluded him in his constant shuttle between Toronto and New York.

The Hirshhorns moved to East 82nd Street in Manhattan to an elegantly appointed house which reflected their taste for antiques and French paintings. Later their suburban home in Port Chester expressed their common love of comfort and fellowship. Lily, applauding his desire "to help artists," steered Hirshhorn to the lofts of her Village cronies. Gatherings with Philip Evergood, Robert Gwathmey, and Frank Kleinholz at a Thanksgiving dinner brought patron and artists together; but even in familiarity, Hirshhorn never wholly lost his wonderment.

Hirshhorn and Lily clashed in matters of art when she attempted to incline him toward Impressionism. At a gallery she openly disapproved of his choice of four paintings by Nicolas de Stael. Hirshhorn did not argue. Alone, he returned to the dealer and purchased four more, at prices varying from $1,200 to $4,000. The value of the deStaels jumped to ten times what Hirshhorn paid for them. From then on Lily no longer assisted with his collection. He flared when a catalog for an exhibit credited his loans: "From the collection of Mr. and Mrs. Joseph H. Hirshhorn." Indignantly he refuted any hint that Lily had influenced his acquisitions. "I don't ask the advice of anybody," Hirshhorn declared. "I don't care if my grandfather or my friend or anybody likes it."

To stay closer to his family and be near the mines at the same time, Hirshhorn decided to build a home beside Lake Huron on Bootlegger's Bay, so called from the time it did port service for rum-runners in the Prohibition years. He approached Philip Johnson to design one that would cost $25,000. To fit the small budget, the architect offered to adapt an existing plan, but Hirshhorn was determined to have something resplendent. Johnson then designed one for $200,000.

"Oh," Hirshhorn demurred, "I don't want anything that fancy."

Johnson modified the plan and Hirshhorn built the house without disclosing the cost of construction.

When it was finished, he asked Johnson, "Philip, why did you design me this particular house?"

"What do you mean?" said Johnson in surprise. "You told me you only wanted to spend $25,000."

Hirshhorn shrugged. "You ought to have more sense than to believe me."

Looking at him, Johnson was aware he was only half joking. "He couldn't help himself," the architect observed later. "He just had to have it cheaper."

In the course of visiting the house during construction, Johnson detected an extraordinary change in his client's demeanor. Hirshhorn's eyes danced and he vibrated with excitement. He was nurturing a dream and at one point, unable to contain himself, he burst out.

"I'm not interested in industry and manufacturing," he said. "I'm interested in discovery, resources: that's creative. It takes imagination. It took a lousy $30,000 to get the Blind River project started and now there's maybe $10 billion in wealth there. The new town, Elliot Lake, will have twenty thousand people making their living—mills, railroads, schools, the works. And I helped build it. Now," he paused, his eyes gleaming, "I want to build a town."

The idea intoxicated Johnson. To plan a city was an opportunity rare in the life of an architect. Caught up in mutual enthusiasm, Johnson remembered, their separate dreams "egged each other on."

Hirshhorn commissioned the architect to design Hirshhorn City alongside Lake Huron.

They chose the site and Hirshhorn bought the land on Highway 17 at the cut-off to Elliot Lake, about 8 miles east of Blind River. Johnson made topographical maps and a model which detailed a school, medical clinic, firehouse, town hall, houses of worship for three faiths, a motel, and a shopping center with a western-style arcade. From the railroad station, the approach afforded an unobstructed view of the town nestling against a mountain. The focal point of the plan was a museum for the Hirshhorn art collection and an office tower dominating a plaza which was to be dotted with sculpture. When Hirshhorn saw the model, he jigged in delight around his hotel suite and cried, "We gotta do it!" He wanted to rush out to buy "a big Picasso." He did commission a Henry Moore and a Jacob Epstein—"a big one."

The dream burgeoned. A foundation funded with Algom Mine stock would establish an institute for mental hygiene, free to children because, Hirshhorn asserted, "Many youngsters lack a sense of balance. We'll be better people if they understand what makes them tick." With the town plaza in mind, he stepped up his purchase of modern sculpture and of antiquities, including Etruscan, Greek, and pre-Columbian. He envisioned art as a living force in the community, and expressed his conviction with the fervor of an evangelist.

"This is going to be an aesthetic town—laid out for growth," he rhapsodized. "It'll have a big square, like in Italy, with sculpture and a museum, too, with paintings. Maybe the miners won't be different because of the beauty but their kids will."

Engineers and surveyors were ordered in to lay out the town according to Johnson's blueprint. Bulldozers growled and cleared the terrain for four apartment blocks which were to rise first and provide 300 dwelling units. Before any construction could commence, trenches had to be dug for the infrastructure—"A silly neologism," Johnson said wryly, "which means water supply and sewage systems and roads." The capital investment would be huge, about $30 million, which didn't seem to concern Hirshhorn. What did give him pause was a tense atmosphere growing up around the project. It emanated from Blind River.

Hirshhorn was puzzled. There was enough precedent for naming a town after distinguished mining men—Timmins, a native Canadian; and Schumacher from Cincinnati. To deny the honor to "a little kid from Brooklyn," he felt, would be arrant prejudice. There had to be another reason, a material cause. Hirshhorn cudgeled his

Hirshhorn, in his graduating class from P.S. 145, Brooklyn, sits directly in front of the teacher. (1914)

The family in 1935. Seated are Rose Berman (*left*), Jennie's mother, and Amelia Hirshhorn (*right*), his mother. Jennie and Hirshhorn are standing. The children (*left to right*) are Naomi, 4; Robin, 12; Gene, 9; and Gordon, 6.

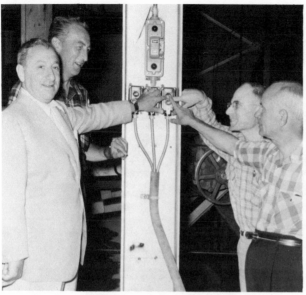

At an informal ceremony on August 28, 1955, a press of the button starts the $6,000,000 Pronto Uranium Mines plant into production. *Left to right,* Hirshhorn, mine manager Paul E. Young, geologist Franc R. Joubin, and company president William H. Bouck.

Abram Lerner (*left*) and Hirshhorn (*right*) visit Henry Moore in England in 1962. (*Charles Gimpel*)

Hirshhorn stands beside Larry Rivers' portrait "Cockeyed Joe." (*Cal Hood*)

Hirshhorn in Canada, 1956. (*Barrett Gallagher, Fortune*)

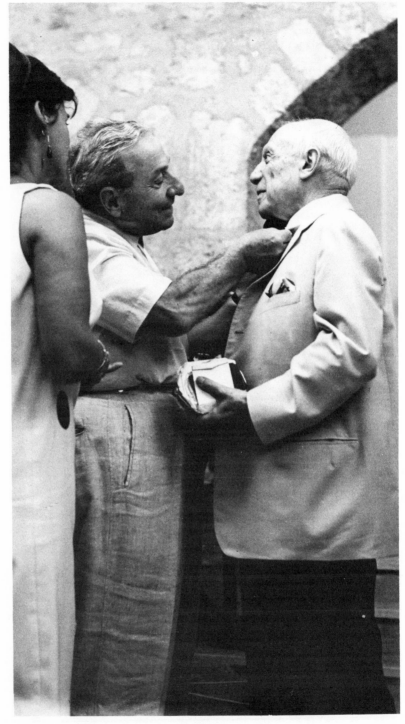

Hirshhorn straightens the tie he gave Picasso. The jacket
was also a gift.

The paintings and sculpture pictured on these two pages were bought in one day in 1957. (*Hirshhorn Museum and Sculpture Garden, Smithsonian Institution*)

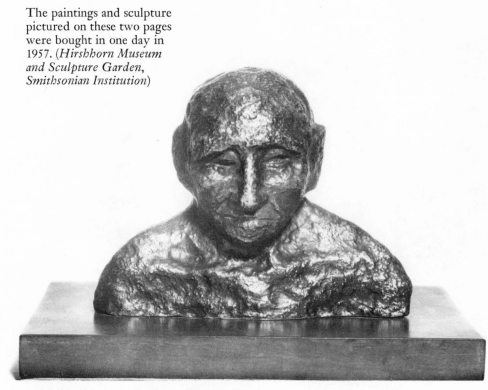

Pablo Picasso, *Head of a Man*, c. 1905. Bronze, 6⅝″ × 8¾″ × 4⅛″.

Robert Motherwell, *Blue Air*, 1946. Oil on canvas, 41½″ × 27⅞″.

Georges Braque, *Hesperis*, 1939, cast 1955. Bronze, 16¼″ × 8¾″ × 3½″.

George Luks, *Girl in Orange Gown*, late 1920s. Oil on canvas, 36″ x 30″.

George Bellows, *The Sea*, 1911. Oil on canvas, 34″ × 44″.

Thomas Eakins, *Miss Anna Lewis*, c. 1898. Oil on canvas, 32⅞″ × 27⅞″.

I. Rice Pereira, *Two Becomes One*, 1951. Front plane: mixed media on glass; back plane: casein on gessoed panel, 22⅜″ × 18⅝″.

Hirshhorn with a model of the museum. Abram Lerner stands behind him. (© *Arnold Newman*)

President Johnson and Hirshhorn at the ground-breaking of the Museum in 1969. (*United Press International Photo*)

The airlift from Round Hill, 1974.

An early air view of the
Hirshhorn Museum
and Sculpture Garden.
(*Lee Boltin*)

Portrait of Hirshhorn taken by his daughter, painter Naomi Caryl,
in Los Angeles, 1978.

memory but it remained shrouded until August when he received a phone call from a representative of Blind River requesting an appointment.

Hirshhorn recalled the lumber town before the uranium rush, when bacon and eggs served up in generous portions were 75 cents. As the bonanza brought throngs to the restaurants and bars, the same dish, slimmed down, cost $4. Hirshhorn had condemned the greed of the locals, reproaching them for robbing the men who came to work the mines. He had let it be known that, in addition to culture, people in the new town of Hirshhorn would be getting a fair shake at the shopping center.

On Labor Day 1954, a Blind River delegation of fourteen appeared to request that Hirshhorn abandon his vision of glory. The businessmen of Blind River wanted no competition for their boom dollars. Hirshhorn was nonplussed. "I only wanted to help Canada," he explained. The townsmen made quite clear they wanted no more of his help; and he realized he "couldn't impose it on them." The men departed and with them went Hirshhorn's dream.

"Building the town would have been a financial nightmare," said Philip Johnson in retrospect. "I don't think he cared so much as he wanted to symbolize in a physical way what his big dream was. At bottom always practical, he actually lost nothing. I don't think we had to cancel one order for materials; just a few days of bulldozing to clear the land for the apartments." A note of regret crept into Johnson's voice. "He always talked as if he were beginning a great adventure. I loved to work with Joe, and I would again. Who wouldn't?"

Later, Hirshhorn and Joubin donated a $250,000 community center to Elliot Lake. The W. H. Collins Memorial Center, completed in May 1958, was dedicated to the man whose geological map solved the mystery of "Location X." His widow, age eighty-four, attended the ceremonies as guest of honor. Hirshhorn did not. He lay abed in New York nursing a cold.

■ ■ □ □

Early in 1955 Hirshhorn had released a report prepared by Joubin which updated the activity in the entire Blind River region. On the basis of drilling at intervals of 1,500 feet—normally probes were made at two and three times that distance—Joubin's geological findings presaged deposits underground of 150 million tons of uranium ore. Its high grade found in the shallow Pronto shaft confirmed expectations in the deeper strata of the upper bars of the "Z," all of a uniform quartz-pebble conglomerate. One contract from the government's Eldorado Mining issued to Pronto called for $55 million of uranium concentrate to start delivery in the fall. Published in the *Northern Miner*, which circulated throughout the world, the report reached Oscar Weiss, representative of Rio Tinto in Johannesburg. He phoned London.

"What," he inquired, "are we doing about this?"

His query, forwarded to Gillanders and Derry, elicited the response, "We know all about it."

Weiss, however, decided to see for himself. Within three days he entered Hirshhorn's office in Toronto and introduced himself. "Rio Tinto must have this," he said firmly.

From that moment, events moved swiftly. Weiss telephoned J.N.V. (Val) Duncan in London. The president of Rio Tinto hastened to Toronto. Hirshhorn called Dean Acheson in Washington to be told that Rio Tinto's brokers, Benson and Lonsdale, whose senior partner was Sir Mark Turner, were "top drawer." In February, Hirshhorn and Val Duncan sat at breakfast in the King Edward Hotel and with their coffee reached an agreement.

Hirshhorn canceled the application to Washington for a Callahan stock issue. Eventually, the corporation made an agreement with Pacific Lighting and Gas Development for a pipeline to deliver gas from the Arctic Islands to Canadian and U.S. markets.

Hirshhorn summoned Joubin and Bouck to his suite. Bluntly, he put the question to them. "How much equity do you want to give up in return for financing?"

Joubin wanted to pick up his chips and walk away. He had no taste for managerial responsibilities. "We're halfway to the nut house now," he muttered. Nevertheless, he viewed the Algom not as one enterprise but as five independent units: Pronto, Quirke, Nordic, Buckles, and Northspan. "I want five bullets in my gun," he said, "not just one."

Rio Tinto of Canada Ltd. purchased one-third of the Algom Quirke Mine on the north and of the Algom Nordic on the center limb. Rio Tinto Management Services Ltd. took on the technical direction.

On schedule, Pronto produced its first 1,500 daily tons of ore in September. For the occasion, Hirshhorn gave a reception for the Earl of Bessborough. His Lordship, the chairman of Rio Tinto, arrived from London to stay at the house completed only four months before for Hirshhorn and his family. However, Lily and the children were not present. Hirshhorn and Lily had parted the year before and on his visits to Manhattan, Hirshhorn had resumed his single state, this time in the Ritz Towers.

Solitary but rarely alone, Hirshhorn was introduced during one excursion in New York to Brenda Hawley, a flesh-and-blood link to one of the Bourbons he had reverenced in his youth. Brenda was the grandniece of Collis P. Huntington whose son, Henry, bought *The Blue Boy* by Gainsborough which hung in the Huntington Museum in California. Tall, blond, lacquered, and vulnerable, Brenda while still in her twenties had been wife, mother, and widow. More recently she had divorced Julius A. Heide, Jr., heir to the candy millions, and was living with her parents on West 23rd Street. Hirshhorn wooed her with euphoric dash and gardens of flowers.

Early in June 1955, as "Canada's biggest mining mogul" conducted a group of financiers and bankers on a tour of his uranium properties in the Blind River area, the Toronto newspapers headlined the news of a breach of promise suit brought against him by Eluned Humphreys. Formerly a stenographer in his employ and listed as president of Rhodes Exploration and Finance of Canada Ltd., one of his companies, Miss Humphreys was privy to his records and books. Whether she enjoyed other intimate knowledge was unconfirmed. Don Smith, the geologist, recalled an evening he had dined with Hirshhorn in his King Edward Hotel suite. As they sat with their drinks, Miss Humphreys emerged from an adjoining room, snatched the bottle from Hirshhorn, snapped, "You've had enough for one night!" and retired.

Hirshhorn refused to respond to the action and presumably the suit was settled out of court. Miss Humphreys left Canada precipitately for California where, reportedly, she married before migrating to Spain. Questioned about the episode, Hirshhorn remarked rather wistfully, "Her typing was excellent."

Whenever the subject of infidelity arose, Hirshhorn was unequivocal. "There never was another girl," he asserted. "I wasn't that kind of guy. I'm a man's man"—hastily adding—"I'm also a woman's man. If I had to make a choice, I'd rather do business with men."

One close observer spoke sympathetically of Hirshhorn's woe. "He didn't like the idea of playing around. To risk a clandestine meeting may have given him a jolt, but he didn't really enjoy it."

To meet the Earl of Bessborough, Hirshhorn invited two hundred guests, a baroque admixture of titled sophistication and bush crudity. Canada's Prime Minister, Lester Pearson, Sir Denys Lowson, former Lord Mayor of London, Dean Acheson, and members of the Atomic Energy Commission mingled with miners, geologists, engineers, and Gillanders and Derry, whom Hirshhorn referred to as "the rock doctors." Drinks flowed from the garage which was converted into a bar guarded by a collie and two blue-eyed Persian cats. After strolling over the broad lawns sloping toward the lake, the guests entered the L-shaped glass house to dine on steak and lobster and to eye the art densely covering the inner white walls. Hirshhorn strode among his company clad in heavy boots and thick lumberman's pants and plaid shirt, generating high spirits and low formality. One arm about the towering old Earl, he steered the Queen's uncle through the crowd making introductions. Drawing near his public relations director, Hirshhorn presented him. "Meet Professor Ed Parker"—and indicated the aged nobleman—"I want you to meet my illegitimate son." Encountering Stan Holmes, Hirshhorn hooked his arm and swung the young geologist round to Bessborough. "Earl," he crowed, "I want you to meet the kid"—and addressing Holmes—"Hey, kid, tell 'em about the ore. Tell 'em—tell 'em how sexy it is!"

The opening of the Pronto Mine and Mill was celebrated on October 15 with a banquet in Blind River's hotel. The menu was printed in miner's jargon. The mill circuit (dinner) consisted of Pronto primary feed (appetizer), solid reagents (Northern Ontario turkey with dressing, cranberry sauce, vegetables, and salad), precipitate (apple pie and cheese), and solutions (beverages). The evening's program, broadcast over the Canadian radio network, was chaired by W. H. Bouck, president of Pronto. W. A. Hutchison, heading the official opening committee, welcomed the guests; Franc Joubin told the Pronto story; W. J. Bennett, president of Eldorado, spoke of Canada's atomic energy program; P. T. Kelly, Ontario's Minister of Mines, delivered the government's congratulations to the uranium industry; and A. W. Manby of Ontario's hydroelectric commission spoke of the future of atomic power. Hirshhorn's comments, appropriately titled "Money and Mines," dealt with just that.

In the next five months the knots in the Hirshhorn plan came untied. In the Blind River beds lay 80 percent of all the uranium in Canada, 20 percent of the entire western world's. Besides Hirshhorn's nine mines, four others—Denison, Can-Met, Stanleigh, Stanrock—emerged from the claims rush. Together they provided the government's Eldorado agency with over $1 billion in uranium. Reserves calculated to last at least forty years were valued at an estimated $12 billion. By agreement, Hirshhorn transferred to Rio Tinto of Canada his nine mines in Blind River and his consolidated fifty-seven companies for prospecting, developing, and mining which comprised his empire of uranium, gold, silver, zinc, lead, iron, and oil. They represented an equity of $74 million. Excepting Pater, a copper mine, the other eight mines—Pronto, Quirke, Nordic, Milliken, Buckles, and Northspan, a combine of Lacnor, Panel, and Spanish-American—held orders from the government agency aggregating $631,910,000 for uranium delivery by 1962. In exchange, Hirshhorn received $48 million plus over 50 million shares of Rio Tinto of Canada and chairmanship of the board. He deemed it "a good ticket." Among the earliest consequences was Rio Tinto's guarantee to the Bank of Montreal, the Chase National Bank, and to Morgan, Stanley and Company for a $90 million loan for the immediate development of Northspan.

On one of his regular weekend rounds of the New York art galleries with Robert Lehman, the head of Lehman Brothers chided Hirshhorn. "You should have given us a chance to buy your company," he said.

"You wouldn't have gone into it," Hirshhorn mollified him. "Besides," he added, "Lehman Brothers wouldn't have given me such a good deal."

Lehman smiled. "You're right; we wouldn't."

Rio Tinto provided its board chairman with a fine new office on Bay Street. He promptly covered the walls with paintings. Backed by the House of Rothschild, the stock of Peach Uranium vaulted to $28. The value of Joubin's 100,000 shares, his 10 percent of the original Hirshhorn enterprise, rose to $2.8 million. Joubin "picked up his marbles" and stepped out of Rio Tinto. He entered the United Nations foreign service and departed for Patagonia. He felt the need to leave "the squirrel cage" of Canada where his phone never ceased to ring and promoters accosted him on the street with "every imaginable kind of proposition."

Hirshhorn too was harried by wild speculators. His greatest difficulty was convincing them that speculation was "a scientific art" and not a roulette wheel. At the same time he stoutly maintained that while "in the mining and oil business you're creating wealth, what's so fascinating is that it's ten to fifteen percent brains and about eighty-five percent luck."

A young Irish immigrant invaded Hirshhorn's office to enlist his support in getting started. "Come on," the newcomer challenged Hirshhorn, "what's your gimmick? I want to emulate you."

Hirshhorn, removing the cigar from his mouth, replied, "I had $4 million when I started. How are you fixed?"

Early in March 1956, parties of the first and second parts assembled in the nineteenth-floor office of Technical Mine Consultants. Platoons of solicitors came bearing reams of contracts prepared for the climax of uranium's 110-year drama. The lawyers shuffled the mounds of papers and X'd the dotted lines for Sir Mark Turner and Val Duncan to affix their signatures below those of Hirshhorn, Joubin, and Bouck. Forty agreements had to be rendered. The enormousness of the transaction charged the air. Hirshhorn, unable to contain his excitement, signaled to Ed Parker. They withdrew and went down the corridor to the men's room. Peeping under the panel of the booths to make certain they were alone, Hirshhorn executed a gleeful buck-and-wing and burst into uncontrollable laughter.

"Imagine me!" he chortled. "The little Hebe from Latvia making this deal with the Royal House of England!"

Abruptly the laughter faded and Hirshhorn's face changed. Joy struggled with uneasiness. He was still the new kid on the block.

In May, the moment his divorce from Lily was final, Hirshhorn raced into his third marriage. He and Brenda sailed for Europe aboard the SS *Coronia* to spend their honeymoon in their new house on Cap d'Antibes, fronting the water. Hirshhorn also bought 77 acres in Vallbone overlooking the Mediterranean, midway between Nice and Cannes. Following three months of holiday, they commuted between their apartment on Fifth Avenue—where Brenda "cooked breakfast for the Rothschilds"—and the suite in Toronto's King Edward Hotel, and often to the Riviera.

Shortly after Hirshhorn was proclaimed "Canada's Man of the Year" in 1956, T. C. Douglas, Premier of Ontario, took the floor in the legislature to say, "When he gets a $206 million contract with the Canadian Government to develop uranium in Ontario, he is a first-class free entrepreneur. The Liberal Party is not calling him a fraudulent racketeer now." Douglas was referring to the 1951 outburst by Alex Cameron in the Saskatchewan congress. "How did it happen," Cameron had raged, "that Saskatchewan permitted these valuable uranium concessions [in Athabasca] to fall into the hands of these racketeers?"

Emmet Hughes reported that British opinion of the Blind River exploit added up to: "Hirshhorn is called just a promoter, sometimes considered a dirty word. Where would Canada be without promoters? People will try to belittle him; in a way he's a great man."

William Bouck summed it up simply. "Joe was just too smart for a lot of sharpers. They don't like him."

On the train to Blind River one day, Hirshhorn turned to Ed Parker and said quite pleasantly of his Bay Street detractors, "I've shown those bastards. I've made them all millionaires."

To commemorate his uranium killing, Hirshhorn presented his daughter Gene with two antique pins. By conditioned reflex, she had them appraised.

"It had become so hard to accept anything from him without suspicion [of ulterior motives]. I wore the pins, enjoyed them, but I had first to go through all of that. It was part of the pastime of 'knocking Daddy Joe.' I honestly believe," she mused, "that he doesn't know how to deal with us. He's still insecure about money. He doesn't throw it away, not even on himself. It's invested; it works all the time. His income in royalties is enormous. But there's more to it than logic. If he asks, 'How are you?' God forbid you tell him you're not fine. All he'll say is, 'That's too bad.' He figures the next thing you'll say is, 'Can you give me . . . ?' I'd love to talk about important things. He can put things together about politics, the economy, about lots of things. He's brilliant. But he says, 'I don't know; forget it.' You'd think we were going to pick his pocket. It's too bad. He's a fascinating man. And I can't share it."

■ ■ □ □

In his office Hirshhorn celebrated the sale of his manifold mines to Rio Tinto with a huge frosted cake inscribed in confectioner's sugar with *E Pluribus Unum*. It sat in pink and green splendor on the center of his desk. Off to one side rested the prototype of Hirshhorn City in clear Lucite, its model buildings topped with black. Intermittently, Hirshhorn pierced the chatter and laughter of his staff and guests with bursts of song—"I'll be loving you always. . ." while his eyes, alighting fleetingly on the model, clouded. The Rio Tinto deal had materialized half his dream. The unrealized part lay in Lucite before him.

Hirshhorn had climbed to a plateau beyond his childhood ambition. Board chairman of Canada's Rio Tinto, he owned one of the largest blocks of stock in the company. Through Dean Acheson he had obtained a favorable tax ruling and had paid $9 million to the Internal Revenue Service. The walls of his Bay Street office were filling with recently acquired art. The nuclear arms program was expanding; all was well with uranium production. Twenty-six companies had contracts from Eldorado for $1.6 billion worth of the element, a third to be delivered by the end of 1958.

With nothing much to do but attend monthly board meetings, Hirshhorn found it difficult to shackle his enormous energy. He rescheduled his week to spend three days in Toronto and four in New York on art-buying binges, or on junketing with Brenda to Antibes.

In July 1958, shuttling back to France to rejoin her, Hirshhorn boarded a DC-7C at Idlewild (JFK) Airport. Four hundred and sixty miles out to sea, the drive shaft of one propeller cracked and broke. The plane shuddered and yawed and dropped 15,000 feet before the pilot regained enough control to level off in denser atmosphere at 6,000 feet. Rather than continue across the Atlantic, the captain radioed all air and surface shipping to stand by for emergency aid and tried for the U.S. Naval Station at Argentia, Newfoundland. For four and a half hours the crippled plane traveled north up the Atlantic coast.

To divert forty-four fellow passengers and nine crew members, Hirshhorn took to the aisles to sing and dance. He jollied the several children on board and cracked jokes. Among the travelers were Lucia Chase, director of the American Ballet Theatre, Eleanor Lambert and her husband, Seymour Berkson. He reported to his newspaper, the *New York Journal-American*, that Hirshhorn "generally made the whole thing seem a picnic as nerves relaxed and tension eased." When the disabled plane touched down, and the pilot's voice on the loudspeaker said, "That's it, folks!" the passengers cheered. A half-hour later they boarded a replacement aircraft and continued onward to Lisbon.

Jauntily, Hirshhorn made little of the exploit. "After all," he said, "my business is oil and mining. That's a gamble sometimes, too." Arrived at Cap d'Antibes, he crumpled and took to his bed to be nursed by Brenda for three days.

At his newly organized International Mines Services Ltd., Hirshhorn "tinkered with a few odds and ends," developing a silver mine, exploring the Arctic Islands, bringing in two natural-gas wells on eastern Lake Erie, and prospecting eighteen mines in Canada and the United States. His activity extended abroad to mining tin in Cornwall, England, and an aborted exploration for minerals in Saudi Arabia.

Since the spectacular success of Preston East Dome, Hirshhorn had favored naming his properties with the initial "P"—Peach, Pronto, Prairie Oil, Pango, Place Gas, Panther, Penelope, and Prado. A ceremonial occasion in honor of Governor-General Vincent Massey found Hirshhorn taking his turn according to protocol on the reception line. "Protocol!" he chirped. "Good name for a mine!"

Everyone in the IMS office, from its president to the elevator boy, shared in Hirshhorn's ventures. He bought stock in their names for which they paid, and when the market went up, they sold half, according to his instructions, getting their money back. "With the rest," Hirshhorn advised, "do as you like."

Presiding at Rio Tinto's board meetings, Hirshhorn lolled in his chair, puffing a cigar and listening to his conservative colleagues at their interminable deliberations. To jolt the talk to an end, he would wave his cigar and say, "Let's cut the baloney and make a decision." The meeting adjourned, Hirshhorn broke into song—"Toot-Toot-Tootsie, good-bye . . ."—and exited with a buck-and-wing. Periodically invited to meetings of the home office at Barrington House in London, Hirshhorn enlivened proceedings for himself by asking Henry Moore to lunch at the big circular table with the directors. The sculptor was totally unknown to them, and Hirshhorn spent the hour impressing Moore upon his compatriots. "He's a great man, very talented." At one conclave, Hirshhorn looked at his watch, excused himself, and departed. He returned shortly with eight maquettes by Moore purchased nearby at the Hanover Gallery and distributed them to the board members.

Ultimately he found himself at odds with company policy. "They weren't interested in exploration," he complained. "I only discovered that later. But I always wanted to know what was around the corner. Once a thing was going and everything was fine, I didn't bother with it. They liked to play safe and buy into things. I wanted to shoot crap."

His frustration mounted as he watched nuclear power tack uncertainly and the Atomic Energy Act of 1954 steer the uranium market onto the shoals of conflicting interests. "Atomic energy shall be directed," it stated, "so as to make the maximum contribution to the general welfare subject at all times to the paramount objectives of making the maximum contribution to the common defense and security." Budgets for developing peaceful uses in industry, agriculture, and public health shriveled in comparison with those of the Pentagon. Explorer missiles and satellites shot into space by the hundreds bearing two-thirds of their payloads for the military. Warheads were stockpiled until the potential for overkill resulted in stalemate and obsolescence. The Atomic Energy Commission allowed its Algom options to run out and extended the time of uranium oxide deliveries, resulting in cutbacks in production. All but one of the Rio Tinto mines in Canada shut down.

As a prop against recession, Rio Tinto of London acquired the Empress nickel deposit in Rhodesia, the Palabora copper mine and other metals, and joined them to its Canadian subsidiary. The effect was to reduce Hirshhorn's share in the company. His disenchantment was complete. In November 1960 he sold all his Rio Tinto stock to the London establishment, unloading 55,903,978 shares at 85 cents.

Describing his move in a characteristic paraphrase of Ecclesiastes, Hirshhorn said, "There's a time to eat and a time to go to bed; a time to wake up and a time to shave. I'm bullish or bearish according to the way the market goes."

The sale yielded $45,818,318.30. In parting Hirshhorn presented an Eilshemius painting to Robert Winters, president of Rio Tinto Canada, and headed for New York.

"I took the money and bought art," he said.

PART TWO

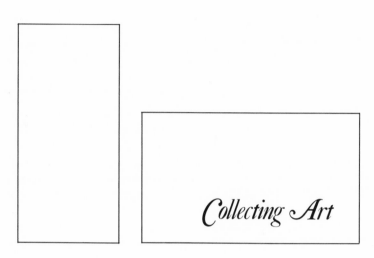

Collecting Art

V More than money went into Hirshhorn's art collection. He spent more than forty years acquiring 12,000 works, half of which he donated to the United States. He had not "ignored the present and plundered the past," as Russell Lynes said of his predecessors and contemporaries, nor had he been aided by agent or war.

Sulla sacked Athens in 86 B.C., flooded its streets with blood, and made off with Aristotle's library. Titus destroyed Jerusalem and transported the sacred Temple treasures to Rome. Egypt was stripped of its heritage by Napoleon. His officer in command of transferring the antiquities to France declared, "Antiquity is a garden that belongs by natural right to those who cultivate and harvest its fruit."

Luigi Palma di Cesnola, United States consul to Cyprus after the Civil War, exported without the knowledge of the Ottoman government 35,373 antiquities, a collection which figured prominently in his appointment in 1879 as the first director of the infant Metropolitan Museum of Art. Henry Havemeyer had Mary Cassatt for a guide in buying art, and Charles Lang Freer had James Whistler to educate him. Albert C. Barnes sent William Glackens with $10,000 to shop for him in Europe. Chester Dale's wife, Maude, a painter, chose the works her husband paid for. Henry Frick, P.A.B. Widener, Benjamin Altman, J. P. Morgan, and the rest depended on the Duveens, Knoedlers, and Gimpels to do the hunting for them.

Hirshhorn never entrusted his purchasing to an expert or emissary. He did his own legwork, attending shows and visiting galleries and the studios of artists. Often buying in lots, he did so according to his own judgment. Whatever the flaws in his collection, the mistakes were his own.

Andrew Mellon, otherwise inarticulate about art, spoke of collecting as if he were making investments. He bought only the Great Masters. He submitted pictures to rigid investigation, yet even so he was duped. He insisted on balancing opinions against his own; on living with a painting before concluding the deal. His dictum: never decide at the point of a gun—a prudent precept which Hirshhorn followed in commerce but not in art. He maintained, "If you've got to look at a picture a dozen times before you make up your mind, there's something wrong with you or the picture. You've got to buy what you believe in."

René Gimpel, the French art dealer and son of a dealer, found American collectors men of little personality who displayed their pictures to visitors like rich children showing off their toys. In contrast to them, he drew in his admirable diary a sketch of his countryman Arthur Veil-Picard. "He came slowly down the long gallery, his hat pushed down on his ears, eyes slitted to kernels, his nose in his moustache, his moustache in his mouth, his mouth in his chin, head down on his shoulders, his whole body sagging into his legs. That's the leading collector in Paris. He has never sold any but a few magnificent pieces from his collection. This peasant from the Pontarlier region, whose rural origin is quite obvious both in his appearance and in a most frightful accent, built up his magnificent collection alone and without benefit of advice."

Hirshhorn possessed the same temperament and qualities. He took chances—"shooting crap"—on his responses to art. He did inquire naively at times about an artist—"Will he make history? Will he be in the book?"—but he inveterately gambled on contemporary art and young talent.

"Sometimes," observed Andre Emmerich, owner of one of New York's venerable galleries, "I think collectors have difficulty in the toilet. Their inability to make up their minds must reflect in constipation. Not Joe."

How explain the phenomenon of Joseph Hirshhorn, the collector of art? With only elementary formal education and devoid of stimulation from his family background, he responded to the beauty of color and form. But he went far beyond any of his contemporaries in the obsessive pace of his collecting and the eventual size of his collection. Francis Henry Taylor, a former director of the Metropolitan Museum of Art, reasoned that acquisitiveness on that scale was "a sort of devil of which great personalities are frequently possessed. . . highly interesting in their own right even had they never collected anything." René Gimpel considered it "easier to enter into the unreal world of the poet than into that of the painter."

Not for Hirshhorn. He refused to be excluded. He sought out artists who opened their world to him and he dealt directly with the artist whenever possible, outdistancing dealers in their own business and meeting them on better than equal terms. He shattered the decorum of gallery and auction room with his uninhibited behavior which ripped away solemnity and pretension. And most wondrously, he disdained the cardinal maxim for preserving wealth by spending capital as well as interest for upwards of $30 million worth of art.

Originally, money meant survival to Hirshhorn. When he achieved wealth, he arrived at the great divide which separates property from position and saw the bridge to gentility supported on its two piers, the near one inherited riches, the far one good breeding. He, a first-generation tycoon without an Ivy League veneer, lacked the credentials to make the crossing, what Francis Taylor called "the eternal conflict between blue blood and yellow gold." Hirshhorn would have his heirs cross over only if he himself preceded them. Ward McAllister's Four Hundred were not inviting Hirshhorn into their midst, but he refused to submit to their snobbery, or to imitate them. Even if Ailsa Mellon Bruce could pay $1.5 million for Renoir's *Pont Neuf*, Hirshhorn would rather have been Monsieur Hazard who a century earlier got the painting for 300 francs ($75).

To build his own bridge to "class," Hirshhorn chose to collect American art. Riotous in personality, energy, and appetite, he gobbled up everything. "Picasso," remarked one artist, "ate up art history and spit it out as abstraction. Joe ate up art and made a collection."

Hirshhorn did not, however, allow his taste for beauty to cloak him in gentility. He dressed and behaved like anyone's uncle and spoke like the proprietor of the hardware store around the corner.

He missionized, distributed copies of Alfred Barr's *What Is Modern Painting?* and Sheldon Cheney's *Modern Art*. When Henry Geldzahler, then the Metropolitan's curator of American painting and sculpture, viewed the exhibit of Hirshhorn's collection of sculpture at the Guggenheim Museum and commented, "The selection falters when the human form is not involved," Hirshhorn dismissed him as "just a kid." He refused to put on intellectual airs or suggest that he was privy to a mystery the general public couldn't unriddle. Quite the contrary; he stressed his humble origins, his childhood poverty, his lack of education. When asked to define those qualities of art which communicated to him, he used no *raffinerie*, said nothing opaque. He described a picture as "speaking to me" when it was "clean" and had "guts." He knew it "was realized" if it "sang" and "made me feel weak." Critic Vivien Raynor thought he did not "try to express anything but wild enthusiasm for his treasures. Certainly," she said, " 'It knocks me cold' may not be acceptable as art appreciation, but it is possible that sensitive talk about something that has become just another industry may now be redundant."

Showing visitors through his house on Round Hill, Hirshhorn would point to several hundred thousand dollars' worth of beauty and laugh, "How do you like my *hazzerai?*" (Yiddish for "junk") and switch the mood to say quietly, and convincingly, "Art has always been a necessity to me. I don't see how people can consider it a luxury." He horrified the establishment. "Just people" were delighted, and their appreciation heightened his own enjoyment. Within him the thought took root that material possessions can be owned privately but the beauty that is art should be shared with the public.

Patterning his invasion of the art world after his assault on Canadian mining, he picked brains. He stole time from business affairs to prowl galleries, and he read art history. He listened intently when artists conversed, and learned to spot crotchets in critics. He passed up what was in vogue and bought what his instincts bade him. The nearest he came to the services of a Bernard Berenson was at the outset during his novitiate at the ACA Gallery with Herman Baron. Until then Hirshhorn's passion had found its channel mainly in printed reproductions. As late as the early sixties, when the New York Graphic Society purchased the publication rights to ten paintings from his collection, Hirshhorn still had hanging over his fireplace on Round Hill a reproduction of Rembrandt's *Titus*, surrounded by a real Picasso, Bellows, and Eakins. It sold for $40, and had been a gift from Norton Simon, who acquired the original paint-

ing for $2.5 million. Hirshhorn later hung the print over the fire-
place in his La Quinta home. He simply liked the picture.

■ ■ □ □

Joseph Hirshhorn and Herman Baron were immigrants and short of
stature, and there ended their likeness. About ten years Hirshhorn's
senior, and of a gentle, poetic bent, Baron disapproved of capitalism,
particularly in art. Gassed and discharged from the army in World
War I, he took his damaged lungs and idealism to upper Madison
Avenue where he and his wife, Ella, opened a shop to sell window
shades and picture frames. Mostly Baron framed the photos of dwell-
ers in Harlem. Once in a while a painting would come for framing
from a resident of the affluent Upper East Side, and Baron would
hang the painting on his wall to contemplate it until its owner called
for it. In the midst of the Depression, he moved to West 8th Street,
down the block from the Whitney Museum, and established the
ACA Gallery, which he dedicated ideologically to Social Art. Although a doctrinaire, he did not deny I. Rice Pereira, apostle of the
dawning school of Abstract Expressionism, an exhibit beside the
muscled workers of Hugo Gellert and William Gropper's political
lampoons.

The ACA was germinal in Hirshhorn's development as a collector. Baron and his gallery introduced him to the inner world of art,
and for almost twenty-five years they threaded through his life, as
did Abram Lerner and Bella Fishko, who became Baron's assistant
when the gallery moved to East 57th Street in 1942 and, upon
Baron's death in 1960, opened her own Forum Gallery. Lerner, who
joined ACA in 1945, twelve years later became curator of the Hirshhorn collection.

Hirshhorn began showing up at the ACA in the thirties. Soon
Ella Baron was telling tales of the little man who rushed up and
down 8th Street and "bought and bought and bought." Asked what
he did for a living, Mrs. Baron, in an awed voice, would reply, "He
has gold mines!"

Hirshhorn was an outsider until Baron welcomed him, as he did
many strays. "One could always go to the ACA when depressed and
sit in the back room," Sarai Sherman, a Greenwich Village artist,
recalled. "Hirshhorn was an old back-room guy." He would show up
of an evening to share Baron's black bread and herring and heed the
good talk, responding to the candor of the artists. "Big people, out-
going," Hirshhorn said, adding ingenuously, "not jealous." Gropper

wondered why Hirshhorn "didn't go into another field, collecting stamps, maybe; but in the thirties, after the Armory Show, the art world was sensational. Maybe," he surmised, "it was organic to him."

Gropper's skepticism did not come between him and Hirshhorn's hospitality. Late Friday afternoons, Hirshhorn would enter the ACA, look about to see if anything pleased him, then pull out a bundle of cash and pay on the spot. Retiring to the back room, he either supped on Mrs. Baron's plain fare—"She was a terrible cook," Hirshhorn moaned—or he gathered up his hosts with any artists who chanced to be there and went off to the Royale Cafe on Second Avenue. Hirshhorn plied them with steaks while he drank in their discourse.

Baron admired Hirshhorn. Sarai Sherman recollected, "It was Hirshhorn's stamina, his daring. He held nothing impossible and therefore everything was possible. He played for big stakes on young artists. He figured what could he lose? He was a gambler, not the Las Vegas type but like the politicians, the big industrialists. In the fifties, people thought him comic; they told him he was buying in the wrong galleries."

Back in 1927, Hirshhorn had made his first "serious acquisition," a red-haired nude by Warren Davies whom Vivien Raynor referred to as "the classic calendar artist." He spent $125. It was one of several pictures he remembered on his bedroom wall in Brooklyn. He purchased others, too, an animal study by Landseer, the Jozef Israëls doctor attending a sick baby, and Bouguereau's *Madonna of the Lilies*. His childhood infatuation lasted until 1932 when he brought Amelia's nephew to America from Riga.

Isac Friedlander, an artist trained at the Rome Academy, found his cousin's audacity appealing—*fegato Italiano*, he called it, an Italian liver. He broadened Hirshhorn's perspective beyond the Salon academicians and Hirshhorn sold his Bouguereau for $5,000 to Michael Meehan, a stockbroker, who presented it as a wedding gift to his daughter. The other Salon works soon followed. Isac also opened his cousin's eyes to the school of American realism and to Louis Eilshemius. Seeing Hirshhorn's home in Great Neck filled with early Italian primitives, Isac twitted him: "How does a nice Jewish man like you come to have this kind of art?" Gradually, the crucifixion paintings were disposed of.

Curiosity soon extended Hirshhorn's interest to the French who were then impressing their stamp on the States. He consulted the John Levy Gallery about Matisse, Picasso, and Rouault. That conservative dealer, from whom Hirshhorn had purchased the Bouguereau, advised him against those painters "who didn't know what they were doing." Hirshhorn, already leaning toward the contemporary, dropped Levy.

Hirshhorn readily reacted to Social Realism. At the ACA, and soon at other salons, he met scores of artists and cut his "eyeteeth" on David Burliuk, Philip Evergood, Robert Gwathmey, Herman Rose, and the Soyers, Moses and Raphael, all of whose works he began to collect by the dozen. Yasuo Kuniyoshi and Jack Levine were little known when Hirshhorn bought their paintings. As his experience deepened, he entered the world of Max Weber and inclined early toward the abstractions of Arshile Gorky.

"Every time I presented a fresh talent and he turned out to be a hit," said Bella Fishko, "Hirshhorn had already bought at an earlier show. John Chambers, an unknown from Canada, one of my first at the Forum Gallery, later made it, but Joe had several long before."

The dedication and perseverance of artists filled Hirshhorn with wonder and their poverty pained him. Other rich men bought Renoirs and Monets, "but," Hirshhorn told Aline Saarinen, "those artists were long since past having to worry about paying their children's doctor bills. These guys did have to worry; they had to worry plenty. I'd take them out and buy them proper nourishing food and lend them money. And I'd buy their pictures."

Though he, himself, would snack hurriedly at the Automat, Hirshhorn felt a pang seeing Arshile Gorky go through the cafeteria's revolving door clad in a winter overcoat and bedroom slippers. "I helped him in my cockeyed way," Hirshhorn told a reporter; "bought drawings in the early days. . . . You couldn't help them; you couldn't give them money."

"Artists," the interviewer reminded him, "are very interested in money."

"No," Hirshhorn contended, "they don't care about it. They care only about their work."

Still, he wouldn't buy what he didn't like. "I once tried to persuade him," said Fishko, "telling him the artist was poor and in need. He pulled out a couple of hundred dollars and told me to give it to him without saying whom it was from. He just didn't like that artist's work."

Hirshhorn's wealth galled some of the Social Artists. A few at the ACA smoldered at Hirshhorn "slumming like Otto H. Kahn, buying pictures at low prices which left little for the artist after the deduction of the gallery commission." A capitalist patron of class-conscious talent, Hirshhorn did not escape the dudgeon of their left-wing philosophy. This was not without its comic overtones when one of them said, "If a guy is in the stock market, what would it cost him to give a few shares to the artist?" They pestered Hirshhorn for tips, and he yielded.

"Suddenly," Raphael Soyer recalled, "everybody was in stocks—Gwathmey, Avery, I, too. But Sarah, my wife, was against it. 'Mines have explosions,' she argued, 'and people get hurt, even killed.' I pulled out. The others lost their money. It was funny to see Baron, the radical, open the *New York Times* every day to look at the stock market report. Mesabi Iron—he was interested in Mesabi."

And for good reason. The Mesabi was one of Hirshhorn's more spectacular successes. To show his appreciation to his mentor, he lent Baron $2,500 to buy the stock. It soared. With the proceeds, Baron repaid the loan and moved the ACA to East 57th Street into what was formerly the Marie Harriman Gallery, above that of Pierre Matisse and Ferargil, next door to Valentine and across from Durand-Ruel, Curt Valentin, and Parke-Bernet before it relocated on Madison Avenue. Situated on the street of golden galleries, Baron and the ACA made it across class lines.

As a patron of the Village Da Vincis, Hirshhorn explored a milieu as densely populated as Antwerp where in 1560 artists outnumbered bankers two to one and butchers four to one. Sarai Sherman likened his monomania to mushrooms "which sometimes grow and sometimes don't; but when they do come out, you can't stop them. They keep coming up." Another painter likened Hirshhorn's intuition to that of an internist. "He could touch the body and know what the hell's going on," said Irving Block. "I recommended an artist, a student of Arshile Gorky, who is one of Hirshhorn's passions, and he wasn't impressed. 'Your friend,' said Hirshhorn, 'is a good painter but he's not a thinker.' I brought his attention to a sculptor and he said, 'I don't like him. You may be right and I may be wrong but he's dead.' Later, I saw Hirshhorn was right. The sculptor showed no growth. There *was* a deadness." Conversely, once he was gone on an artist, Hirshhorn kept buying him. "It was very personal," said Pierre Matisse, "like admiring a woman. When he liked something, he liked to have it."

Louis Eilshemius was only one example of his enduring infatuations. In 1939 Hirshhorn bought his first Eilshemius at the Kleeman Gallery. In the next eleven years he acquired hundreds of oils, watercolors, pencil drawings, and chalks, some during visits to the five-story house on 57th Street where the artist lay dying. As recently as 1975, Hirshhorn paid $1,200 for an Eilshemius landscape.

The first picture Hirshhorn bought at the ACA was a Philip Evergood. To frame it, he went to Fourth Avenue to the shop of Lazouk, a former ballet dancer, only to discover Evergood at work there as a framer for $25 a week.

"Evergood was a darling human being," said Hirshhorn, using a favorite endearment. "I said to him, 'You're a very talented man [Hirshhorn's other choice compliment]. Why don't you come and see me on a Saturday at One Fifth Avenue.' I made him quit his job. 'Listen,' I said to him, 'you go ahead and paint and I'm going to buy some of your art.' I bought a lot of his drawings and paintings. [Sixty-eight were in the gift to the museum.] He painted strange faces and things. Once I took the subway up from Wall Street to 57th Street. I saw people sitting in the subway and Evergood had caught their expressions. He sang, and he was also a good drinker. He was a darling man."

In 1938 Evergood accompanied Hirshhorn to the Preston East Dome Mine in the Porcupine and stayed four days, painting nearly all the time. They shared quarters and Evergood recounted how Hirshhorn woke in the middle of the night to pace the room and cry out, "They're trying to kill me!" Two major works by Evergood resulted from this trip: *Madonna of the Mines* and *Wheels of Victory*, the latter a $2,000 prize-winner in the 1944 "Portrait of America" exhibit.

In his early days, Raphael Soyer carried his canvases to the Whitney Museum for possible sale, and from there down the street to the ACA for display. "No museum director came to my studio," said Soyer with quiet irony. "Joe did. He was the only one to buy directly from the studio."

At the suggestion of Milton Brown, the art historian, Hirshhorn walked up one flight from the ACA, when it was on East 57th Street, to the Egan Gallery to see the work of Herman Rose and spent $3,000 on his pictures, including *Skyline*, painted the year before, in 1949. It hung in the inaugural show at the museum in Washington. The money permitted Rose to switch from Sunday painting to daily easel work. A year later Hirshhorn visited his studio. Rose was away. Hirshhorn looked about and purchased a similar amount. In 1952 Dorothy Miller presented "Fifteen Americans" at the Museum of Modern Art, exhibiting Rose beside Clyfford Still,

Edwin Dickinson, and Mark Rothko. Before the show opened, Hirshhorn bought another group of Rose's work and met the painter for the first time in the basement of the museum.

"He was more than a patron to me," said Rose. "He was very personal. He came to every show I had and bought five or six each time. He must have about seventy-five."

Ten years later, Hirshhorn bought enough of Rose's work to enable the painter to travel and see the art of Europe. At his Zabriskie Gallery exhibit, Hirshhorn, upon departing, paused at the elevator to congratulate Rose with an exuberant college yell.

"I was stunned," Rose said. "All I could think to do was yell back, 'Three cheers for Joe!' "

Late one Saturday night in 1952, Joseph Solman was preparing his show at the ACA and helping Abram Lerner hang the pictures, when Hirshhorn dropped in and picked the best four.

"How much?" he asked.

"Two thousand," said Lerner.

Without a word, Hirshhorn paid. It was the first real money for Solman, who until then had been selling parimutuels at the racetrack for six months in order to buy the next half-year to paint. Four years later, with his family, he was able to visit Europe to study and work.

At times Hirshhorn was erratic to the point of eccentricity. He visited the 9th Street studio of Chaim Gross in 1951, departed with forty watercolors, and was not heard from until he returned the portfolio without explanation. Encountering the sculptor at an exhibit, Hirshhorn said, "Chaim, I'm coming to see you," and did not appear for several months, by which time Gross had moved to his 12th Street studio. The sculptor was carving in stone. Hirshhorn shed his coat, peered about, stabbed his finger at five pieces in stone and at a child's figure in ebony. Gross named his price and Hirshhorn, cutting it in half, donned his overcoat with a curt, "You want it?" Gross took it, delivered the half-dozen works to the office downtown, and was paid on the spot.

When Gross next heard from Hirshhorn, the sculptor had moved again. Hirshhorn phoned Gross at his 105th Street studio to say he wanted his portrait done. Once a week at 7 A.M. the chauffeured limousine called for the artist and drove him to Hirshhorn's office. During the sitting, they chatted and munched sandwiches as Hirshhorn questioned Gross intimately about his family life. One morning about ten o'clock, Hirshhorn said, "I'm tired." They piled into his limousine and streaked up to a gallery where Hirshhorn bought $6,500 worth of primitive art in ten minutes. During the sittings, Hirshhorn ordered portraits of his daughters Joanne and Amy, 15-inch full figures and small heads. When Gross delivered the pieces, Hirshhorn pulled out a wad of money and began peeling off twenty-dollar bills into the artist's hand. "I told him, Enough!" said Gross, "but he just kept on peeling."

Beginning in 1949, Hirshhorn spent time with Willem De Kooning. Often they lunched together. "When he was sober, he was the kindest man," said Hirshhorn, "a great artist and a darling human being. When he was drunk, he was terrible." Hirshhorn owned over forty oils and drawings by De Kooning, including early ones such as *Seated Man* (1939), *Special Delivery* (1946), and *Woman* (1948). He kept buying De Koonings consistently. In 1965 the artist painted three doors.

"He said he wanted $25,000 and I paid him," said Hirshhorn. "The museum has them, and the others too. His pictures bring six figures today. In 1974 the doctor warned him about his liver, and he stopped drinking. He came to the opening of the museum sober as a church."

Hirshhorn went to Los Angeles in 1960, where Lerner told him to look up Irving Block to get the lowdown on the west coast art scene. Block, "a private painter" at the time, worked in films. Hirshhorn invited him and his wife, Jill, to dinner and questioned him closely. Block responded without mentioning himself, preferring to maintain his "amateur standing." Jill, however, spoke up.

"You should see Irving's work," she told Hirshhorn. "He's a wonderful artist."

Discounting a wife's enthusiasm, Hirshhorn nevertheless consented. At his cottage in Laurel Canyon, the painter set up an easel and a chair 6 feet in front of it. Hirshhorn moved the seat to a distance of 20 feet.

"The works are small," Block explained.

"Look, kid," said Hirshhorn, "don't tell me how to look at pictures."

Block propped several on the easel, each 6 by 8 inches. Without a word, Hirshhorn took them in hand and sat on the floor.

"You're pretty good," he said. "Let me see more." He chose a goodly number and turned to Block. "How much you want for them? And don't cheat me." Block quoted a moderate sum. Hirshhorn paid it, saying, "You should raise your price. You're a good painter."

Over the next nine years, after purchasing more of Block's work at the Ankrum Gallery, Hirshhorn asked to inspect additional ones at his home but there were none. Block had joined the faculty of Northridge College in the San Fernando Valley and had little time to paint.

"When I have a sabbatical—"

"I'll get you one," Hirshhorn cut in, and back in New York phoned Block. "What's your annual salary? Take a year off. I'll pay for it. You arrange it with the school and just paint."

"What," Block asked breathlessly, "do you want in return, Joe?"

"Oh, I'll take some paintings."

Block received his grant in two equal payments from the Hirshhorn Foundation and was cautioned to silence. "If this gets around," said Hirshhorn, "I'll be nudnicked by a lot of people."

"Don't you want some letter of agreement?" Block asked.

Affronted, Hirshhorn demanded, "What's the matter, don't you trust me?"

"It's the other way around," Block assured him. "How do you know what I'm going to do with the money?"

Hirshhorn laughed. "That's ridiculous! I think I'm going to adopt you, kid."

In that year, Block painted steadily, turned out a lot of work, and blossomed. When Hirshhorn showed up again, he asked to see what he had done. "It's all at the Ankrum," said Block. "You can have anything you want, Joe." As far as Block was concerned, Hirshhorn could have taken "the whole kit and kaboodle." Hirshhorn was embarrassed. "All those stories about his beating the artist down!" Block later related. "My experience has been opposite. He always added to the price I named."

Kenneth Snelson, the constructivist sculptor, voiced the same sentiment somewhat differently. "Hirshhorn wants artists to love him. That's probably the reason for his attraction to contemporary art. People have to be alive to love him. He doesn't haggle any more than a museum does. He's genuinely interested in what he collects, unlike others who sell as styles change. [The vogue of the sixties declining, Robert Scull unloaded his collection at Parke-Bernet and realized a substantial profit.] I don't know what Hirshhorn sees when he looks at my work. He'll say, 'That's terrific, kid!' I don't talk to him on any other level. He's willing to take a chance on love. If I didn't like him, I wouldn't deal with him. And he feels it. It's great to have such a character in the world."

Untiringly Hirshhorn ferreted out new talent. At the Krasner Gallery he bought *Small WC #13*, *WCH #14*, and *WCA #32*. It transformed the outlook of sculptor Nancy Grossman.

"Nobody told him, yet he bought it," she said. "I was twenty-three, living in a storefront and illustrating children's books. I had no precedent. I didn't even know anyone who was represented by a gallery and sold. It provided money to buy material and time to do more work. I've been living on my art since."

Carol Anthony was another. As late as 1974, Hirshhorn bought five of her works from an exhibit at the Greenwich Country Day School. He had never seen her work before.

At the age of seventy-four, Hirshhorn climbed six flights to the studio of Peter Passuntino on La Guardia Place in New York City's Soho and bought five monotypes. Descending, Hirshhorn stopped on the next landing. He knocked on the door as a young man mounted the stairs.

"Any paintings in there?" Hirshhorn inquired.

The young man unlocked the door and ushered him inside. On a bed in one corner a pair of bare feet jutted from a blanket. The young painter drew forth several canvases from which Hirshhorn chose four.

"How much?" he asked.

"Five thousand," said the artist.

Without a word, Hirshhorn made for the door. At three thousand he was still on his way and the price went to one thousand as his hand reached for the knob. At that, the blanket on the bed heaved violently. The feet disappeared and the cover fell away as a young woman shot upright.

"You can't do that!" she cried. "We have a child only five years old."

Hirshhorn advised the artist that a check would be in the mail the next day. Turning to the bed, he drew a hundred-dollar bill from his pocket and handed it to the young woman. "For your child," he said, and left.

On the way down he knocked on the door of Leon Golub's studio but received no answer. He would have tried all the other floors but the hour was getting late and Olga awaited him in Greenwich.

Usually upon arrival in his Toronto office, he was greeted by the works of artists spread around the floor and against the walls, ready for his inspection. He would authorize an associate to purchase the pictures of one artist or pay an annual stipend to another who showed promise.

Interviewed on Canadian television in 1960, Hirshhorn lauded the work of Jack Siegal, an unknown Canadian, whose painting he had hung in full view behind him. During the interview, Hirshhorn puffed on his cigar, blew smoke at the camera, and looking directly into the lens apologized casually. "I hope the smoke doesn't get in your eye." He invited the camera to follow him and focus on the paintings. Mentioning Siegal and the others by name, he told his audience confidentially, "Keep your eye on this guy," or "Dwell on this fellow." After the broadcast, Hirshhorn phoned Siegal to inquire how he liked the boost he had received. The artist's rejoinder was to complain that his painting had been hanging askew.

■ ■ □ ▫

His week divided between Canada and the United States, Hirshhorn hurtled through his four days in New York, finishing his business quickly in order to leave most of the time to pursue his obsession. At a corporation meeting he would excuse himself to keep a dentist appointment and depart a half-hour earlier to hunt pictures. Or he would simply say, "Mind if I step out a minute?," grab a cab, and speed to a gallery. Almost always he made at least one purchase.

His enthusiasms, however, were not shared at home. Business and art palled on Brenda. They encroached on her privacy and limited her party life to official functions. She preferred television to exhibit-hopping. Aline Saarinen, preparing her book *The Proud Possessors*, asked to see Hirshhorn, and met him and Brenda at the St. Regis for an interview over a drink and dinner. Soon bored, Brenda interposed, "Let's go dancing."

"She liked the kind of parties she read about in the gossip pages," said Hirshhorn. "I'm not that kind of guy. I never sat around. I'd go to a gallery."

They separated in 1960. Hirshhorn moved into a small residential hotel on Manhattan's Murray Hill.

Racing through galleries with the eye and speed of a hawk, his passage marked by a rush of wind and the predator's cry, Hirshhorn, like an elemental force, left changes in his wake. To buy five Walt Kuhns, he swooped down on a staid, leisurely establishment whose owner represented few artists. "In a half-hour," Aline Saarinen wrote, "that dealer's life changed; he was developing a tic." More hardened merchants, she said, recovered only after a long rest.

Abram Lerner was in his first week at work at the ACA when "this little tornado stormed in and said, 'You be a good boy and I'll take that one, that one, that one, and that one.' " New on the job and alone in the gallery, Lerner "just stood there waiting for the keeper to come." He phoned Herman Baron, who recognized Hirshhorn from Lerner's description and authorized the transaction.

Hirshhorn's impatience sounded harsh as he jabbed a finger and rapped out, "This, this, this, and that one. How much?" and swiftly computed the deal himself while the startled attendant was still fishing out her list to quote prices, her hand trembling as she laboriously made out the bill. "She's very nervous," Hirshhorn observed. Told he had frightened her, he exclaimed in puzzlement, "Why? I was very nice. I bought something." One aide compared him to a tank, complex, tough, unbridled. "He could also be considerate, sweet," said Fran Weitzenhoffer, research librarian for the collection, "even gentle."

In the days when the bell closed the Stock Exchange at noon on Saturdays, Hirshhorn pursued paintings the rest of the day with a flying squad of gallery-hoppers whom he marshaled, among them Eddie Cooke of Century Lighting, Ben Heffner, an attorney, William Weintraub, a public relations man, Maurice W. Haft, a garment manufacturer, and Albert Dorne, who later headed the Famous Artists School. After lunch at the Sherry-Netherland, they trotted off to nearby galleries, auctions, museums, and the studios and homes of Milton Avery, David Burliuk, Philip Evergood, Chaim Gross, and the Soyers. The troop tasted Hirshhorn's ardor as he made instantaneous buys and exhorted them to do the same. He presented Avery's works to his companions, several of whom later acquired additional ones on their own.

One Saturday early in the forties, Hirshhorn dropped in on Avery, who was then on hard times. Hirshhorn peered about the studio. He pulled out a wad of hundred-dollar bills, peeled off 120 of them, pressed them into Avery's palm, and swept the studio clean of forty paintings. In the center of his studio, Avery stood stunned by the windfall, staring from the bare walls to the $12,000 in his hand. Regaining his voice, he exclaimed in dismay, "I've been robbed!"

In his buying, Hirshhorn applied a simpler rule than the San Diego dowager who strolled through a Rolls-Royce showroom in London, pointing—"I'll have that one, that, and that one, and those two over there. . . ." She paid $92,000 in cash for seven Rolls and two Bentleys, and called it an "investment," certain that "antiques, especially antique cars," would hold their value. Questioned why he purchased several paintings at a time, Hirshhorn replied, "I can't afford to buy only one."

Ambroise Vollard bought about 250 canvases for 50 francs apiece from a depressed Paul Cézanne. Holding onto the pictures, Vollard in time disposed of them for up to 15,000 francs each. It established him as the wealthiest art dealer in Paris. But Hirshhorn never sold his Averys. He promoted the artist's reputation by his purchases, though Sally Avery, widowed in 1964, resented Hirshhorn's wholesale gain. She overlooked the fact that Avery had lived to see his work command sizable sums at Parke-Bernet auctions. The price of his *Portrait of Mrs. Avery* jumped to $7,000 in 1965 during the same period his *Three Seated Women* went for $8,000. Ten years later, Averys brought prices in multiples of ten thousand.

Only once did Hirshhorn dispose of pieces from his store of art. Struck by reverses in the Philippines at the same time the Rix-Athabasca mines were draining his resources, he put some French Impressionists on the block at Parke-Bernet. He also parted with two Eilshemius landscapes and a small *Family Group* by Moore. A week after the election of President Truman in November 1948, thirty-five items, worth a half-million today, were knocked down at $44,310, including a Monet, Cézanne, Renoir, Degas, Rouault, and Chagall, and several Pascins and a Redon, artists who subsequently reentered the Hirshhorn trove.

The tactics of dealers appalled Hirshhorn. Even as respected a figure as Joseph Duveen had insisted on paying a titled English-woman £25,000 for a family portrait instead of her asking price of £18,000 so he, in turn, could charge £50,000 for it.

Harry Brooks, head of the Wildenstein Gallery, was working for Knoedler when Hirshhorn breezed in to "pick his mind." Brooks suggested Maurice Prendergast's *Girl in Blue* at $10,000.

"How much off?" inquired Hirshhorn.

"The usual—fifteen percent," Brooks replied.

"What about the Eakins?"

Brooks looked at *Miss Anna Lewis*, said $35,000, and anticipating Hirshhorn's question, added, "Also fifteen percent."

Hirshhorn indicated three additional pieces and offered to take all five at one-third discount. A strenuous duel ensued which concluded on a compromise of 20 percent. At the day's end, Hirshhorn phoned to say his interest in the three works had waned but he still wanted the Prendergast and the Eakins—at the same discount, of course. Exhausted, Brooks surrendered.

Already in possession of several Prendergasts and Eakinses, Hirshhorn acquired the latter's *The Violinist* at the Babcock Gallery and returned to Knoedler for the portrait *Mrs. David Jordan*. By 1965 he secured the Samuel Murray cache of paintings, sculptures, and memorabilia which brought his total of works by Eakins to 129.

In September 1946, as yet a comparative newcomer to 57th Street's environs, Hirshhorn's first contact with David Smith occurred through the sculptor's representative, Marian Willard, whose gallery he visited upon the recommendation of Milton Brown. Rapidly he inspected the display, departed, and did not reappear until late October, when he selected the three *Medals of Dishonor* and a smaller bronze, *Woman in the Subway*. He offered $800 for the lot. Dubious of this brash unknown, Willard suggested $900 might be acceptable though that, too, was below the list price and would require the consent of the artist. Smith agreed and Hirshhorn paid $900. Over the next nineteen years the bronzes were joined by twenty-one additional Smiths, including the celebrated *Pittsburgh Landscape*. Friendship between sculptor and patron grew and lasted until the artist's tragic death in 1965.

"Hirshhorn had the appetite of a child, avid and shrewd," commented Pierre Matisse. "He knew when to work a price the hardest, like Helena Rubinstein. He sensed a weakness—when I needed the money." Matisse never argued with Hirshhorn or attempted to direct him. "It was impossible," said the dealer. "It only led to misunderstandings and harsh words. I just gave him his head."

Hirshhorn also knew when to slacken the line. At the Marlborough Gallery he selected five paintings which Frank Lloyd priced at $2,000 each.

"I'll give you $5,000," said Hirshhorn firmly, "not a penny more."

Lloyd sputtered and reddened. "You must be kidding!"

"You're a nice kid," Hirshhorn said and softened. "Let's have a cup of coffee."

The negotiation ended in his favor with a 30 percent discount.

Implacable, Hirshhorn could relent unexpectedly. One ear glued to the phone and stock quotations, his other ear heard the cries of distress from a dealer trying to sell him six color lithographs by Picasso for $34,000. Hirshhorn countered with $20,000. The price descended to $24,000, then $22,000. Hirshhorn demanded they split the difference and make it $21,000.

"Joe!" the merchant wailed. "Do you want to kill me?"

"No," said Hirshhorn hastily, his eyes widening. "Okay, twenty-two."

"When a collector like Hirshhorn spends so much time in the art world," said Max Weitzenhoffer, "he begins to know as much as dealers. At that point he finds it psychologically difficult to pay the full price."

The director of the Gimpel-Weitzenhoffer Gallery cited examples of Hirshhorn's two-way effect on dealers. Weitzenhoffer's establishment sold one client a Louis LeBrocquy simply because that artist had entered the Hirshhorn collection. But because Hirshhorn never received less of a rebate than a museum, generally more, he added to the difficulties of at least one dealer who answered his phone one day to find the secretary of Governor Rockefeller on the other end. "The Governor wants to know," the secretary said, "if he can get a ten percent discount." Charles Gimpel was virtually the sole dealer who could get Hirshhorn to pay the asking price, perhaps because in the tradition of his father and grandfather he did not boost it to unreasonable heights.

The only other dealer who prevailed over Hirshhorn was June Wayne, publisher of the Tamarind prints for subscribers. She recounted how in 1962 Hirshhorn hurried into her studio in Los Angeles, looked her up and down, and said brusquely, "I've got forty minutes."

"What," she asked coolly, "do you have in mind?"

"Are you married?" Hirshhorn snapped.

"What's that got to do with it?" she shot back, unruffled.

Baffled, Hirshhorn got down to business, requesting a subscription—"one of everything Tamarind published." Wayne turned him down. She advised him to approach the artists and buy from them directly, not at subscription prices.

Having materially assisted Herman Baron with a loan, Hirshhorn encouraged other dealers with his trade. In 1955, Harold Diamond made his first sale to Hirshhorn, an I. Rice Pereira. In succeeding years, Hirshhorn bought his first Alexander Calder, *Fish Mobile* (1955), from this young dealer, another Pereira, *Two Becomes One* (1957), Naum Gabo's *Linear Construction #1* (1958), and Antoine Pevsner's *Black Lily* (1959). Three years later Hirshhorn bought five works by Willem De Kooning, including *Queen of Hearts*, from the Martha Jackson Gallery, and in 1964 Mark Rothko's *Number 24*. Hirshhorn was among the earliest to scent the leaders of the Washington School and acquired works by Morris Louis and Kenneth Noland.

In the case of Pierre Matisse, ten years elapsed from the time Hirshhorn bought three Chagalls until 1956 when he reappeared at the gallery. "I don't know," said Matisse, "he must have taken offense at something I might have done, probably over the price. He was going too far and I must have shown irritation. When he came back, it was as if nothing had happened. I was astonished. The atmosphere was pleasant; he kidded and he bought the Marino Marini *Bronze Bull* without bargaining." A year later Hirshhorn bought a

Miró and a Reg Butler and then took the shortcut to another Matisse artist by inviting Loren MacIver to lunch. From Longchamps they went to the painter's studio but his artifice didn't work; MacIver referred him back to the gallery. Hirshhorn bought her *Skylight Moon* and *Spring Snow*, adding them and nine more to his collection. Thereafter he dropped in regularly on Matisse, from whom he acquired a Maillol and an Etrog, several by Balthus and Riopelle, and many Giacomettis and Henri Matisses, including the *Four Backs*.

In 1954, arriving on Saturday from Toronto, Hirshhorn happened into the Curt Valentin Gallery to be confronted by Henry Moore's elegant yet haunting *King and Queen*. Completed the previous year on a commission from the Uris Brothers, Percy and Leon, it had enhanced the lobby of the new office building they had erected at 380 Madison Avenue. The tenants had rebelled at being greeted daily on the way to work by the twin figures, and the embarrassed brothers had sent the majestic Moore to the gallery, where it waited on the decision of Mrs. Albert List, who was seeking her husband's consent to buy it for $12,000.

"Did you make a commitment?" Hirshhorn asked Valentin.

"No," the dealer replied, "it's tentative."

"I'll take it for twelve," Hirshhorn said instantly.

"It's yours," said Valentin.

The value of the Moore, which now stands in the plaza of the museum in Washington, was last estimated at $1.5 million.

The crowded opening of a Theodoros Stamos show coincided with the marriage of his gallery owner, Andre Emmerich. Late that Saturday, Hirshhorn arrived to hear the news and to be presented to the bride. Lifting his voice and shattering the gallery hush, Hirshhorn sang his congratulations, accompanying himself with rhythmic clapping of hands and dancing. "No collector," said Emmerich, "ever expressed himself with such freedom and joy." Hirshhorn bought a group of Stamos paintings and Emmerich, regarding it as a wedding gift, celebrated by shortly closing the shop and going home with his new wife.

At the Felix Landau Gallery in Los Angeles, Hirshhorn's eye went to Gisele Neiman, the attractive assistant. When she spoke, he noticed her accent and asked "in a nice inquisitive manner where I was from and to tease me, talking in Yiddish to Landau's astonishment. In less than ten minutes, Hirshhorn spent $5,700 on four Jack Zajac sculptures." Hirshhorn commented, "I'm not only bullish, I'm Yiddish."

The same common touch stamped his encounter with Jacob Epstein, from whom he had ordered a sculpture. Shortly after being
knighted, the artist came to New York.

"What's doing?" Hirshhorn inquired. "What about the project?"

"I didn't get to it," Epstein admitted apologetically. "I was busy
with other things."

Hirshhorn wagged a finger of rebuke at Sir Jacob. "Yankele," he
chanted, "you're a bad boy!"

Epstein, himself up from the Lower East Side of Manhattan,
understood Hirshhorn perfectly.

While living at the Ritz Towers in 1955, Hirshhorn bought a spate
of small sculptures, including a Reg Butler, at the Emmerich Gallery. Wanting them immediately "to live with," he, Emmerich, and
the gallery assistant loaded their arms and drove to the hotel. They
crowded into the elevator with two tall, distinguished-looking men.
Hirshhorn stared at them towering over him. Freeing a finger, he
poked one of them in the stomach.

"Hey," he said affably, "don't I know you down on Wall
Street?"

With exquisite disdain, they ignored the question and Hirshhorn's existence. Hirshhorn was not to be put off.

"I'm Joe Hirshhorn," he said heartily.

Magically, the pair unbent, their faces wreathed in smiles. "We
didn't know you lived in this hotel!"

Hirshhorn acknowledged their sudden cordiality. It was a type
of snobbery he generally met with sardonic humor, as when Charles
Burns, a banker friend in Toronto, introduced Hirshhorn to a col-
league who boasted of his model farm, his prize produce, the stock
of his herd, and was overproud of his own lineage. "You've simply
got to see his spread," Burns enthused, but no invitation was forthcoming from the hidebound breeder. At parting, Hirshhorn turned
to him with unaffected warmth.

"I'm coming up to see your place, and I'll be there for breakfast," he promised. "But one thing—no bacon, please. I'm kosher."

Pierre Matisse observed his aplomb when Hirshhorn, invited to
lunch at a villa in southern France, entered minus his trousers. His
pants had been soiled and torn on the way there. In jacket, vest,
shirt, and tie, an ensemble of sartorial chic set off by a pair of plaid
swim shorts, Hirshhorn frolicked about and put all at ease over his
own inconvenience.

With the same facileness he made the acquaintance of Picasso during frequent stays at the house on Cap d'Antibes. "I was able to get some paintings with help from him," Hirshhorn remembered. "We had a great time together. I taught him to do a buck-and-wing. He liked my jacket, so I gave it to him. Fitted him perfectly."

Hirshhorn varied his attire as much as his deportment. Ordinarily, his clothes favored sobriety: white shirts, Dunhill suits of gray or black, the ever-present clip-on bowtie. Unpredictably, he would switch to a sport jacket of screaming plaid. In the same way, humility changed to flamboyance, pugnacity replaced politeness, guile faded into innocence, the transformation so swift as to seem unpremeditated. In business, even the perceptive adversary mistook his responses for real feelings, misapprehending his true purpose. When it came to dispelling tensions or lending a hand, his graciousness and courtliness were ineffable.

On his rounds, Hirshhorn once entered the Forum Gallery to be introduced by Bella Fishko to a lofty lady from Winston-Salem. Fishko was having difficulty thawing her rich client, who confused aloofness with dignity and taste. Grasping the situation, Hirshhorn broke into "Carolina Moon" and circling the visitor's waist, waltzed her around the gallery. Winston-Salem melted.

Time was when Hirshhorn made his presence felt in a restaurant by dressing down the maître for his undistinguished menu, the poor table, and worse service. Having reduced the man to thoughts of suicide, Hirshhorn would hand him a twenty-dollar bill and say, "Forget it."

Later, Hirshhorn could forsake such performances. Entertaining his staff at the 21 Club with filet mignon and champagne, he tucked a napkin in his collar, ordered himself a mushroom and barley soup, and consumed the dish closest to his favorite "stoup," a stewlike soup his wife Olga prepared for him at home.

■ ■ □ □

Olga Zatorsky Cunningham entered Hirshhorn's life in 1961, the same year he gave up smoking and purchased the Round Hill estate in Connecticut. Separated from Brenda in January and living in the hotel on Murray Hill, he had awakened in the middle of the night attacked by heartburn. "The switchboard operator was off somewhere. For almost four hours I literally climbed the walls. I got over it finally but I made up my mind." In the morning he dumped two and a half boxes of Corona Belvederes. From smoking thirty to thirty-five cigars a day, he quit cold.

In March he moved to Round Hill in Greenwich. The Tudor-esque château of stone and brick roofed with Ludovic russet tile stood on the summit of 22 acres overlooking Long Island Sound to the east. The gardens and lawns, front and rear, he transformed into settings for 144 pieces from his treasury of sculpture, and the 23 rooms served as a repository for hundreds of paintings and drawings. Besides a tennis court, a swimming pool, and a gardener's cottage, a five-room apartment topped a five-car garage.

One day, shortly after moving in, Hirshhorn called a local employment bureau. A woman answered.

"Services Unlimited."

"This is Mr. Hirshhorn. I just bought the Sinclair Robinson house on John Street. I want a chauffeur. I don't care whether he's white or black. I'll pay a good salary."

His "ordering a chauffeur like a loaf of bread" disconcerted the agency woman. Figuring him for a busy man, she determined to demonstrate her exemplary service. The woman was Olga Cunningham.

A native of Greenwich, Olga was born in 1920, the third child of Nicolas and Barbara Zatorsky, who migrated from the Ukraine early in the century. At Greenwich High School, Olga had won the singles tennis championship and swimming awards and had fallen in love with her English teacher. A year after her graduation they married. By the end of twenty-three years, she had three sons, a divorce, and a flourishing employment agency evolved from a swimming instruction class, a nursery school, and a baby-sitting service. She lived five miles from Round Hill in an old Victorian farmhouse where she had reared John, a sculptor, Graham, a Wall Street broker, and Dennis, an environmentalist.

Piqued by Hirshhorn's manner, Olga decided to handle his request personally. From her file she selected a suitable candidate, checked his references, and phoned Hirshhorn.

"Mr. Hirson, this is Mrs. Cunningham."

"My name isn't Hirson," he barked. "It's Hirshhorn—H-I-R-S-H-H-O-R-N!"

His brusqueness stunned her. "I know him better now," she said, "and I sympathize with people who meet him for the first time." She arranged for Hirshhorn to interview an applicant the next morning at nine. At 9:15 her phone rang.

"Mrs. Cunningham," said Hirshhorn severely, "how dare you send me a man who arrives for an interview drunk?" In the midst of her apologies, Hirshhorn cut her short. "Mrs. Cunningham, how old are you?"

Matching his directness, Olga replied, "I'm forty-one. How old are you?"

Automatically, Hirshhorn answered, "I'm sixty-two."

Actually he was sixty-one. He had always thought he was born in 1899. Not until 1975 did he learn that he was a year younger when he was shown the passenger manifest of the SS *Cedric*, the ship which brought him to America in 1907. It listed him as seven years of age.

Olga submitted chauffeurs for his approval and Hirshhorn would keep one for a week or two, then dismiss him and phone for a replacement. He found Olga's voice "youthful and interesting; she was very bright and answered fast." After several exchanges, he asked, "Why don't you come and visit me?"

"Of course," replied Olga, "but I'll have to charge you my regular consultation fee."

He approved of her businesslike manner. She arrived, they talked, swam in the pool, and lunched. He continued to fire chauffeurs and hire chauffeurs. Occasionally Olga herself acted as his secretary. Before long they were seeing each other regularly, and a courtship ensued.

In 1962 Hirshhorn's doctor ordered him to the White Plains Hospital in Westchester County, New York, for a gall bladder operation. As he came out of the anesthetic, Olga was at his bedside. His first act was to ask for the stock quotations. Scanning the newspaper, she called them off.

"No, no!" Hirshhorn stopped her in exasperation. "You've got them all wrong—" and he corrected her from memory.

His divorce from Brenda became effective in 1963 and Hirshhorn married Olga the following year. She disposed of her business, Services Unlimited, and in answer to an ad placed in the *Greenwich Times*, Bill Sullivan was engaged as superintendent and later as the newest chauffeur. He and his wife, with two of their children, came to live over the garage.

In 1964 Hirshhorn had acquired another house in La Quinta, near Palm Springs, California, and in 1970 his present winter home in Naples on the Florida Gulf Coast. Ten years later he bought Olga a Valentine, a motorboat they named *Oatmeal*, since he was fond of his childhood cereal and she of the cookies. Shortly after, Hirshhorn replaced it with a houseboat which they dubbed *Oatmeal II*. Hirshhorn always paid cash for his purchases.

"Property," he said, "is like a suit of clothes."

At times Hirshhorn seemed to regard marriage as if it were the stock market, to be entered for growth and dropped, if possible, before its value fell. He passed off his exchanges with a quip.

"I've been married four times. Three threw me out, one out of a seven-story window. I landed on my feet instead of my head because I had an umbrella in my hand. This is positively the last one."

Underneath the waggery lurked a sense of defeat.

Years after their divorce, Brenda spoke of her relationship with Hirshhorn. "He has a lot to give. People don't know but one side of him"—adding pensively—"I was a café society girl. We met just a little too soon."

At a costume party whose theme was "Come As You Were," Brenda appeared as Madame du Barry. The *New York Times* reporter inquired why she had made that choice.

"I always wanted to be a courtesan," she joked, "not a wife."

When he read the paper, Hirshhorn was furious.

But he was capable also of gallantry. Over three decades Hirshhorn paid court to the Appleton sisters, Marie and Helen, from the days of the Whitney Museum on West 8th Street. Helen married but Marie steadfastly tended the sales desk at the museum, and when the institution moved to West 54th Street and on to Madison Avenue and 75th Street, she continued to dispense postcard reproductions, publications, and gentility. The sisters were "kinfolk" of the benefactor who had endowed Harvard University's Appleton Chapel; their great-grandmother was "a close friend of Henry"— Thoreau, that is. They lived in Brooklyn Heights and doted on parties for artists.

With a black beret on her white head, Marie was tall, willowy, quintessentially aristocratic. At parties, Hirshhorn would sedately kiss her cheek and invite her to dance, managing gracefully though his head reached only slightly above her waist. He teased her. She thought he was "the cutest thing." Each Christmas a box of candy from Plumbridge arrived with Hirshhorn's compliments. Marie adored the gesture, and the chocolates. Abruptly in 1965, the boxes stopped coming.

"You know what he sent us this year?" She looked perplexed. "A book—a book of pictures by David Duncan."

In November 1974, Helen died. "One month earlier," said Marie, "and she wouldn't have gotten to the Hirshhorn Museum opening in Washington."

■ ■ □ □

In the forties, Hirshhorn took to proselytizing visitors who crossed his threshold. As late as the sixties he converted Ray Stark, the film producer, to collecting art. He spent two days accompanying his neophyte on a shopping tour and took charge of negotiating his purchases of a Henry Moore and a Reg Butler.

Hirshhorn was himself led through the loftier reaches of the art world by Robert Lehman. The head of Lehman Brothers inherited a hoard of paintings from his father, Philip, along with his zeal to make of it "the finest private art collection in existence." Watching him execute his design, Hirshhorn came to know the financier for "a gentle, sensitive human being." He esteemed the banker's scholarship and "his encyclopedic knowledge of the art market" which exceeded the connoisseurship of the entire board of trustees of the Metropolitan Museum of Art, which he joined in 1941.

In the presence of superior knowledge, Hirshhorn in his usual way assimilated his companion's experience. Stopping only for a quick lunch at the Plaza, or a quicker one in the drugstore at the corner of Madison and 56th Street, they wound in and out of Lehman's haunts to expose Hirshhorn to a completely different perspective on galleries. He saw the owners of Knoedler, Valentine, and Carstairs defer to the collector. He kept his eye on Lehman as he bought a Rouault; and Hirshhorn purchased three at the Pierre Matisse Gallery—*Clown in an Interior, Hommage au Gilet Rouge,* and in 1944, *Christ and Fisherman.* Lehman invited him to the house on West 54th Street, back of the Museum of Modern Art, where hung the treasures coveted by the Metropolitan. Awestruck by the Rembrandts, El Grecos, and the abundance of Spanish, Flemish, and Italian rarities, Hirshhorn nevertheless did not follow Lehman down the road to the Old Masters.

"I was buying contemporary art," said Hirshhorn. "He thought I was crazy. I told him I didn't live in the past, that I was a contemporary man. He accepted that. My association with him didn't hurt."

Lehman, too, profited from their alliance. His firm participated with Hirshhorn in the British Columbia Oil deal and in Prairie Oil royalties.

In 1964 the Metropolitan Museum of Art, in electing a new president, bypassed Lehman after his almost two and a half decades of valuable trusteeship. Lehman resigned. To secure the Lehman collection, Thomas P. Hoving, the museum's new director in 1967, had the trustees do some furious thinking. They created a chairmanship and offered it to Lehman as an inducement to return to the board. Seriously ailing, he accepted the "honor." Two years later Lehman died and left the collection to the Metropolitan with the proviso that it be installed, intact and permanently, within a replica of its 54th Street setting.

Hirshhorn, who witnessed the snub and its effect upon Lehman, filed the incident away for his own instruction.

Museums imposed unbearable restraints on Hirshhorn because the art on exhibition was not available for purchase. Auction rooms were another matter. They permitted his enthusiasms and excitement free rein. "He behaved," said publicist Ben Sonnenberg, "as if he were a member of the Borah Minnevitch Harmonica Rascals."

Parke-Bernet auctions resemble Broadway openings. Ticket-bearing collectors, dealers, and artists drive up in limousines and cabs. Hugging the evening's "program," the catalog which contains coded notations of the items previously assayed and soon to be put on the block, the participants alight to greet earlier arrivals gathered on the sidewalk. They exchange pecks on the cheek and shoot guarded sallies like tracer bullets to search out each other's targets in the coming sale. All is charm and dissembling.

On the evening of May 27, 1976, into their midst Hirshhorn charged to hail the first familiar face in the crowd. "You son-of-a-gun," he yelled, "don't you dare bid against me or I'll kill you!" He was like Marcel Duchamp drawing a moustache on the *Mona Lisa*. Tremors radiated in all directions. To a question about his interest in the evening's proceedings, he shook his head mournfully. "I don't have any money," he sighed. "I'm here only to look."

During the auction he flouted decorum as usual, jumping up in excitement after a buy and crowing, "My name is O'Brien! I'm just a poor ballplayer out of left field from Yonkers! " He bid and bought a Tobey for $6,000. A second got away at $6,500. A third went for twenty, and a fourth and fifth for twelve and eight—all "too high." A Calder started at $15,000 and he muttered, "That takes me out of the picture." It was knocked down for nineteen. In each case his withdrawal disclosed his judgment and thrift.

Up came an Arshile Gorky. Bidding opened at $50,000 and went up in increments of $5,000. In less than two minutes the auctioneer rapped his gavel. Hirshhorn got it for $140,000. The audience burst into applause. "I didn't expect it to go that high," Hirshhorn grumbled, the Gorky being the primary reason he was there. Ten minutes later he shouted "$15,000!" and a Josef Albers was his. Just as readily he applauded the buys of other bidders, leaping to his feet and crying, "Great!" Compared with his conduct, theirs was furtive, as if to buy a work of art were an act of cosmic intrigue.

Hirshhorn cleared the air of mystery to reveal the auction for what it was, simply a market.

The show over, the crowd drifted out mid chatter and farewell kisses. A circle of gossip buzzed around Hirshhorn. Someone pressed in to congratulate him noisily on acquiring the Gorky and moved on. "He knows as much about art as I know Latin," Hirshhorn said. Asked how much Latin he knew, he laughed. "Three words," he said. "E Pluribus Unum. I learned that from a nickel."

Some artists carried their disapproval of Hirshhorn to absurd extremes. "We used to sit around," said Frank Kleinholz, "and when we ran out of talk, we'd jump on Joe."

One painter whose work appeared eighteen times in the collector's catalog declared, "He's not in *my* collection," and of Hirshhorn's febrile activity, "They [the collector and his curator] should have had someone advise them. They should have been ahead of the others [in the field of Abstraction]. They got the leftovers. The elite laughed at them."

That same artist failed to see his self-contradiction in saying, "The impression is that museums get the best work. That's far from the truth. A thing that will sell easily is going to go to a collector who can afford it. Even the dealer doesn't get the best from an artist. I'll have a show but keep the best that I like for myself. This applies to most artists. So the artist selects and the dealer selects, and a collector or a museum doesn't get the best."

Equally absurd was Hirshhorn's disillusion with some artists. To him it made no sense for an artist to be an anti-establishment ideologue and at the same time be avaricious, invest money in real estate and the stock market, live in a country home, and rail at dealers and collectors for victimizing him.

The artist's *bête noire* was the Internal Revenue Service. A law in 1969 governing gifts to museums permitted tax deductions of the cost of materials only—canvas, paints, and frames. The art value was disallowed.

Helen Frankenthaler, wishing to make a contribution to her alma mater, Bennington College, brought her problem to Hirshhorn. If he bought three of her paintings, he would own the art and Bennington would get cash, which would be her gift. All was arranged. Hirshhorn accompanied her to the storehouse with her dealer, Andre Emmerich. Carefully they selected the three paintings and agreed on the price, amounting to $40,000. At this point, things got muddled. Either Frankenthaler in gratitude had promised Hirshhorn a small painting as a bonus, or he, upon departing, pointed to a gouache on the wall and said, "I'll take that thrown into the deal." She was offended. The negotiation foundered. "She got very mad," said Hirshhorn. "We didn't talk for a long while."

Some regarded Hirshhorn's "love affair with art" as an admission of psychological guilt externalized in collecting—"doing good for others," and reflexively "doing himself good." Aline Saarinen wrote of one detractor who stated that Hirshhorn's "buying of socially conscious art [in the late thirties] with its bloated capitalists and gaunt sharecroppers was good for Hirshhorn's conscience. More accurately," said Saarinen, "it was in agreement with his conscience. There is nothing specious in his identification of himself with 'the little man.' The fact that he is worth millions simply makes him 'a little man' who has happened to make good."

When Hirshhorn began referring to his art objects as his "children," he implied tacitly, subtly, that an artist not represented in his "family" was unimportant. Which parent does not cherish his progeny above all others?

"Okay," said Larry Rivers, "he bought a lot and there was a certain strength in the relationship. But the period of being poor, being fed by him, is over. He always gave you the feeling he came out bitter. He wanted to buy but he wanted a devastating percentage."

Among the first in the early fifties to recognize Rivers in his many guises, Hirshhorn acquired thirty-one oils, drawings, collages, and sculptures, often snapping them up as they dried: *Molly and Breakfast* in 1957, the notorious *Billboard for the First New York Film Festival* in 1963, and *The Greatest Homosexual* the following year. Also in 1963 Rivers went to Greenwich to paint Hirshhorn's portrait. He stayed several days, working in the library as Hirshhorn went through "his customary changes from nervous pace to relaxation," most of it on the phone. For hours Rivers struggled to capture his subject, until, frustrated, he laid his brush down on the paper covering the Oriental rug.

"Goddamnit!" he exploded. "I don't know what's the matter. I can't do anything with your eyes."

"Is that what's bothering you?" Hirshhorn inquired. "Let me tell you," he informed Rivers seriously, "I have two different eyes, one shrewd and one kind eye."

In a half-hour Rivers completed his task. Hirshhorn titled the portrait "Cockeyed Joe." Later, Rivers commented, "There's some truth in it, a combination of looking at you with a jaundiced eye and worrying what you're thinking of him. I wanted to do another," he went on, vaguely dissatisfied, "but Hirshhorn thought it was only for business."

Hirshhorn praised Rivers vociferously. At that Parke-Bernet auction in 1976, when a Rivers went for $37,000, Hirshhorn stood up to shout his delight. A man, leaning over from behind, inquired, "Did you buy it?"

"No," Hirshhorn quipped. "The Louvre."

His neighbor looked puzzled. "Lou who?"

In discussing Rivers, Hirshhorn exclaimed, "He's the most talented painter we have around today. Crazy as a loon and wastes his energy, but he's great—and *m'shugah.*"

"The hostility toward Hirshhorn is honest," observed Sarai Sherman, thirteen of whose works were in his collection. "But saying 'Down with Hirshhorn' is provincial. You should be down on yourself. He dunned me out of my price—paid $2,000 instead of $12,000. I was angry; still am; but it's a love-hate. I don't know today whether I'm in the Museum of Modern Art only because he was willing to give up my *Motorcyclist;* but he did, and I'm there. Of course, he had to have another in exchange—for nothing—and a good one. And I gave it to him. But it was up to me, wasn't it? It was the law: What's in it for me?

"You can't attack Joe. You have to attack the system. He did what he did and you can't put the onus on him. He was down and he was up. He never went around crying the blues. Why hang it on him? Everybody tries to work the same thing. He gave his collection 'to the people.' It's the way of the gambler, to keep the game going. It's the way of the street. I don't believe that bullshit about America gave it to him, that it's the only place it could have happened. He did it himself. Nobody gave him a hand up. He's wise enough, smart and courageous, to put it out in the open."

■ ▪ □ ▫

Hirshhorn's art purchases increased with his fortune and his confidence. The chart of his first decade of buying, beginning in 1930, showed 10 to 60 items annually. The graph peaked to 140 for the first time in 1942, and fluctuated during the next ten years up to 200. With his uranium coup, it erupted in 1955 to 700. In 1961, after the sale of his Rio Tinto holdings, his acquisitions rose to 757, a quantity he duplicated in 1964. The record high in his forty-four years of collecting was 960 items in 1968, following the announcement of his gift to the United States.

In his first twenty-five years as a collector, Hirshhorn amassed 2,485 pieces of art. By the time the museum opened in 1974, he had almost quadrupled that amount, adding 9,522 pieces, which represented 79 percent of the total 12,007. The bequest to the Smithsonian Institution consisted of half that number.

The fury of his collecting turned tyrannous. Possessions glutted his households, offices, and warehouses. No one had seen all the collection; its scope could only be guessed, not graded.

To bring it under control, he established the Hirshhorn Foundation in 1956, and he acquired a curator. Besides providing the conventional tax shelter for his treasures, the foundation disbursed several subsidies to artists and published *The Story of the Armory Show* by Milton Brown. Otherwise it was dormant, though it objectified for the first time his concern for the collection's future. He began to envision "an active museum in which also would be a salon for younger painters, giving them a chance to show."

Failure to make Hirshhorn City a reality had touched something in him deeper than mines and stock promotions. It had grazed his mortality. The ex-messenger boy on his errand through life had recognized he was speeding toward the inevitable and needed to lift himself from nonentity, else, like Melville's Bartleby the Scrivener, he would end up in the "dead letter office."

Pythagoras said, "Men are like God in only three things: knowledge, music and painting." Thus, a man, after years of getting and spending, might reach out, according to John G. Bowman, chancellor of Pittsburgh University, "to connect his life with something he thinks is eternal." Pliny the Younger wrote to his friend Annius Severus, "I have lately purchased a statue of Corinthian bronze. . . . I did so not with any intent of placing it in my own house but of fixing it in some conspicuous place in my native province, preferably in the temple of Jupiter, for it is a present well worthy of a temple and a god. Pray, give immediate orders for a pedestal to be made. I leave the choice of marble to you but let my name be engraved upon it, and if you think proper, my titles."

Similarly Hirshhorn wanted to ensure himself immortality while he was still alive. "You know," he once confided to Abram Lerner, "you can't come back. You can't make a deal."

Hirshhorn's friendship with Lerner had begun in 1945 when Lerner joined the ACA Gallery. Younger by thirteen years, short as Hirshhorn and slighter in build, Lerner was gentle where Hirshhorn was volcanic, reasoned instead of instinctual. More important for Hirshhorn, he belonged to that mystical league of the artist.

A native product of New York and its art schools, Lerner graduated in 1935 from New York University into the Federal Art Project as a muralist. He painted throughout his ACA days, participating in several group exhibits. He would accompany Hirshhorn to other galleries and auctions but never urged the purchase of a particular item; he found it sufficient to say, "Joe, you ought to see this show," and invariably Hirshhorn selected the prime works. In 1955 Lerner quit ACA. Funded by the Hirshhorn Foundation, he spent two years in Europe studying and painting. Returning, he took employment at the Artists' Gallery before assuming the curatorship of the Hirshhorn collection in 1957. The following year he held his one-man show at the Davis Gallery, but with mounting curatorial duties, painting became his recreation.

Over the years, the two men drew closer and Lerner advanced from chamberlain to confederate. Sometimes, witnessing Hirshhorn's mass procurement, Lerner was hard put "to separate the collector's desire to acquire from his love of art." Hirshhorn would phone to inform him of ten or twelve pieces newly purchased, exulting, "I did some damage today." Lerner chided him for overbuying, overspending. He tried to persuade him that certain works were superfluous or unworthy, while others were necessary additions to the collection. Respectfully, Hirshhorn listened to his opinions and advice but his purchases were motivated by independence, predilection, willfulness, or power, and Lerner argued eloquently to no avail. Helpless to prevent Hirshhorn's "mistakes," he sometimes made his own.

Lerner first performed his duties in Hirshhorn's place of business at 165 Broadway in the heart of the financial district. He occupied a desk beside a secretary who, to his horror, had been coding the flood of paintings with a sharply pointed pencil on the backs of the canvases. The other occupant of the office, George Courtney, wrote a Spencerian hand, spoke with a Guys-and-Dolls tongue, and condescended to pay for the art while diligently registering the stock certificates showered upon him by Hirshhorn and attending to the invoices from brokers. Few professional records had been kept of the incoming pictures and sculptures—title, date of acquisition, price, provenance, and filing of photocopies.

Instituting a catalog system, Lerner contended with two obstacles: distractions from Hirshhorn's hurricane of phone calls, and a secretary named Margo. Young and nubile, Margo troubled her mother deeply because she stood little chance of meeting anyone marriageable in that office. In 1959 Hirshhorn saw the wisdom of separating his collecting from his Wall Street activities and moved Lerner and Margo to 24 East 67th Street. The change increased her mother's fears—"Cooped up in that apartment, just you and that man!"—and Margo departed. In her stead, Lerner obtained the assistance of Doris Palca, a young mother of two children, who could be entrusted with the key to the treasure trove and could be depended upon to cope with the Holmes burglar alarm. In 1962 the office moved to 11 East 68th Street off Madison.

To Hirshhorn, the four rooms on the seventh floor were "my art office." From floor to ceiling, paintings covered the walls and were stacked along the corridor from the front room to the kitchen. Small Daumiers lined the mantel in Lerner's office among art objects from eleven civilizations. Picasso's *The Arm* rested on Palca's desk. A visitor to the kitchen, where stood the Xerox machine, opened a cupboard to discover a Joseph Cornell box. Wrapped in flannel, a Brancusi bronze head, as yet unmounted, lay in a carton labeled "Rat Poison." In the bathroom the shower curtain was always drawn— "No one was supposed to look behind it." It hid a clay bust of Hirshhorn by Laura Ziegler. He had tired of posing and the sculptor had returned to Italy. It sat in the tub and one of Palca's chores was to sprinkle it daily to keep the clay moist. Never completed, it went to the warehouse.

Problems in keeping accurate records arose from the hopelessness of staying abreast of Hirshhorn purchases. When Lerner accompanied him to the galleries, the curator returned with notes of the acquisitions. But Hirshhorn, arriving home after a trip alone to Europe, would be followed by 250 pieces of art, some directed to the warehouse, others to the art office or Callahan Corporation, the villa on Cap d'Antibes, the apartment on Park Avenue, or home in Greenwich. "He bought," said Palca, "like the Red Queen in *Alice* counted: One-plus-one-plus-one-plus-one-plus . . . ; and when Alice protested, 'I lost count!,' the Queen snorted, 'You just can't add!' Joe liked to buy the way people breathe. It gave him delight. He had no doubts about his opinions and he never wavered."

After Congress ratified the gift to the Smithsonian, Fran Weitzenhoffer and Cynthia McCabe signed on as researcher and curator respectively in 1967. An art library was started which grew to several thousand volumes, and the enlarged staff and rows of files removed to six rooms on the fifth floor of 135 East 65th Street to be joined by librarian Anna Brooks, curators Inez Garson and Frank Gettings, photographer Walter Rosenblum, and secretary Rita Jaros. Security necessitated moving most of the pieces from the office to the warehouse and registrar Myron O'Higgins was stationed there to record the incoming avalanche of artworks. By the time the gift went to the museum, the collection occupied most of four lofts at Morgan Manhattan Storage on West 21st Street.

"When I first came," Lerner said, "I knew every painting personally. I could look at each one and recognize it. But now," he added ruefully, "I don't know them anymore."

Hirshhorn maintained phone contact throughout the day, exchanging intelligence about purchases and deliveries. His computerized mind stored information precisely and up to the minute, often ahead of events. Seeking a moment's respite during the day, or on his way home, Hirshhorn stopped off at the office "to enjoy art." Stockbrokers buzzed in pursuit as he sat chatting with Lerner, who set before him works submitted by dealers and artists. A rush of phone calls routed the serenity from the mid-Manhattan retreat and though Hirshhorn stayed only a half-hour, the office vibrated long after he departed.

Lerner marked catalogs of auctions for Hirshhorn's attention and went along to witness the excitement he generated when his desire for a work sent bids spiraling in thousand-dollar units. Lerner estimated that in the decade ending in 1967, Hirshhorn spent $5 million for the works of twenty-one sculptors, from Archipenko to Zogbaum, including Grooms, Manzù, Moore, Nadelman, Picasso, Rickey, Rodin, and David Smith. He was said to be keeping the sculpture world solvent almost singlehandedly.

Payment for art made out of Toronto involved intricate billing and shipping instructions. One invoice went there and duplicates were sent to the art office and to Hirshhorn in downtown New York, where George Courtney groused as he issued the checks.

"He thought I was crazy," Hirshhorn chuckled, "spending money like a madman. He wanted to know what I needed it for, what I was going to do with it. But, after all," said Hirshhorn defensively, "he was working for me and it was my money!"

A notice arriving from the transport company required that the covering invoice first be traced in order to account for each item. The bill might list seven pieces and the crate be two short, the shipment being tardy, incomplete, or directed to another terminus. In 1961, the delayed receipt of two sculptures by Henry Moore and Picasso instigated a police search for the missing express truck. The

vehicle on its way to Manhattan had been hijacked and driven to a
remote pier in Jersey City. The thieves had broken into the crates
expecting a haul of sweaters, shirts, and purses, only to find a hunk
of bronze with a hole in it and another which looked to them like
battered junk. In Lavender Hill Mob style, they fled, abandoning
truck, Moore, and Picasso, which the police recovered unharmed.

At the downtown office George Courtney sustained "a pain in
the backside every time some guy walked in with a picture—or a
half-dozen. One day," he related, "they walked in with an eight-foot
statue by some Italian. It arrived at the building from Italy—or
maybe it was Epstein. Couldn't get it in the elevator. About two
hundred people gathered to watch. I was supposed to be handling
securities, and there I was wrestling an eight-foot statue. I had to get
it out or there'd have been a riot on Cortlandt Street. I gave the cop
five dollars to disperse the crowd. Finally, the moving people gave
up and took it to the warehouse."

"It" proved to be Jacques Lipchitz's monumental *Figure*—87½
inches tall. Its correct destination was Greenwich, where it went to
stand as a sentinel on the lawn of Round Hill.

From his beachhead on Cap d'Antibes, Hirshhorn blitzed the
galleries of Paris, London, Rome, and Zurich every month. On one
four-day maneuver, Abram Lerner and his wife accompanied him
and returned to New York in a state of exhaustion. Hirshhorn not
only bought, he looked, sensing the stasis in Europe and the ascend-
ancy of American art with its ferment, impertinence, and violence.
He had absorbed "The Eight" of the Ashcan School, and the best of
Social Realism. His Nadelmans, said Katharine Kuh, were on the
way to being "the largest and most representative collection of the
sculptor's work in existence except for the group left to the artist's
son." Hirshhorn moved into the New York School, acquiring Motherwell (1957), Baziotes (1958), Pollock (1961), Gottlieb (1963), and
Rothko (1963). In 1957 he bought Stuart Davis's *Rapt at Rappaport's*
and *Tropes des Teens* at the Downtown Gallery. Later, at the Whitney
Retrospective, he saw *Odol—Its Purities*, a bottled product painted by
Davis in 1924. It had presaged Pop Art by four decades and the artist had promptly renounced the experiment, having "decided the
whole thing wasn't worth it." Hirshhorn was disposed to tread war-
ily among the Campbell soup cans and Brillo boxes and their succes-
sors, the Op Art, Structuralism, Conceptualism, Minimalism, and
the "inward-eye" intellectualisms of the stormy sixties.

The reputation of the collector and his trove spread as color
reproductions of his prizes appeared in art journals and magazines
such as *Fortune* and *Life*. His loans to exhibits vied in number with

those from museums, outstripping other collectors and putting a strain on Lerner's time and staff. To the Royal Ontario Museum Hirshhorn lent an eighth-century Etruscan bronze, reputed to be one of the most important extant. In 1955 Moore's *King and Queen* crossed the border to the Toronto Art Gallery. Canadian customs phoned, interrupting Hirshhorn in the middle of a deal, to levy an import tariff on the sculpture. "Hey!" Hirshhorn yelled to an aide, "They want me to pay duty on the Moore. Do something! Get that law changed!"—and slamming the instrument into its cradle, continued negotiating on his other phone. Nine months later, Canada's tax on the importation of contemporary art was repealed. It had taken the U.S. Congress thirty years to put through a similar bill in the Tariff Act of 1930.

The action in Canada's parliament drew the attention of Governor-General Vincent Massey. He invited Hirshhorn to meet with his cabinet, who requested him to expand his art loans for Canada's cultural benefit. In 1957, with fanfare and official pomp, *Some American Paintings*, eighty-four from the Hirshhorn collection, opened at the National Gallery in Ottawa whence the show toured for ten months to Montreal, Toronto, Stratford (Ontario), and Winnipeg.

A self-styled "Einstein of archeology," Eli Borowsky, offered Hirshhorn a group of "rare erotic ivories." Hirshhorn deemed them more appropriate for a museum and suggested they go to the Royal Ontario. Borowsky's price was $500,000. "Wonderful!" said Hirshhorn. "Take half and count the rest as your gift to Canada." Borowsky demurred. His contribution, he said, was already in the price, reduced to a half-million, which he needed before his option ran out. To a dinner arranged for prospective donors, Hirshhorn was invited as the star guest from whom was expected at least half the purchase fund. Instead, Hirshhorn volunteered to underwrite the option for a year, provided the assembled Canadians evinced a desire to develop their culture by raising the half-million. When no more than a trickle was forthcoming, the matter was dropped.

In 1970 Toronto erected a new municipal hall and the city elders thought to beautify the plaza with a Henry Moore. When the sculptor asked for $150,000, their ardor cooled. They called for help from Hirshhorn. Fifteen years earlier he had lent the Toronto Art Gallery three of his great Moores—*King and Queen*, *Glenkiln Cross*, and *Reclining Woman*. He prevailed on the artist to cut his price almost in half and the sculpture was installed. Subsequently, Hirshhorn helped foster the Henry Moore Center for 20th Century Art which the city of Toronto established in November 1974.

In January 1959, the American Federation of the Arts selected thirty paintings by ten modern masters from the Hirshhorn collection and toured the exhibit to twelve cities through the south, midwest, and the west coast. In May, the Detroit Institute of the Arts presented *Sculpture in Our Time*, consisting of 213 works from the collection: 38 by Daumier, Degas, Renoir, and Rodin representative of the nineteenth century; and 175 by 53 more artists, from Kenneth Armitage to William Zorach, embodying the twentieth century. Of the total, 108 proceeded on an eighteen-month itinerary of museums and art centers in Milwaukee, Houston, Los Angeles, Colorado Springs, Toronto, Minneapolis, Kansas City, and San Francisco.

Further renown attached to the Hirshhorn collection from another tour sponsored by the American Federation of the Arts, this time 88 paintings comprising *A View of the Protean Century*. Initiated in October 1962 in Manhattan at the Knoedler Gallery, the show traveled through eighteen cities and concluded at the Brooklyn Museum in April 1965. The loan policy continued after Hirshhorn committed the collection to the Smithsonian. Before the museum opened, in 1969 alone, 200 paintings and sculptures by 17 artists participated in 16 major retrospectives and group exhibits across the United States and abroad.

Round Hill in Connecticut, which George Courtney dubbed the "Palazzo," provided a lyric setting for the sculptures. They dotted the gardens and lawns surrounding the manor, nestled among the trees, and lined the driveways. Besides those which decorated the interior of the house, scores of paintings, sculptures, and African art filled two rooms on the second floor where also were stored piles of lithographs, engravings, and prints; and the third floor was fitted with racks to stack canvases, and with solander boxes for drawings.

On October 2, 1962, the Hirshhorn sculpture exhibit opened at the Guggenheim Museum. Art historian H. Harvard Arnason, vice-president for art administration of the Guggenheim, termed it "the most comprehensive collection of modern sculpture in existence." Drawn from 800 in the Hirshhorn hoard, the display of 444 works spanned the nineteenth and twentieth centuries. Among them were 9 by Arp, 5, by Bourdelle, 37 Daumiers, 17 Degas, 9 Duchamp-Villons, 17 Giacomettis, 13 Lipchitzes, 11 Maillols, 26 Manzùs, 11 Marinis, 12 Matisses, 51 Moores, 10 Picassos, 6 Renoirs, 14 Rodins, and 7 Medardo Rossos. Alphabetically, the list went from Archipenko, Brancusi, Hajdu, Hepworth and Laurens all the way to Zadkine, Zogbaum, and Zorach—altogether 128 artists. The exhibit lasted until January 13, 1963. Sir Herbert Read wrote to Hirshhorn,

"I have seen many collections but never one that could rival yours in completeness, in quality and in display. It is a great achievement and I hope it will remain intact for the enjoyment of generations to come."

At the close of the show, 300 pieces went to the warehouse and 144 returned to Greenwich, where they remained until transferred eleven years later to Washington. Art lovers flocked to the Hirshhorn estate, and the curious turned Round Hill into a tourist attraction. Olga Hirshhorn put her administrative talent to work and limited public viewing to groups organized for charities. Subsequent shows aided Sarah Lawrence and Barnard colleges, Lenox Hill Hospital, the New York Medical Center, and Temple Beth Sholom of Greenwich.

One afternoon in September 1965, a thousand men and women turned out to benefit the National Cystic Fibrosis Research Foundation, Westchester Chapter. For four hours visitors roamed the Round Hill grounds with Hirshhorn acting as part-time guide. Leading one group through the house, he remarked confidentially, "This is the dining room. When I can afford it, I eat here." The crowd viewed everything, from a 2-inch bronze figurine Hirshhorn picked up for a dollar at the flea market in Nice, to the 7 by 9-foot *Burghers of Calais*, which cost $250,000.

"Fabulous! Incredible!" exclaimed one woman. Another, emerging from an arbor full of Rodin, Giacometti, Moore, and Manzù, sniffed reprovingly. "Why did Mr. Hirshhorn clutter up his rose garden with all those statues?"

The catalog for a fund-raising show to benefit Public TV's Channel 13 contained a pensive envoi by Abram Lerner. "Although," wrote the curator, "the new museum in Washington will display many of these pieces in an architecturally impressive setting, it is doubtful that the sculpture will ever be seen in the same way as here in Greenwich where the tranquil rural background provides an exquisite setting for some of the most famous sculptures of the 20th century."

The last exhibit at Round Hill took place in October of 1973 for the benefit of the Greenwich Arts Council. In ten years, almost 175,000 persons passed through the grounds.

■ ■ □ □

Eventually, Hirshhorn came to the realization that "the collection doesn't belong to one man." It had to go to a museum. According to John Walker, "It was axiomatic that the undertaker and the museum director arrived almost simultaneously." Or the collection had to be sold. Both notions were repugnant to Hirshhorn. They stirred him to conjure up a third possibility.

"I want my own museum!" he announced.

Lerner concurred. With Hirshhorn he favored New York as the site. Meeting Chaim Gross, Hirshhorn aired his thought. He asked the sculptor to be on the lookout for a suitable building. Gross located the Cornelius Vanderbilt mansion on Fifth Avenue and 86th Street, close by the Metropolitan, but Hirshhorn didn't bother to inspect it, and the building passed to the YIVO Institute for Jewish Research.

In 1960, on one of his forays into Los Angeles, Hirshhorn was interviewed by Henry Seldis, art critic of the *Los Angeles Times*. The following year, Seldis journeyed to Greenwich to view the sculpture, at which time Hirshhorn mentioned he was thinking of moving to Palm Springs and turning his Connecticut residence into a museum. Seldis described Greystone, the Doheny estate on the edge of Beverly Hills, owned by a Chicago realtor named Henry Crown who planned to demolish the château on the promontory and subdivide the 18½ acres of gardens for a housing development. On Hirshhorn's next trip to Los Angeles, he, his daughters Gene and Naomi, Seldis and his wife picnicked on the grounds, which Hirshhorn found ideal for displaying his sculpture. Seldis recruited the aid of Taft Schreiber, an officer of Universal Films and an art collector. Together they sang the west coast's virtues. In New York, they maintained, another collection such as Hirshhorn's was not to be found, perhaps, within a radius of 400 miles; but in Los Angeles it would be unique. To adapt the Doheny castle to museum needs would require only $500,000.

Hirshhorn met with Mayor Leonard Horwin of Beverly Hills and a deadline of October 1, 1964, was set for consummating the project. Henry Crown was prevailed upon to hold off his realty development until State Senator Thomas M. Rees (later Congressman) consulted with Governor Pat Brown. With executive approval, Rees moved to amend the California State budget, and Sacramento appropriated $1 million to purchase Greystone and to rent it to the proposed Hirshhorn Museum for one dollar a year. Additional funds were voted for maintenance.

Vociferous objections were raised by Max Chotiner, a prominent neighbor of the Greystone site. "This is destroying the residential community," he argued. "People of Beverly Hills won't use the museum. It'll attract tourists." The local *Beverly Hills Times* canvassed the area and found that most property owners preferred a museum to another housing development.

Despite added opposition from the Doheny heir, the Pasadena Art Museum, and the Municipal Art Gallery, as well as from county officials who saw the proposal as competition for the Los Angeles County Museum, the Beverly Hills City Council met, and in August of 1964 voted its approval. The plan was assured.

In January a Los Angeles councilman was dispatched to La Quinta to interview Hirshhorn regarding the art collection. He questioned its value, wanted to know if Picasso was a communist, and topped off his investigation by disparaging Jews. Incensed, Hirshhorn phoned Seldis.

"Get that bastard off my back!" he shouted furiously. "I don't want any part of this."

He canceled the project. The state subsequently leased the property to the American Film Institute.

Offers began to rain on Hirshhorn. The city of Baltimore proposed to add a wing to its museum for the collection. A letter from the Smithsonian Institution expressed interest. Robert Moses and Bernard Gimbel submitted a plan to house it in Flushing Meadow in a pavilion of the New York World's Fair. Zurich bid for it with the proviso that Hirshhorn sell off part of the collection to pay for the building. Mayor Teddy Kollek asked that it be donated to the Jerusalem Museum. Governor Rockefeller and Congressman Ogden Reid made overtures for Westchester County. And Sir Vincent Massey, Governor-General of Canada, requested it for Ottawa, but Parliament declined to fund construction.

From Florence, home of the Medicis, came an invitation from Mayor Giorgio Lapira. To Hirshhorn, he sang the praises of the tower of Galileo with its spectacular terraces fit,for sculptures and its harmonious location overlooking the city of the Renaissance, to which the collection would be the dramatic modern counterpart. His aria ended, the Mayor caroled, "Everyone visits Florence!" He made it sound so alluring that Hirshhorn flew with Lerner to Italy. A few minutes by car brought them to the tower, which was reached from the highway over a narrow, unpaved road winding up the mountainside. Mayor Lapira, Italian to his hair roots, said to be a Christian-Democrat who stood left of the Communist Party, also stood the same height as Hirshhorn. They lunched congenially. With the coffee, cookies, and candies, they discussed Lapira's proposal.

"That road up the mountain," Hirshhorn pointed out, "you'll have to build a new one."

"Eh!" said the Mayor with an Italianate shrug.

Hirshhorn turned to Lerner. "What does he mean—Eh?"

"It means it's logical," said Lerner. "It also means perhaps."

Barely had Hirshhorn digested that when Lapira informed him of the 15 percent tax on the importation of artworks. Quickly the luncheon concluded and with it the likelihood of Florence.

In his New York office, Hirshhorn received a phone call from the British Embassy in Washington. Her Majesty, Queen Elizabeth, had instructed her ambassador to talk about the art collection. An appointment was arranged and David Drummond, Earl of Perth, came up from the capital to confer with Hirshhorn. He visited Greenwich. Upon receipt of his report, the Queen offered Hirshhorn 10 acres in Regent's Park plus a museum to cost up to $7 million. It was the equivalent of being situated in the middle of Central Park. Hirshhorn responded favorably and the architects rushed to their drawing boards.

Lerner was unhappy. He wanted the museum in New York. Indefatigably he searched and found the old Astor Library on Lafayette Street across from the venerable Cooper Union on the border of Greenwich Village. Recently vacated by the United Hebrew Immigrant Society, the building appeared well suited to the collection. The purchase price was $550,000. By March 1965 the contract was drawn and ready for signatures. Hirshhorn called in Philip Johnson to inspect the building. The architect judged it structurally inadequate to support the mass of sculpture. To buttress the floors and make them safe would require $6 million worth of reconstruction. "That," said Hirshhorn, "together with the annual maintenance would have busted me." The sale was not consummated. The building went to Joseph Papp's Public Theater.

Earlier in the year, Governor Rockefeller had taken to breakfasting with Hirshhorn in Greenwich on Saturday mornings. The State University at Purchase in Westchester County was nearing completion and the Governor was pressing his proposal to house the collection in a museum which would occupy the focal spot on campus.

"He liked bagels and cream cheese, and eggs with smoked salmon," Hirshhorn recalled. "He's a nice man and I was honored. I went to his home and I saw his collection. We got along beautifully. But Purchase, New York! I never heard of it!"

Hirshhorn did not reject the Governor's offer out of hand. He conferred with Lerner. They weighed the alternatives. Hirshhorn could present the collection to an established museum and relinquish his identity, or he could risk the expense of a personally endowed institution. There was also the Queen's award in England. By 1965 thousands were traveling overseas each year. In London, gateway to Europe, Americans as well as Europeans would see the art of their century. Then there was the campus of the State University of New York, in Purchase, where the collection would provide a didactic experience daily to a student body projected to reach 20,000, and would create generations of habitual museum-goers. Any one of the options, varying in attractiveness, would solve Hirshhorn's dilemma. But none was ideal.

At that moment Washington called. S. Dillon Ripley, secretary of the Smithsonian Institution, asked for an appointment to meet with Hirshhorn.

The Museum

VI But for Sidney Dillon Ripley, the Hirshhorn art collection might never have gone to Washington, and once there, it would have wandered in the labyrinth of the federal bureaucracy and been forgotten. Ripley's diplomacy beggared Talleyrand's, and his outlook was Copernican. His specialty was ornithology of the Far East. He sighted like a hawk and worried like a hen. Bald and reed-slender, with his extraordinary height and faint scholarly stoop he suggested a skeptical crane. Grandfather Ripley had helped lace the nation with railroads. Ripley's mother had organized a women's auxiliary to support the Museum of Modern Art in New York when it occupied a Madison Avenue brownstone and a German shepherd dog guarded the door. She imbued her son with a lively and abiding love of art.

Ripley left Yale at fifty-one to assume the secretaryship of the Smithsonian Institution in February 1964, bringing with him an encyclopedic knowledge of science, art, and the humanities. He had spent eighteen years at the university as professor of biology and ecology, and four years as director of its Peabody Museum of Natural History. He had served on the staffs of Philadelphia's Academy of Natural Science and the American Museum of Natural History in

New York, had written four books, and had done a hitch during World War II with the Office of Strategic Services. This last was to stand him in good stead in his new post. He well knew the Smithsonian, "the nation's attic," which contained millions of curios, among them a dinosaur's skeleton, George Washington's false teeth, Lindbergh's "Spirit of St. Louis," the 44.5-karat Hope Diamond, and a 17½-foot beard, the longest on record. He could recall his horror as a temporary curator at the Institution in 1942 when he found in the clutter of its Natural History Hall #10 a painting by Albert Pinkham Ryder with its pigment cracking, and many other canvases coated with dust, left to the National Collection of Fine Arts by John Gellatly and Harriet Lane Johnson, niece of President Buchanan.

Poring over legislation governing the Smithsonian, Ripley came upon the congressional act of May 17, 1938, by which the United States had accepted the Andrew Mellon gift. It provided that the President assign a site on the Mall for a museum of contemporary art as a counterpart to the National Gallery and its Old Masters. A contest for the design of a modern museum had been held in 1946. Eero Saarinen won the $7,000 prize but the plan was quietly scotched by the Capital Planning Commission, whose most influential member, William Delano, uncle of Franklin D. Roosevelt, delivered the dictum of Frederick Law Olmsted: "Let no touch of modernity sully the Mall." No trace remained of the Saarinen model or drawings.

Ripley mused on this as he read *The Proud Possessors*, written by Aline Saarinen, widow of the slighted architect. He thought of the vibrancy of the Museum of Modern Art in New York, of the opportunity the Smithsonian had missed in the forties to grab "a piece of the action" for Washington. He envisioned the Institution, its tradition one of scholarship and research for the "increase and diffusion of knowledge," as an "open university." During his incumbency the Smithsonian would brush away its cobwebs with innovations of a performing arts division, extensions into neighborhood museums, and fresh uses for the Mall in annual festivals of American folklore. He concentrated initially on two actions: to dust off the National Collection of Fine Arts and with $100,000 "stimulate it to remove its light from under a bushel"; and to search out a private collector of contemporary art.

"The only way to make up for lost time," said Ripley, recalling the year he became Secretary, "would be to take a giant step by finding someone who had already done it." And he remembered the account in *The Proud Possessors* of Joseph Hirshhorn, who sounded like his man. Mellon, Frick, Freer, and Dale collected Old Masters but Hirshhorn was the first to put his chips on the artists of his own era.

Ripley phoned Roger L. Stevens. The counsel on the arts to President Johnson was chivvying contributions to build the JFK Center for the Performing Arts. He told Ripley that he had been in London at the Savoy Hotel when Hirshhorn was there at the invitation of Queen Elizabeth to hear the proposal for housing his collection in Regent's Park.

"Convince him," said Ripley, "that our need is greater."

Stevens set out to find a conduit to Hirshhorn while Ripley, by way of Charles Cunningham, director of Chicago's Art Institute, called on Abram Lerner. In the "art office" he browsed through the farrago of works, noting the Daumier figures casually lining the mantel. Like jewels in Cartier's window, they hinted of countless gems within. Back in Washington, Ripley dictated a letter on June 15, 1964. Adroitly mixing national pride with good sense, Ripley told Hirshhorn, "The Smithsonian Institution has a lively interest in establishing an American equivalent to the Tate Gallery [in London] emphasizing American contemporary art. The National Gallery of Art with its emphasis on the arts of Europe and the past leaves the Capital and the nation with no proper equivalent to the Tate. The need for such a museum here has been widely recognized. . . . We would be most happy to explore the concept with you."

As related by Ripley, in September an appointment with Hirshhorn was arranged through Mrs. Permilia Reed, with whom Ripley took tea in Greenwich and then together drove to Round Hill "for more tea." The meeting was brief and friendly. Ripley contented himself with not "talking turkey," simply commending the Smithsonian to Hirshhorn. Unacquainted with the Institution's art archives, Hirshhorn remained cool. Ripley realized he needed to muster aid.

In conference with President Johnson on the matter of saving Washington's Renwick mansion before the wrecker's ball leveled it for a parking lot, Ripley seized the moment to voice the hope that the Smithsonian would bag the Hirshhorn art collection, valued then at $40 million. Observing the President's eyes glitter, Ripley's spirits lifted.

Early in the new year, Hirshhorn's attorney, Sam Harris, phoned from New York to pursue Ripley's letter of June 15. Harris arrived at the Smithsonian "Castle" on the Mall accompanied by Max Kampelman, a partner in his Washington office. They sat in Ripley's parlor on the third floor and Harris spoke of the bids from England, New York State, Israel, and elsewhere.

"Would Mr. Hirshhorn consider giving his collection to the Smithsonian?" Ripley inquired mildly.

Harris paused before answering. "He would want his name on the museum," he said.

"That," Ripley replied without hesitation, "is simply the identification of a building, not an impediment to other gifts."

Cogitating further, Harris asked, "On the Mall?"

"I don't see why not," said Ripley.

"You mean," Harris said, suppressing his astonishment, "a Hirshhorn Museum on the Mall?"

"This is 1965," Ripley replied, underlining his words deliberately, "and I think America has grown up."

Ripley stressed Washington's lack of a contemporary art museum, reiterating that London had the Tate, New York the Museum of Modern Art, and Israel the Billy Rose Sculpture Garden. Only Washington had none. Hirshhorn's attorney listened intently and departed.

Learning of the friendship between Hirshhorn and Abe Fortas, Ripley suggested to the President's confidant that a timely sign of interest from the White House would do immeasurable good. Fortas, who trusted Ripley's appraisal of the collection, told the President and Mrs. Johnson that in view of Hirshhorn being wooed by such formidable rivals, some tactful persuasion, perhaps a luncheon by Lady Bird, could tilt the suit in favor of the Smithsonian.

A nervous swain, Ripley did not rest. He knew the First Lady's keen interest in acquiring a Thomas Eakins painting for the White House collection during the Johnson incumbency. To hone her zest for the luncheon, he got word to Elizabeth Carpenter, her staff director and press secretary, that Hirshhorn possessed the largest group of works by Eakins in private hands. In a second letter to Hirshhorn he drove home three crucial points: under the Smithsonian the collection would retain its independent identity; annual attendance of 12 million on the Mall would assure the collection the greatest possible prominence and more accessibility than any other place in the world; and it guaranteed the collection against change and interference. To illustrate the Smithsonian's capability, he cited the Freer Gallery, which was built in 1906 at a cost of $1 million. Charles Land Freer left $200,000 to endow curatorial salaries and $1,958,591.42 for the operation of the gallery. Through prudent investment, the endowments had appreciated five times.

"Mrs. Johnson," Ripley concluded, "is herself keenly aware of the importance of your collection to the nation. She would be happy to discuss this with you and Mr. Lerner at luncheon, and I hope you will be able to arrange to visit both the Smithsonian (especially the Freer) and the White House."

The communication warmed Hirshhorn. It also provided Sam Harris with the rebuttal to Lerner's objection to removing the collection from New York, the locus of art and artists. "New York," said the attorney, "gets a million tourists a year; Washington gets twelve," and he and Hirshhorn went off to meet Ripley and Stevens and to discuss the site of the museum.

Stevens would have liked it on the bank of the Potomac adjacent to his projected Kennedy Center. The old Patent Building, which was to be restored as a museum and archive, was suggested. But only the Mall produced unanimity among the four men. They settled on Constitution Avenue at 9th Street, fronting the National Archives and hard by the National Gallery. This choice of location was to prove an obstacle.

Early in May a letter arrived at Round Hill from the White House. Mrs. Johnson wrote, "Just a note to say how much I am looking forward to seeing you on May 21st at 12:30." Others would join them for lunch but not until 1 p.m. "The two of you know and care so much about art, I wanted us to have a little time to ourselves just to see the paintings of the White House."

On accepting the invitation, Hirshhorn incorporated in his reply to the President and Mrs. Johnson a set of conditions outlined by Sam Harris. They spelled out the understanding according to the conversations with Ripley: the collection would be housed in a modern museum to be erected on the Mall; it would be maintained, preserved, and developed by the Smithsonian and operated under a board of trustees in accordance with plans and proceedings to be agreed upon by the Institution and himself. In addition to the collection, Hirshhorn would contribute $1 million in cash to fund further art acquisitions.

He went on to say, "I would, of course, want binding assurance that the Museum would bear my name in perpetuity; that it would be adequately maintained and operated in such a manner as to assure the fulfillment of my objective of a better understanding and appreciation of modern art."

This letter of May 17, 1965, contained the basic terms which emerged after debate and refinement as the statute which Congress enacted two years later. On May 19 the Board of Regents of the Smithsonian empowered its secretary, subject to acceptance of the gift by the President, to submit legislation to designate the Mall location and to authorize planning for construction.

Accordingly, on May 21, Dillon Ripley, Sam Harris, Abe Fortas, Roger Stevens, and their wives assembled for lunch in the upper dining room of the White House. Thirty minutes before they arrived, the Hirshhorns had entered the Southwest Gate to be greeted in the Diplomatic Reception Room by Mrs. Johnson.

"We had a delightful time," she recorded in her diary. "He enjoyed seeing the White House collection and I love showing it to people who enjoy it."

The Hirshhorns viewed the paintings which had been culled with curatorial aid by Jacqueline Kennedy from the haphazard and often tasteless gifts foisted upon past Chief Executives, and augmented by Lady Bird Johnson. The prime pieces were Winslow Homer's *Surf at Prout's Neck*, Mary Cassatt's *Young Mother and Two Children*, Thomas Moran's *The Three Tetons*, and portraits by Samuel F. B. Morse, Thomas Scully, and Douglas Volk. All the while they gazed at the paintings, Mrs. Johnson remained silent about the Eakins she wished Hirshhorn would bestow on the White House. She had "charged Roger Stevens, Dillon Ripley, and Abe Fortas with that hope because," she said, "I am the world's poorest salesman."

The President met with his Cabinet in a nearby conference room as the guests sat down to *tournedos béarnaise* companioned by a domestic red wine. Conversation touching discreetly on the prospect of the museum carefully refrained from any mention of how Hirshhorn would make the gift or the mode of its acceptance. Had the subject arisen, Fortas was prepared to choke it off as premature. The objective of the luncheon was only to assure Hirshhorn that the United States desired the collection. The rest was up to the President. The terms being agreeable, Fortas was certain Hirshhorn would consent.

As dessert and coffee arrived, Sam Harris unobtrusively passed a paper to Dillon Ripley. The Secretary retained his composure as he read the contents of a letter in which Governor Rockefeller proposed that a New York State bond issue provide $10 million for a Hirshhorn museum at the university campus in Purchase. Before Ripley could respond, President Johnson entered. Introduced all around, the President took a seat beside Hirshhorn, addressed him familiarly, joshed him, and let out all the stops of his personality with gracious subtlety.

"He was seductive," Fortas remembered. "In all my political experience, he was the greatest salesman. He had a selling job to do and he did it magnificently."

The President thanked Hirshhorn, and to Mrs. Johnson's relief,

as she reported in her diary, he boldly said what she had been wanting to say and couldn't. "It was wonderful the people of the United
States were going to be able to enjoy his [Hirshhorn's] artworks, but
it would be downright selfish if the White House itself didn't get an
example. Mr. Hirshhorn could appreciate Lyndon, I think. They
both are aggressive and strong."

Bearlike, the President loomed over the little man and put his
arm around his shoulder. "Joe," he said, "you don't need a contract.
Just turn the collection over to the Smithsonian and I'll take care of
the rest."

Hirshhorn almost succumbed on the spot. "Once the President
puts his arm around your shoulder," he said later, "you're a dead
cookie. He was a powerful man. I knew then there was going to be a
deal."

Even so, Hirshhorn automatically plugged into his instinctive
shrewdness. He turned to Harris. "What do you think, Sam?" he
asked.

And Harris, borrowing a verse from the Hirshhorn canon, replied, "We ought to think about it."

"You leave it to me," the President told Hirshhorn earnestly,
"to see that the conditions are fulfilled," and making his apologies, he
went on to keep his executive schedule.

After the luncheon, Dillon Ripley declared to the others, "This
is the greatest art gift that's been made to the United States since
Andrew Mellon gave what formed the nucleus of the National Gallery in the thirties."

"That is, if it *is* made," thought Mrs. Johnson, noting the day's
events. More optimistically, she ended the entry, "Something happened today that may be of utmost importance to the nation's Capital. . . . This Hirshhorn gift may open a great chapter. We will
see."

Abe Fortas sensed Hirshhorn's feeling toward the President and his
Lady, the sincerity of their declarations, their personal warm desire
for the collection. Before leaving him, Fortas reassured Hirshhorn.
"You don't have to worry about this, Joe," he said. "Just do as the
President says."

Sam Harris protested. "To hell with that, Abe!" he exclaimed.
"You're a lawyer and I'm a lawyer. Johnson's just been elected with
a Congress overwhelmingly Democrat. You know, with his power
and everything else, he could kick the bucket tomorrow; he could be
run over or killed in a plane accident; and it's not inconceivable that

his power might decline. It's happened before. We've seen in history presidents come in, and at the end of their regimes they haven't been as powerful as they were at the beginning." His objections gathering force, Harris finished, "Over my dead body are you going to get this collection without the conditions written into the contract and a statute passed."

A couple of days later, Hirshhorn heard from the President. Hirshhorn, he wrote, "remained much in his thoughts" and he urged Harris and Kampelman to communicate with Richard Goodwin and Bill Moyers of his staff to "discuss further developments." Said LBJ, "I know how eager Mrs. Johnson is especially to see your collection and I hope that she will find it possible to get to Greenwich soon." He made no reference to Hirshhorn's letter of May 17.

Ripley began to feel anxious when drafts of a bill and a presidential message to Congress, for all their magniloquence, failed to satisfy the attorneys for Hirshhorn and the Smithsonian. A feeling, not unfounded, haunted them that Hirshhorn might change his mind. Abe Fortas, privy to the President's thinking, strongly favored an exchange of letters of intent. Sam Harris considered that inadequate, and so did the Smithsonian's James Bradley and Charles Blitzer, who desired the earliest possible transfer of title. Upon his appointment to the Supreme Court, Justice Fortas withdrew from the negotiations and turned White House liaison over to Harry C. McPherson, special assistant to LBJ. All guns then trained on Sam Harris. "I clung to the agreement [contained in the May 17 letter] to the bitter end," he said.

Scouting ahead for a design concept, Ripley consulted Nathaniel Owings of Skidmore, Owings and Merrill, head of the President's Pennsylvania Avenue Commission for the rehabilitation of the Capitol Triangle. Ripley frowned on the architect's propensity for marble magnificence and pantheons. Ripley complained, "Rembrandt belongs in the marble hall; contemporary art belongs in an area of understatement." To Hirshhorn, Washington appeared to be stalling and his uncertainty returned.

Early in June, a clipping from the (London) *Sunday Observer* delivered to the White House revealed that Hirshhorn was in England as house guest of the Earl of Perth. The *Washington Post* got wind of the story. Despite attempts by Ripley, Bill Moyers, and Richard Goodwin to persuade the editor that publicity at this time was inappropriate, the newspaper published a full account of the Smithsonian's negotiations and the federal government's "fierce competition for the multi-million-dollar treasure trove." The *Post* said,

"Hirshhorn was considering accepting an offer by the British Government in which a special museum would be built in Regent's Park.
. . . With President and Mrs. Johnson watching every development
. . . Washington officials are holding their breath."

Feted by the British Arts Council, Hirshhorn listened to its serenades and inspected a model for the museum. To Ripley's relief, Hirshhorn did not commit himself. "I love England and I do business here," he told the Britons. "But I love the United States and I belong there. Let me think about it."

When Hirshhorn read the disclosure in the *Washington Post*, his embarrassment triggered anger. He suspended further discussions.

■ ■ ◻ ◻

That was Ripley's long hot summer. In July 1965, from his home in Connecticut, he wrote to Richard Goodwin, "I feel we are losing ground with Joe Hirshhorn." His glumness derived from knowing that Governor Rockefeller was a regular visitor to Round Hill with Congressman "Brownie" Reid doing a "snow job" on Hirshhorn about the State University transforming Westchester County into a cultural enclave. "We have been down to see Hirshhorn," continued Ripley, "he has been up to Litchfield to our farm to see us. He is a most sentimental attractive guy. He is in love with his collection. He wants to feel it is as much loved wherever it lands."

Ripley fired inducements from every angle to convince Hirshhorn that the collection belonged in Washington—the millions of visitors the Smithsonian drew to the Mall; the vivid effect the collection would have by expanding the horizons of Congress, which was just then contemplating a proposed Arts and Humanities Foundation; the potential growth of the capital art scene to equal New York. In a burst of visionary eloquence, he told Hirshhorn, "You would have a whole world of your own to set on fire!"

Ripley's fervor, however, was no substitute for loving attention. He reminded Goodwin that Hirshhorn had not yet received an acknowledgment of his letter of May 17 to the President and Mrs. Johnson. What Ripley suggested was "a friendly, personal, nonbusiness, sincere, holding operation letter." He needed time and Hirshhorn needed what could only be described as "cozening and not direct power or political leverage."

"There is a chance," said Ripley, "Mrs. Johnson might come up into this area again late summer or autumn. It would be wonderful if she could come and get over to Greenwich while she is in the neighborhood and just radiate her charm and sincerity."

Six days later, the Hirshhorns received from the White House a First Family album of unpublished photos "personally selected by the President and the First Lady." The following week Mrs. Johnson scheduled a shopping trip to New York and settled in at the Carlyle Hotel with her daughter Lynda Bird and Bess Abell, her social secretary. Learning of her presence in Manhattan, Olga Hirshhorn consulted her husband and phoned to invite Mrs. Johnson to Greenwich. Lady Bird promised to squeeze the visit into her next day's program.

The morning of Friday, August 6, President Johnson signed the Voting Rights Bill at a ceremony in the Capitol which his wife watched on television in New York. After lunch she left the hotel and headed for Greenwich accompanied by Lynda Bird and Bess Abell. They had only one hour to spend with the art, for which Mrs. Johnson reproached herself. She felt Hirshhorn's cornucopia "should be savored slowly, luxuriously, like a candlelit banquet instead of gulped like a hamburger," but she wanted to get back to Washington to be sure her husband got away for a weekend's respite at Camp David. At 3 P.M. the limousine wound up the driveway of Round Hill, past rhododendrons and tall elms, to halt before *The Burghers of Calais*. Awaiting them were the Hirshhorns, the Lerners, and the Harrises.

The greetings over, Mrs. Johnson captivated her host, saying, "I really know nothing about art. I'm prepared to learn." Hirshhorn was affected. "That was honest," he recalled, "and I respected her."

He showed his guests around the gardens and lawns, identifying the scores of works and their sculptors. Every few minutes Bess Abell murmured to Lady Bird, "If we're going to catch that plane, we have to leave. . . ." Mrs. Hirshhorn brought refreshments, which Mrs. Johnson "snatched up and kept walking, none of us willing, least of all me, to stop and think about planes and food." Inside the house she looked longingly at portraits by Eakins, "very commanding with something of the quality of the Flemish masters." Finally, in a whirl of security men and good-byes, the party departed for the White House and Camp David.

Several years later, Mrs. Johnson took time to revisit Round Hill. "She remembered a lot of things I had told her," said Hirshhorn in astonishment. "I couldn't get over it."

Negotiations gathered momentum after that. Lerner began to prepare lists and descriptions of paintings and sculptures and obtained estimates of fair market values from auction firms, dealers, and insurance companies. But no sooner had Ripley plugged one hole than a leak sprang elsewhere.

Owings, contributing his time and that of his staff to the construction of a model, had devised what he thought was an ingenious museum entrance off Constitution Avenue, raising the street grade, lowering the level of the garden, and masking the exterior with banks of grass and overhanging trees. Lerner and Harris greeted it with hearty dislike. The attorney proposed a design competition which evoked in Ripley the specter of 1946 and the ditching of Saarinen. He tried to allay Harris's fears. The design intended, he said, to "create a congeniality and rapport with the works of art. In the spirit of our time, the design [was] properly a departure from the traditional." He invited inspection of the model.

"Maybe Joe would like to look at it in Greenwich," Ripley urged. "No one, but *no one* is trying to twist anyone's arm!"

Abram Lerner bluntly called the design "a bombshelter." He wrote to Ripley with tempered irony, "I am sure Mr. Owings is quite convinced of his approach—and he may very well have his finger on the avant-garde pulse—in a subterranean way. But the 'stylish' solution is not necessarily the best and your own reference to a Sassanian tomb is quite to the point."

In presenting the model to Hirshhorn, Ripley tried to avoid "the idea of descending levels to get away from looking down into a pit or catacomb."

Hirshhorn expressed his unembroidered feelings to Owings. "You're not going to bury me underground," he snapped. "You can bury yourself."

At this stage, Owings' partner, Gordon Bunshaft, took over. He, Ripley, and Owings met for what the latter termed "a straight out-and-out talk" with Hirshhorn to work with him and make him feel part of the solution. Bunshaft, a member of the Commission of Fine Arts, brought to light the fact that the site chosen for the museum had been previously allotted by the Capital Planning Commission to a sculpture garden and skating rink. Ripley came up with an alternative. Due south across the Mall, on 7th Street and Independence Avenue, stood the old half-used Armed Forces Medical Museum, a ward of the Smithsonian. In 1955, the AFMM headquarters had been relocated at the Walter Reed Army Medical Center, and part of its specimens and exhibits was already incorporated into the Center's Pathology Museum. A year later, the AFMM's library had been moved to the National Library of Medicine of the National Institutes of Health in Bethesda. Ripley offered to accommodate the remainder of the medical archives in temporary space in the Arts and

Industries building ("a special inducement") until completion of the facility at Walter Reed. The War Department acquiesced. But allocating the evacuated site to the Smithsonian for the Hirshhorn Museum would require congressional approval.

The White House Budget Bureau, meanwhile, brought Ripley's attention to the fast-approaching deadline for preparing the 1967 budget. The Secretary temporized. The museum "was a delicate matter . . . not to be hurried." Bunshaft was "designing a small but very stylish building" and would be in consultation with Hirshhorn. Ripley hoped to "conclude some sort of agreement with Mr. Hirshhorn before the end of the year."

The strain intensified and took its toll on Hirshhorn. Before his sixty-fifth birthday, he suffered a heart attack. Hospitalized for four weeks in La Quinta, he spent another month in his California home and two weeks back in Greenwich. A letter of sympathy from the President advised him in mid-September that "rest and thinking about things far removed from everyday life were indispensable." LBJ had followed the same prescription during his own illness. He went on to say, "Lady Bird told me so much about your great collection. Her visit to you was one of the high moments of the past year for her. She has stirred a very considerable interest in it in me. We have you in our thoughts and we pray for your early deliverance from your present trial."

The President's note, mayhap its prayer, worked wonders with Hirshhorn. "Your letter," he wrote to LBJ a week later, "came as a pleasant surprise. I was touched. . . . Mrs. Hirshhorn and I would love to have you visit with us any time at your convenience to show you the art collection. . . . Mrs. Johnson is a darling and has completely charmed me. She is the most perfect wife a President could have—and as you know, she has become interested in modern art. Be careful. This interest can be contagious—you had better watch out!"

The next month, their positions reversed, the President found himself confined to Bethesda Hospital after an operation to remove his gall bladder. Consolation arrived from Greenwich.

"At Temple, on Yom Kippur," Hirshhorn wrote LBJ, "our congregation joined our Rabbi in prayer for your well-being and speedy recovery. My wife and I are delighted to see you up so soon. Keep it up. We all need you and love you."

Lady Bird thanked Hirshhorn for his solicitude. She reported that her husband was "recovering quite well . . . at the Ranch, enjoying the sunshine, scenery and as near serenity as it gets."

From that moment, negotiations governing the art gift went

forward in tranquillity. They continued unaffected by a letter from Governor Rockefeller which promised to bequeath his *Grande Nue Assise* by Matisse to the museum on the SUNY campus if Hirshhorn's group of Matisse sculptures went there. Ripley was not overly disturbed even when the *Washington Post* scooped the story of the gift on May 12, 1966, five days before the signing of the agreement. The *Post*'s correspondent in New York had phoned Hirshhorn, who said he had decided to give his collection to the United States. Asked by a reporter about London's offer of Regent's Park, he replied, "I've promised the Earl of Perth I'll lend my paintings to England once the collection is established in Washington. But England will have to take care of them. The last time I lent a Morris Louis to a London exhibition it came back with a hole in it. Soon after they asked me for a Giacometti and I turned them down."

That same day Hirshhorn confirmed his commitment in a personal communication to the President. "I am delighted that you and Mrs. Johnson have encouraged me to arrange for the establishment in Washington of a museum and sculpture garden to help achieve our common objectives and contribute to the improvement of our cultural environment. It has now been agreed that the Hirshhorn Foundation and I will donate our collections to the Smithsonian Institution."

President Johnson responded saying, "Yours is an act of patriotic generosity which will be treasured by this and future generations of your fellow men. . . . Mrs. Johnson joins me in expressing our profound appreciation of your contribution to the nation."

Creeping euphoria began to envelop Ripley and Harry McPherson. The bill to Congress was drafted. In preparation for its presentation the following week they alerted Senator Jennings Randolph, chairman of the Committee on Public Works, and Senator Stephen M. Young, chairman of the Subcommittee on Buildings and Grounds; and Representatives George H. Fallon and Kenneth J. Gray, chairmen of the House's parallel legislative bodies.

"Everyone we saw," McPherson reported to the President, "was enthusiastic and offered full support. Ripley told each one that 'Mrs. Johnson was the decisive factor. Hirshhorn is crazy about her and the President.' If we were to strike a medal for the occasion, Mrs. Johnson and Dillon Ripley should get it. Because of them—and because of Hirshhorn's affection and respect for you—we have beat out Rockefeller, the Queen of England, the Governments of Israel, Canada and the State of California."

■ ■ □ □

At noon, on May 17, 1966, Hirshhorn and his wife, Olga, followed President and Mrs. Johnson from the White House out to the Rose Garden. Forgathered were Vice-President and Mrs. Humphrey, Ripley, Harris, Lerner and their wives, Supreme Court Justice Fortas, Roger Stevens, and Harry McPherson. Present, too, were Secretary Stuart Udall, whose Interior Department controlled the real estate; and Robert McNamara, Secretary of War, whose department had relinquished the site. In front of this assembly, the President signed his message to Congress urging the adoption of the measure to effect the acceptance of the gift.

"This is a magnificent day for the Nation's Capital," said President Johnson, "and for the millions of Americans who will visit Washington in the years to come. . . . I know that Joseph Hirshhorn will go on seeking out the best in modern paintings and sculpture for years to come. But, he will never have a finer hour than this; for today he offers the fruit of a lifetime in the service of art to the citizens of a grateful nation. Now we must build a museum worthy of the collection and worthy of our highest aspirations for this beautiful city. Washington is a city of powerful institutions, the seat of government for the strongest nation on earth, the place where democratic ideals are translated into reality. It must also be a place of beauty and learning. . . ."

In his finest hour, Hirshhorn spoke simply and briefly. "I'm deeply touched," he said. "You know, I'm an American, and I'm giving this to the capital of the greatest nation in the world. I'm glad to be able to do it."

Dillon Ripley remarked that the new museum would make Washington "the number-two art center of the country. No one would want to disclaim New York's number-one position, although," and his eyes twinkled in his solemn face, "there is room for two such places. Artists seem at last to have discovered Washington." Later, he asked Hirshhorn, "Will you miss your collection?"

"I feel wonderful," Hirshhorn enthused, fortified by a couple of sherries. "I don't feel any sense of loss at all. In fact, I'm going to go on collecting like I always have. My only regret is that I can't go back to the beginning and start all over again. It's been an adventure. Nobody in the world had a back garden like that." His forehead furrowed sadly. "I feel like we've given away six thousand children. But we're going to live near here—to be close to the children like mama and papa should."

Ripley, the biologist, smiled. "You want to see them reproduce?"

"We want to see our children grow," Hirshhorn replied.

A newsman inquired why he hadn't left his art collection to Canada. "Nobody asked me," Hirshhorn replied crisply. "I love Canada and it's been good to me. But some of the people are asleep up there."

From Ottawa came word of wounded pride, of officials crestfallen at not having been in the bidding; others were relieved at not being faced with the cost of housing and maintaining the collection. Hearing that Judy LaMarsh, Canada's secretary for cultural affairs, was ready to spend $6 million for one Leonardo da Vinci, Hirshhorn offered to obtain for her ten world masterpieces for that sum. He stated his willingness to lend his art to celebrate Canada's centennial—"if somebody up there asks for it."

Solicited for comment, James Harithas, curator of Washington's Corcoran Gallery, said, "The collection is staggering. It will have an enormous effect on the museum scene. It will embrace many of the things the Corcoran and Phillips and the Gallery of Modern Art have been trying to put together. We are all very pleased but it will be difficult to compete."

The *New York Times* questioned Hirshhorn as to why he had presented the collection to the United States. "Well," Hirshhorn said, "a lot of people wanted it. But I'm an American, and I'd have been called a traitor. What I accomplished here in the United States, I couldn't do in any other country. It belongs here." Crediting the President and "his darling and charming wife" as the major influence in his decision, Hirshhorn hugged and patted the tall man. "I've adopted him," he said of LBJ. "I love him."

President Johnson bent to Lady Bird and kissed her tenderly. The ceremony was concluded.

Thus, said the *Washington Post*, "ended one of history's greatest cliff-hangers."

At least one man knew otherwise. Inside Dillon Ripley's head reverberated *Paragraph Ninth* of the agreement he had just signed. It stipulated:

> In the event that legislation containing provisions substantially as set forth in *Paragraph Second* hereof is not duly enacted by the Congress of the United States and duly approved by the President no later than ten (10) days after the close of the 90th Congress, or in the event that said Museum and Sculpture Garden shall not have been constructed and completed as provided in *Paragraph Third* within five years after such legislation shall have been enacted and

approved [by 1971], this Agreement shall be null and void and the proposed gifts by the Donor and the Hirshhorn Foundation shall not be consummated.

Looking back, Ripley saw that only the first mile had been covered. Ahead lay a long rutted road.

■ ▪ ☐ ▫

The Hirshhorn Museum bill reached Congress and began its tourney known as the legislative process, filtering through committees and agencies, bringing the bureaucracy into play, stirring the purest and basest motives. The Hirshhorn, the first museum proposed for the Mall in almost thirty years, encountered the weight of criticism, private prejudice, animus, conflicts of personality and ego, loyalty, self-interest, all to test the endurance of proponents and adversaries. Every aspect came under fire. The museum site was contested, its name opposed, its donor disparaged, its sponsor investigated, appropriations delayed. A subcommittee protested the measure was rammed down its throat. Senator Richard Clark of Iowa, ignoring the President's pledge and the signed agreement, demanded that the name of Franklin D. Roosevelt be substituted for Hirshhorn's. Another cited Andrew Mellon, who chose anonymity by calling his gift the National Gallery of Art, whereupon Senator Robert M. La Follette declared that kind of self-effacement pretentious; it presumed the gallery to represent the nation and not merely Mellon himself.

Within a short time charges and countercharges brought the museum to the brink of extinction. Accompanied by faint rumblings of bigotry, a storm broke over Hirshhorn symptomatic of the rage of the sixties. Some of it may have ricocheted off Lyndon Johnson. In April 1966 Johnson polled a majority for the last time; his popularity declined rapidly to where the premonition of Sam Harris proved to be dire prophecy.

On May 19, 1966, Representative George W. Fallon introduced HR-15121 with similar acts proposed by Representatives Kenneth J. Gray, Donald J. Irwin, and Thomas M. Rees. Senator Jennings Randolph, for himself and Senators Stephen M. Young and John Sherman Cooper, tendered S-3389 to the Senate, where Birch Bayh spoke for the measure. He asked for unanimous consent of the body to insert in the Congressional Record the remarks President Johnson made upon accepting the Hirshhorn gift. There was no objection. The bills, read twice by their titles, were referred by House Speaker McCormack and the Acting President of the Senate to their respective committees on Public Works and to the Senate's Committee on

Rules and Administration. The opposition preceding their passage and following the President's signature was remarkable only for its virulence.

None but Hirshhorn and Lerner had ever seen the entire collection, but based on the exhibits of hundreds of its sculptures and substantial samplings of its paintings, art critics and historians had judged that it was, in Senator Bayh's words, a "significant gift." Suddenly and unaccountably the collection's rating toppled.

The day following the introduction of the bills to Congress, Sherman E. Lee addressed a letter to Lady Bird Johnson objecting to the President's recommendation to Congress. "The recent action," wrote the director of the Cleveland Museum of Art, "seems to me ill-advised and inimical to the national interest in the fine arts. . . . Its acceptance ill accords with current standards of wisdom and professional knowledge in the arts. It is a mistake to accept a collection of contemporary art formed by one man. . . . One presumes that the proposed monument will be designed to display the Hirshhorn collection in its entirety or nearly so. Anyone who knows the contents of the collection knows of its personal and quixotic nature and of its considerable variation in quality. . . . I feel that a truly National Museum of Contemporary Art should be founded on a carefully developed program employing the best available professional advice and that it should bear the name of the nation."

The president of the Federation of Citizens Associations of the District of Columbia voiced misgivings which sounded mild and reasonable until he quoted the minister of All Souls Unitarian Church who, hearing that the sculpture garden was to be located on the Mall, exclaimed, "I cannot think of a greater tragedy. We should then view the Capitol from the Washington Monument and the Washington Monument from the Capitol as if through a modernistic cemetery."

House and Senate committees heard a succession of witnesses oppose making room for the Hirshhorn Museum by the removal of the Armed Forces Medical Museum, known to the *Washington Post* as "a strong candidate for the ugliest building in Washington." Doctors, formerly attached to the Armed Forces Institute of Pathology (AFIP), sailed into the committee rooms on a sea of letters and telegrams from medical men and pathologists all over the country protesting the interference with the museum's scientific functioning and the eradication of a historic landmark.

Paul R. Cannon, Professor Emeritus of Pathology at the University of Chicago and consultant to AFIP, addressed the House panel, and Frank W. Townsend, of the San Antonio State Tuberculosis Hospital and former director of AFIP, spoke to the Senate group. In almost identical language they appealed for the right of visitors to see "actual specimens [and] feel the full impact of viewing a lung infiltrated by cancer, a brain damaged by hemorrhage or a human heart with coronary thrombosis."

Representative Durwant G. Hall, committee member and physician, having served as assistant Surgeon General during World War II, called the AFIP his alma mater. "I think, " he said, "it's important to keep medicine, and military medicine in particular, on the Mall."

"The gentleman is opposed to moving," Chairman Gray inquired, "even though it might be to improved quarters?"

"Yes," Dr. Hall insisted, "I truly would."

A. Clark Stratton, acting director of the National Park Service, settled the question of destroying a historic landmark by clarifying the Interior Department's citation. He stated: "The evaluation of national significance rested primarily on the importance of the museum collections and secondarily on the distinction of the structure. . . . If the collections were moved, we should not regard the building as retaining national significance. . . . We would view the landmark status as accompanying the collection regardless of its location."

Dillon Ripley encouraged committee members to visit Greenwich to satisfy themselves as to the vastness and value of the Hirshhorn collection. Some did in mid summer. Meanwhile, as inflation followed in the wake of the $30 billion Vietnam budget, the price tag on the museum jumped from $10 million in May to $13 million in July. Sam Harris apprehensively sounded out Richard Goodwin. The White House aide suggested an appropriation of $15 million. "That's a helluva lot of dough," said Harris, voicing qualms about an "austerity" Congress. "In my opinion," Goodwin assured him, "they will be enamored of the idea of a modern museum."

At the end of August, Senate Public Works authorized construction of the Hirshhorn Museum and Sculpture Garden at a cost of $15 million plus an annual $1,388,000 for maintenance and operation, and together with Rules and Administration reported S-3389 favorably out of committee. The Senate passed the bill on September 1.

The House delayed action until mid-October to prepare a companion bill authorizing $7.5 million for construction of the AFIP addition to its main building at Walter Reed. Elections approached; Congress itched to adjourn. Ripley hung on tenterhooks as House

Public Works held the museum bill in suspension, and the AFIP measure remained locked in the Senate's Armed Services Committee. Passage of both bills by this 89th Congress was essential to the Smithsonian timetable, which would need both sessions of the 90th Congress to process appropriations for planning and construction and meet the completion deadline of the museum by 1971. Not until October 18, with a nudge from the Executive Mansion, did Armed Services clear AFIP at its final meeting. Only then did HR-15121 break the jam in the House. Unanimously approved, the bill went to the White House for signature.

The Hirshhorn Museum measure caught up with the President in Johnson City, Texas, where he signed it into Public Law 89–788 on November 7, 1966. The *New York Times* reported that the Act represented "President Johnson's boldest stroke as a patron of the arts, a personal triumph, a national victory over foreign bidders, and an inestimable enrichment of Washington's cultural resources."

Aline Saarinen, who had written admiringly of Hirshhorn in *The Proud Possessors*, was outraged. "Joe," she cried, "took the Government as it's never been taken before." She blamed Ripley for overselling the President and Mrs. Johnson instead of bargaining shrewdly and persuading Hirshhorn to give his choicest treasures to form the base of an anonymous "National Collection of Modern Art." She condemned the public grant of a building named for Hirshhorn and criticized his indirect control of the museum through his right to handpick its director.

Questioned about this, Sam Harris derided the idea of Hirshhorn putting anything over on the United States Government. "They were all grown boys," he said. "They knew what they were doing. They wanted the collection. They were only one of a great number of people and institutions that wanted it."

A conflict-of-interest issue arose when Gordon Bunshaft was awarded the design contract while being a member of the Commission of Fine Arts. Bunshaft dismissed the complaint with a shrug. Ever since its establishment in the 1890s "to protect and develop the environmental character of Washington," the commission consisted of an architect, a sculptor, a painter, a landscape artist, and three laymen. As commissioners, they received no compensation. As professionals they did much of the work in the capital, the founders knowingly constituting the commission in this fashion to control the look of the city. "While I was occupied with the Hirshhorn Museum," said Bunshaft, "[John Carl] Warnecke, the architect, was doing the Kennedy tomb; Theodore Roszak, the sculptor, was on another assignment; and Hideo Sasaki, the landscape artist, was all over the place."

The Smithsonian appointment of Abram Lerner as director of the museum agitated the museum community, chiefly because he had not risen from the ranks. In their estimation he was not qualified despite his two decades of firsthand knowledge of the collection, ten years as its curator, and his lecturing on art and teaching at Brooklyn College. He did not, however, have a Ph.D., which put him in the company of two distinguished museum directors and scholars, John Pope-Hennessey of the British Museum, and Kenneth Clark, formerly of the National Gallery in London, both self-educated in art history.

But the basic controversy, said Charles Blitzer, a Smithsonian official, stemmed, as it does in all bargaining, from someone always winning the advantage. "Who did in this case?" he reflected on the deal. "It was a name on the Mall against the acquisition of a unique collection. The same and better were offered by England and New York State."

In the increasingly heated climate, art critic Vivien Raynor delivered a comparatively temperate appraisal shortly after President Johnson enacted the law. "Half the pictures and sculptures I have seen are excellent," she declared. "The rest are mediocre, including a sprinkling of choices I would call unfortunate. But a just estimate can only be made relative to other collections, and those in museums have been carefully weeded—as the junk-filled basements would testify. The point is, Hirshhorn has bought as a private individual, unprotected by the tastemakers 'union.' It's a fantastic gesture this man has made; it could turn out to be as eccentric as a Watts Tower—and as beautiful. . . . Modern artists [have expressed] consciously or unconsciously that something is desperately wrong with civilization. Hirshhorn is a man of the 20th century; the swath he has cut through its art may well be true history, not the edited kind."

Raynor was not to remain unaffected by the controversy. In the next eight years the conflict burst into flame, leaving few unsinged. By the museum's opening date, Raynor sided coldly with Hirshhorn's opponents.

The fracas took such intense form that at times Hirshhorn felt like withdrawing. He was pained and bewildered by an art world which only weeks before had paid court to him and homage to the collection. Suddenly it looked askance at his "personal" treasures. He wondered what if not "personal" were the collections of Phillips, Mellon, Frick, Freer, and the rest.

■ ■ □ □

With the agreement signed and the bill passed, the "art office" in New York became a beehive of reorganization, transforming itself from private to federal stewardship. The government's General Services Agency (GSA) stamped civil service ratings on curators, researchers, and secretary. Relaxed informality dissolved in regulations. Cataloging the condition of the artworks, providing for their restoration and transfer, making preparations for exhibits, setting up a reference library, all these procedures required expenditures. Fran Weitzenhoffer had to itemize everything down to pencils and paper clips on petty cash vouchers to be forwarded in triplicate form to the Smithsonian auditors. An omission or error could precipitate an accounting nightmare.

When the staff worked nights, the government provided sandwiches and coffee. On one occasion Fran ordered up a bagel and punctiliously filled out a voucher for 11 cents which she clipped to her report. Days later her phone rang. The voice on the other end sent a tremor through her.

"This is the treasurer's office at the Smithsonian," it said.

"Yes?" Fran quavered.

"What," a southern drawl inquired, "is a bagel?"

Though 1967 boiled over with mobilizations for peace on both coasts, race riots in Newark and Detroit, and a two-day Peace March on Washington, it opened joyously for Lady Bird Johnson. On January 10 Hirshhorn fulfilled her longtime wish by presenting her with an Eakins to enhance the White House collection. The portrait of Ruth Harding, painted in 1903, showed a little girl in a white dress and pink ribbon, niece of sculptor Samuel Murray, who was a close friend and early student of Eakins. On the back of the canvas the inscription read: "To Laura K. Harding from Thomas Eakins." Hirshhorn had bought it on January 8 at the Knoedler Gallery for $40,000. Within a few years its value had increased sevenfold.

In the *Washington Post* of February 12, 1967, Sophy Burnham, a local writer on art, stated that Hirshhorn "gets a big tax write-off." Elsewhere in the same issue Hirshhorn stated, "I'm taking no tax deduction on my personal gift. You want to talk about taxes? In 1955 I sold my Rio Tinto interests and paid the U.S. $9 million on my long-term capital gain."

Bunshaft's design of the museum sculpture garden and reflection pool roiled the National Capital Planning Commission. The garden and pool, equal to two sunken football fields, measured 80 by 450 feet with pebbled walks 45 feet wide on each side. Their trench traversed the Mall north from Independence Avenue. The Commission of Fine Arts approved the plans but the Planning Commission sanctioned them only tentatively because Mrs. James H. Rowe, its chairman, objected to the bisection of the Mall. The conflict was to rage into 1971.

Meanwhile Hirshhorn brightened. In an address to the Women's Democratic Committee in October 1967 at the Shoreham Hotel, he said, "I think I'm out of the woods." Cheerfully, he asserted that there was "no question whatever that Mrs. Johnson [would] attend the 1969 opening of the museum—I'll invite her myself!" He prognosticated that ground-breaking would take place early in 1968.

Almost at the same moment, Dillon Ripley was voicing apprehension to the President that the project had arrived at "a grave moment of decision." As a counterinflationary move, the House Appropriations Committee had deleted the AFIP from the Army budget. Ripley feared its elimination would affect the Hirshhorn. The Republicans would pounce on spending for a museum— "Modern art in time of war!" Ripley's alarm proved groundless. The House approved the AFIP item in December.

It was the Smithsonian budget which was in serious danger of being struck down. To request the remaining $14.1 million of the appropriation for the Hirshhorn in one sum would swell the Institution's annual allowance by an unwholesome 65 percent. Yet without the total amount, Ripley had no authority to contract for construction, which meant that the museum could not be completed in the agreed time. The deadline for decision was April 11. Harry McPherson referred the problem to the White House Budget Bureau with the behest that LBJ was "determined that nothing be left undone that will help secure the bequest. We must not lose the Hirshhorn gift," McPherson adjured the Bureau.

The Budget Bureau recommended that Ripley use the same formula as the new FBI and Labor Department buildings and request $2 million to start construction of the Hirshhorn Museum along with authority to enter into future contractual arrangements for the balance of $12.1 million. Against Gordon Bunshaft's warnings that this procedure invited trouble, Ripley adjusted his budget and requested contract authority. Congress approved.

With the arrival of 1968 a wistful strain underlay the President's New Year greeting to Hirshhorn. "Dear Joe," it read, "I think we are on the road toward building the Museum. With the budgetary pressures we are facing, it's not easy to convince some members of Congress that they should spend for art. But I think most of Congress recognizes the unique character of this great public opportunity. Lady Bird and I wish you and Olga the best of all your years—this year. You have done so much to make the last two years encouraging and exciting for me."

At the end of March the President halted the bombing of Vietnam and made his historic television address to the nation. "I do not believe I can unite this country. . . . I shall not seek and I will not accept the nomination of my party for another term as your president."

At the end of April, LBJ opened the old Patent Office Building on 8th and G streets to house the National Portrait Gallery, the Archives of American Art, and the National Collection of Fine Arts. Abram Lerner, uneasy about the relationship of the NCFA and the Hirshhorn Museum, said that "duplication and redundancy, monotony and needless expenditure [would] combine to reduce the effectiveness of both institutions." Ripley thereupon designated the resuscitated NCFA as the repository of American works exclusively, with the Hirshhorn devoted to contemporary art and its trends. The refurbished Patent Office, with its Greek Revival architecture, provided NCFA and NPG with twenty-one exhibit areas. Dedicating the new Smithsonian facility that April, President Johnson made the wry comment that if he were not remembered as patron of the arts, he would "like to be known as the uncle of the arts."

The day after the murder of Robert Kennedy stunned the nation, Hirshhorn granted Ripley permission to emend the agreement, to defer major funding for the museum to the 91st Congress and to reschedule completion of construction by the end of 1972. That same day Hirshhorn shopped for sculpture, but when he was done he could not recall that he had bought Dubuffet's *Glass of Water II* and *Transparent Rhythm II* by Agam, both destined for Washington. In June he ordered *Interlocking Vertebrae* from Henry Moore. In a frenzy of acquisition he gathered up in rapid succession Baizerman's

The Miner, Kadishman's *Open Suspense*, Lachaise's *King's Bride*, Pomodoro's *Opposition*, Steinberg's *Still Life with Golem*, and Zox's *Diamond Drill Series*. He kept on buying throughout 1968, a good deal earmarked for the museum though the destination of the works appeared immaterial. Hirshhorn's frenzy of buying seemed to be an attempt to buttress order against chaos, to affirm life through art. By the end of that fateful year he had set his record of 960 additions to his collection. The fever abating, in 1969 he acquired half that number. With time the fever subsided further.

■ ■ □ □

On the morning of January 8, 1969, Washington's winter sun shone on the red and white stripes of a tent erected at 7th and Independence beside the Mall for the ground-breaking ceremony of the Joseph H. Hirshhorn Museum and Sculpture Garden. The assembled dignitaries took shelter from the 40-degree cold in the adjacent Arts and Industries Building to await the President. Members of the Supreme Court and Cabinet, Congressmen, and Smithsonian officials stood among the Wright Brothers' plane, Lindbergh's "Spirit of St. Louis," and the first space capsule, "Friendship," and warmed themselves with coffee, sweet rolls, and bouillon laced with sherry. With Hirshhorn and Olga were his five daughters, some of them busy collecting autographs. Carol Fortas, wife of the Justice, smoked her long slender cigar.

At 11:30 A.M. the President, accompanied by Mrs. Johnson and Lynda Bird Robb, arrived to perform one of his final acts in office. He wore an overcoat "so long," said one observer, "it could have been a hand-me-down from General Pershing." Hirshhorn was protected against the elements by a thigh-length dark mink coat. Clipped to his shirt collar was the customary bowtie, this one dotted white on red. The party issued forth, some to the heated tent, others to join several hundred guests and friends seated and standing in front of the rostrum. The Army band played brightly, the sun glinting on their brass, as the President, Chief Justice Earl Warren, and Hirshhorn took their places. Towering over the lectern, Dillon Ripley opened the formalities.

"In 1780," Ripley said, "in the beginnings of our republic, John Adams wrote to his wife, 'I must study politics and war that my sons may have liberty to study mathematics and philosophy, natural history and naval architecture, navigation, commerce and agriculture, in order to give their children a right to study painting, poetry, music, architecture, statuary, tapestry and porcelain. . . .' Today, in the refinements of the technological world which is upon us, I submit that this is true no more. . . . To survive one must be skilled not only in politics and war but also in poetry, music and mathematics lest the urgent stresses of our environment deafen us to the very meaning of life itself. We risk being dehumanized in one generation, so that every generation must be all things to itself. We can no more afford to ignore art than we can afford to ignore technology. We must be trained for life at all levels of integration. In this setting . . . no building presently planned could add more to the spirit of the place than this one, a fortunate and humane partnership of Joseph Hirshhorn and our enlightened Government."

Ripley introduced Hirshhorn. To enable him to be in full view, a plywood box was placed at the lectern. Hirshhorn stood on it between LBJ (6-feet-2) and Ripley (6-feet-3) and looked to each side. Not one to be stifled by solemnity, he commented, "They should have given me a high-chair." He spoke of "golden moments that have the greatest significance. Today is such an occasion for me. . . ." He told of his early years when the idea was considered absurd that American art would ever become vital in world art. "I guess," said Hirshhorn, "I felt from the beginning that American art had an explosive energy that one day would affect and influence art all over the world. The past twenty years proved it. This is a proud day for me. . . . I was six years old [he was seven] when my mother brought me here from Latvia. I am grateful to that Mama of mine, and I hope she is here in spirit. What I have accomplished here in the United States I could not accomplish anywhere else in the world. . . ."

"When he began to talk," wrote Paul Richard, the art critic of the *Washington Post*, "standing on a box so he could see over the podium, the tie and the mink coat both made sense. There was poverty mixed with money in his voice."

Hirshhorn paid tribute to all those who had made the museum possible, particularly President and Mrs. Johnson, Dillon Ripley—"this amiable diplomat, a charming seducer"—and Abe Fortas—"Where are you, Abe? Stand up and take a bow." He also named Sam Harris and Roger Stevens, and James Bradley and Charles Blitzer. He ended by expressing the hope that the museum would become "a productive center of recreation, education and study for all our people."

President Johnson, the final speaker, connected the start of the museum to the next day's scheduled welcome for the three astronauts returned from orbiting the moon. "Today and tomorrow are memorable days," he said, "for our Capital and for this country.

. . . Each of the events we commemorate these two days—the flight of Apollo VIII and the birth of the Hirshhorn Museum—tells us something about this country and its people. . . . Today and tomorrow we affirm our people's intention to voyage in both directions of human discovery, toward the outer reaches of space and to the inner territory of the human heart. . . ."

President Johnson went on to say that "I share Mrs. Johnson's great respect and affection for Joseph and Mrs. Hirshhorn. . . . I shall take great pride in turning the first spade of earth and dedicating this new museum to 'the increase and diffusion of knowledge among men.' "

The President left the podium, took up a silver-plated shovel, and to the jubilant blare of the band plunged it into the earth to begin excavation. Chief Justice Warren and Dillon Ripley followed suit. When Hirshhorn's turn came, he dug in with such a will that his bowtie unclasped and fell to the ground. He retrieved it and Ripley bent to refasten it on Hirshhorn's collar.

The ceremony concluded after forty-five minutes. The President and his daughter returned to the White House and Mrs. Johnson accepted the invitation of the Ripleys to lunch in the Great Hall of the "Castle" with the Hirshhorns and a number of guests, including Mrs. Robert McNamara, Gordon Bunshaft, and William Walton, painter and chairman of the Commission of Fine Arts. On her black woolen dress Mrs. Johnson had pinned a new gold and diamond brooch, a gift from her husband on their thirty-fourth anniversary. Olga Hirshhorn wore a two-thousand-year-old Egyptian necklace of gold set with blue stones presented to her by her husband for this occasion. "Joe," she told a reporter, "was so happy that when the band struck up, I thought he was going to break into a buck-and-wing."

Asked to comment on the art gift, Abram Lerner delivered an elaborate witticism. "Mr. Hirshhorn," he said, "has the spirit shown by mountain climbers, explorers, and bird watchers," the last being a sly allusion to Ripley, the ornithologist. To Lerner's consternation, the *Washington Post* reporter filed her account of the morning and quoted the museum director as saying that Hirshhorn exhibited the spirit of "mountain climbers, explorers and burglars." The error, due possibly to her overindulgence at lunch, was corrected by the newspaper the next day with an apology.

With the ground-breaking came the first public view of the exterior design of the museum. The model of the building disclosed a cylindrical structure resting on four legs and "floating" 15 feet above a plaza. Reporters vied with each other to describe it, likening it to a "a gargantuan bagel . . . the Pentagon with the corners knocked off . . . a magnificent pillbox from the Maginot Line . . . the biggest tomb since the Pyramids."

Ada Louise Huxtable, architecture critic, delivered her judgment in the *New York Times.* She denounced "the biggest marble doughnut in the world. . . . The new museum," she wrote, "will line up solidly and formidably with the crushing phalanx of marble mausoleums devoted to the endless aspects of American art, culture, history and technology shepherded along both sides of the Mall by the Smithsonian. . . . Hirshhorn frankly considers his Museum a happy testament to the fact that in the United States of America a once poor Jewish boy can get his name on the Mall. . . . The scale is megalomaniac and the style is colossal funerary. . . . It may turn out to be a splendidly engineered tomb . . . only Louis XIV could have called *intime.*"

Tartly Bunshaft retorted that "she doesn't like Washington; she doesn't like the Mall; she doesn't like poor men getting rich." He recounted a trip he took a year earlier with Huxtable to the Johnson Library he designed in Austin, Texas. "Nobody was sympathetic to Johnson at the time," he said. "On the plane she started on Johnson and I thought, Oh boy! this is going to be something! When we got there she was flabbergasted and she wrote a marvelous article, a eulogy. If she were reviewing that same building at the time of the Hirshhorn, she would have beaten it to death because monumental buildings were out of fashion in the press. Those fashions come and go. It's hard to tell whether the students or the faculty or the critics create these fashions. It was a terribly anti-monumental period; so she tore the Hirshhorn to pieces."

The wrecker demolished the old Army Medical Museum. As the bulldozers rumbled in to scoop up the rubble and clear the area, a letter to the *Times* from New Haven foreshadowed further onslaughts. It noted with chagrin that the Huxtable denunciation of the museum's design had received little support. "Since architects," wrote George DeF. Lord, "are understandably reluctant to criticize the work of fellow architects, it looks as though the opposition to this monstrosity would have to come from the ordinary citizen and his elected representatives in Congress."

■ ■ □ □

Gordon Bunshaft designed a marble face for the museum in pale travertine or alternative white from Rome. "Everything was in order, looked perfect," said Bunshaft, "until it went out for bids in May." Congressmen from marble-producing states joined the Marble Institute of America to clamor for a native product. Representative Philip M. Landrum of Georgia dismissed Italian marble as "an esthetic idiosyncrasy." The Institute's Donald A. Hagerich allowed "if the Government insists it must have Roman travertine, okay; but we insist it must be fabricated in this country," a reasonable specification until Bunshaft learned that the GSA budget had lumped quarrying with fabrication and that domestic labor for cutting and finishing marble could not compete with Italian costs. After seven weeks the bids came in, up an inflationary 6 percent. Construction costs already had jumped 20 percent in 1968. "We were about $1.5 million over," said Bunshaft. He returned to the drawing board and in August flew to Cap d'Antibes to show Hirshhorn his adjustments in design. Bunshaft eliminated the public restaurant and kitchen and reduced the ground floor area by 40,000 square feet. The sculpture garden shrank and gravel substituted for dark flagstone pavement. Marble facing was out, replaced by a granite-chip concrete, propitiating native industry and approved by the Commission of Fine Arts. Before the new drawings were ready, it was December and costs had jumped again.

Piracci Construction Company of Baltimore submitted the bottom bid. Shortly afterward it requested a correction upward of $754,375, claiming a secretary "erroneously omitted the item for architectural concrete." Norair Engineering, the second-best bidder, protested, demanding the original figure be adhered to. Norair charged Piracci with "buying in," a practice common to firms that contracted with the Defense Department by which they put in for "unanticipated costs." Another month lagged until the General Accounting Office was "satisfied that the evidence established the existence of the alleged mistake." Piracci's ultimate price of $13,799,138 was still below Norair's by $1.7 million. Nonetheless, it was $899,138 above the funds appropriated by Congress for construction, $2.1 million having been committed to design, clearing the site, and other preliminaries. At lunch in New York, Bunshaft broke the gloomy news to Hirshhorn. It meant further reductions in the structure—no fountain in the plaza, no stairway and underpass to connect the sculpture garden with the plaza. "It made Hirshhorn ill," said Bunshaft. "He went out and bought something for $30,000." The "something" was the Picasso bronze *Kneeling Woman Combing Hair*.

An additional appropriation was out of the question. Dillon Ripley suggested to Hirshhorn that he apply his million-dollar endowment for future accessions to bailing out the building. Hirshhorn agreed. He then supplemented his original gift with an additional million dollars' worth of art. Bunshaft was able to retain the fountain and underpass. Instead of the marble, he specified a special agate granite which "gets pinkish when wet." Later he admitted, "When it gets really wet, it gets dirty gray. Horrible. Travertine would have been warm and elegant, but," he shrugged, "there was no money."

Construction began in March. In the words of Charles Blitzer, "Nothing that could have gone wrong didn't." The asymmetrical cylinder of the building prohibited the use of duplicate forms for pouring concrete. The concrete would not pour easily because special reinforcement rods required an unusual consistency. The four "legs" supporting the cylinder were odd-shaped and the contractor had first to build a model and obtain approval from GSA. The model was constructed, correct in shape but not in scale, and was disapproved. GSA demanded it be redone at a cost of $75,000 and precious time. Ripley had to request further extensions from Hirshhorn. Final appropriations, deferred to the 92nd Congress, moved the completion of the museum back to the fall of 1973.

Undismayed, Ripley picked his way through the thickets of Washington. The history of museums had ever been attended by vexations, from the first one founded in the United States in 1773 by the Library Society of Charleston, South Carolina, to the 216 institutions since, particularly the Smithsonian itself, which Ripley administered. James Smithson, an Englishman who had never set foot in the United States, bequeathed his entire fortune to the government in 1829 "to found in Washington under the name of the Smithsonian Institution an establishment for the increase and diffusion of knowledge among men." Nine years passed before the legacy could be pried loose from British courts. Only after Attorney General Richard Rush sailed to London did eleven boxes of gold sovereigns arrive at the Philadelphia Mint to be melted and recoined in the amount of $503,319.48. Congress wrangled for another eight years. "It is beneath the dignity of the country," sniffed John C. Calhoun, "to accept such gifts from foreigners." An anonymous colleague haughtily rejected the bequest, saying, "If an institution of this kind was desired, I would prefer it to be established out of our own funds and not have Congress pander to the paltry vanity of an individual. If they accept this donation, every whippersnapper vagabond that had been traducing our country might think it proper to have his name distinguished in the same way." Only the stamina of John Quincy Adams, Representative from Braintree, Massachusetts, saved the matter from oblivion. His arguments prevailing, the

Smithsonian came into being by Act of Congress in August 1846. Its first building on the Mall opened in 1853, twenty-five years after the gift.

The National Gallery of Art and its donor, Andrew Mellon, underwent rough handling at the time of his gift in 1936. In *Self-Portrait with Donors*, John Walker, the gallery's first curator, wrote, "On the election of Franklin D. Roosevelt, lawyers from the Department of Justice descended on Mellon. Mr. Roosevelt and his followers who had victoriously overthrown twelve years of Republican supremacy looked upon Andrew Mellon as a symbol of all they opposed. They were determined to discredit him. They asserted that he had committed fraud on his Federal income tax return. They attempted to procure a criminal indictment but the Grand Jury flatly refused to indict. A civil trial to collect penalties dragged on, overshadowed his last years. When the court handed down the verdict, a complete vindication of any wrongdoing, Mr. Mellon was no longer alive." The National Gallery opened in 1941.

Aware that the past repeated itself, Ripley retained his equilibrium as he read Gilmor D. Clarke's letter to the *New York Times*. The former member of the Commission of Fine Arts (1932–1950) pointed to the Hirshhorn Museum "as a thoroughly disgraceful intrusion in Washington's central composition of the Mall which would impair its integrity and dignity." Notwithstanding the Smithsonian and the Freer, Clarke declared, "We shall have to leave to those in authority to determine whether any individual by offering to donate a collection of art works to the Nation should be memorialized in perpetuity by having a building . . . constructed in the central area of the Nation's Capital . . . to purchase a place in history."

Mr. Clarke directed a more contumacious note to the *Washington Star*. "The whole project should be stopped," he cried. "The Hirshhorn Gallery has no place on the Mall. I sincerely hope that Congress will take appropriate action to save the Mall from being desecrated."

A letter from F. D. McHugh, a local resident, appeared alongside Clarke's. "Recently," it read, "a commentator—the name escapes me but I think it was James J. Kilpatrick, or it could have been Jenkin Lloyd Jones, or perhaps Jack Anderson—went into great detail showing that the business career of this man Hirshhorn, a Russian immigrant, did not make him particularly worthy of any government honor. There is no record that he ever performed an act or exhibited any special patriotism that would entitle him to monumental recognition."

The two letters elicited a temperate reply in a *Star* editorial.

"Most great public collections in Europe were begun as the strictly private collections of kings, princes, dukes and emperors of highly dubious political and personal moral standards. The tradition has continued in this country. On the Mall itself, Charles Freer, whose name is memorialized in the lovely gallery of oriental art, had a well-deserved reputation as a rake and died of a disease acquired in gaining that reputation. James Smithson, whose name covers everything from the Air and Space Museum to the Zoo, was a bastard, the illegitimate son of the Duke of Northumberland, whose chief motive seems to have been to spite his native land. The Nation is not, as our correspondents imply, erecting a monument to Hirshhorn. It is accepting and suitably housing his gift of a magnificent collection of modern art. In doing so, the Nation is enlarging the art enclave along the Mall. All of this is perfectly proper and completely within the tradition." The editorial did little to still the hubbub.

John Canaday, the *Times* art critic, bored on a Labor Day weekend, wrote, "It would be fascinating to know whether there is anybody in the American museum field who, when the hair is all the way down, really likes the idea of this project going through. If the project isn't doomed, is the situation irremediable? Tell me, somebody."

In response, Ripley's assistant wrote to the *Times*, "The Museum and Sculpture Garden have been under construction since March. Full contract authority and the necessary appropriations have been legislated by the Congress. Completion is assured, scheduled in the fall of 1973."

Ripley expressed his compassion for Hirshhorn. He acknowledged the donor's additional gifts and heartened him with gentle optimism on the twists and turns in the road to the Mall. "I am sure," he wrote, "this all reads like a strange tale to you but I have found there is a way to get things done in Washington despite the system—it just takes longer, a lot of know-how and the grace of patience."

These attributes in Ripley were soon to undergo a severe test. A disgruntled employee of the Smithsonian had embarked on a crusade to stir the press and to instigate an audit of the Institution by the GAO, the first in more than a century. The investigating House Subcommittee met for almost nineteen hours to hear testimony which filled 1,032 pages in two volumes.

▪ ▪ □ ▫

Robert Hilton Simmons, in his mid-forties, arrived in Washington in 1965 from his birthplace on Cape Cod by way of the University of

California/Berkeley and the merchant marine. Of medium height, stocky, square-jawed, his dark eyes gazed out of a baby-round face with the fixed stare common to seamen. He gravitated to the Smithsonian's National Collection of Fine Arts, where he contracted to prepare an exhibit of Henry O. Tanner's paintings. In a letter to the *Washington Star*, Simmons charged the Smithsonian with irregularities. From a memorandum he fished from the wastebasket of an NCFA curator, he learned of a picture in the collection by the sixteenth-century Flemish painter Jan Massys having been exchanged for one by the eighteenth-century American artist Benjamin West, the former putatively valued at $35,000, the latter at $10,000. Simmons carried this tale to the Internal Revenue Service, which referred him to the Federal Bureau of Investigation. The FBI took no action. The NCFA terminated his contract.

Feeling personally wronged, and believing he was defending the public interest, Simmons met with his Congressman, Hastings Keith, who brought his constituent's complaint to the attention of the GAO. The Comptroller General cited "various questionable policies and practices in Smithsonian financial management." The Board of Regents of the Institution expressed its confidence in the policies and leadership of its secretary who, with five museums under his care, "each with a different approach," instituted regulative procedures to govern the sale of works by NCFA thereafter. However, Simmons continued his offensive. In 1970, as three bills for expanding the Smithsonian were pending in Congress, he planned a two-pronged assault. He attacked the Hirshhorn Museum and Sculpture Garden in the press, and he prepared Representative Keith for congressional action. Foraging in Canada, Simmons returned with his armament.

Clark Mollenhoff fired the first barrage. The *Des Moines Register* Washington Bureau Chief and ombudsman to President Nixon called for an IRS examination of the Hirshhorn gift. "This is the greatest stonewall job ever done in this town. . . . Because this is art, the scandals get lost on the society pages. . . . The truth is, this isn't a gift, it's plain theft. . . ." The least that could be done, Mollenhoff recommended, was to get Hirshhorn's name off "that building."

Several months later columnist Jack Anderson published the story of a "blue-eyed sixty-seven-year-old retired nurse" of Bonita Springs, Florida, who had taken investment counsel from her lickerish lawyer and consequently would not be attending the opening of the Hirshhorn Museum because she could not afford the bus fare to the capital. "She lost her life's savings," wrote Anderson, "through a stock hustle by Joseph Hirshhorn whose name will now be honored alongside those of George Washington and Abraham Lincoln."

As the GAO inquired into the Smithsonian's "misuse of funds and faulty purchasing procedures," Representative Keith pressed for a full-dress hearing. The Subcommittee on Library and Memorials, the appointed guardian of the Institution, convened on July 16, 1970, in Room 2257 of the Rayburn Building to discharge "the responsibility of Congress to oversee all Federal activity and spending" and to show solicitude, somewhat belatedly, for its ward.

In the course of two weeks, Dillon Ripley and the heads of the Institution's fourteen bureaus detailed their forty-one activities in thirteen buildings, seven located on the Mall. According to statute, the Smithsonian Board of Regents included the Chief Justice of the Supreme Court, the Vice President, and several Senators. The Institution employed 3,147 persons in multifarious occupations ranging from the care of 80 million artifacts, which increased annually by one million, to astrophysics, the humanities, and festivals. During Secretary Ripley's administration the budget had tripled from $15.4 million in 1964 to $50 million in 1970. Two items in the Smithsonian audit suggesting misuse of $40,095 in one instance, and in another of $3,835, were attributed to differing accounting systems used by the Smithsonian and the GAO. Measures were already in operation to correct faulty procedures. Astringently, Congressman John Brademas from Indiana commented, "When I think of what goes on over in the Department of Defense, my blood does not boil very much about the Smithsonian's shortcomings. . . . I do hope some of the zeal displayed in the GAO can also be pointed in other directions where the pay-off might be far richer from the taxpayer's viewpoint."

Sherman Lee reiterated to the committee the misgivings he still harbored about the Hirshhorn Museum ever achieving first-class status. Abram Lerner testified that Lee had never seen the Hirshhorn collection and, besides, was a specialist in Oriental art. Nonetheless, the Cleveland Museum director was of the opinion that a museum such as the Hirshhorn would form had poor prospects of growth due to "the specific nature of its contents." He went on to say, "I am more concerned now with what the design of the building does in terms of its encroachment on the Mall by means of the sunken sculpture garden. This really hurts the Mall. . . . This is the nose of the camel under the tent which may provide an excuse for future encroachments."

Representative Jonathan Bingham of New York, a panel member, stated that "just within the hour I have spoken with William Walton, Chairman of the Fine Arts Commission, and have so received word that the Fine Arts Commission has approved the design without dissent, having obtained some modification of the plans for the sunken garden across the Mall so that it will not interfere, in their judgment, with the sweep of the Mall."

Anticipating Sherman Lee's criticism, Dillon Ripley requested an opinion from H. Harvard Arnason, art historian and former director of the Walker Art Center. Arnason, closely acquainted with the Hirshhorn collection, had published a book on its sculpture and written the catalog for the painting exhibits sponsored by the American Federation of Arts. His letter to Chairman Frank Thompson, Jr., was placed in the record.

"Hirshhorn," it said in part, "has built up the most comprehensive collection of American painting of the 20th century in existence. This includes representation of every major American painter of this century, frequently with many examples of each painter's works. The collection also includes a great number of examples by lesser artists or by artists such as the Social Realists and regional painters of the Thirties and Forties who are now out of fashion. These artists are nevertheless an important part of the history of modern American art, and without them any picture of American art of this century would be incomplete."

Of the sculpture, Arnason wrote, "In my opinion and that of most other specialists in the field, [it] is the most important collection of modern sculpture in existence. I do not believe any museum of modern art, including the Museum of Modern Art in New York, possesses as comprehensive and important a collection."

When Robert Simmons appeared for the hearings, Committee Chairman Thompson addressed him. "I have just gotten your statement," said the New Jersey Representative. "Witnesses before Congressional committees have at least limited immunity from suit. . . . In the case of your statement I would just caution you that if there is any question in your mind as to any allegations in it, you might be wise to consult counsel with respect to whether or not you should read them at this time." To which Simmons replied, "I have consulted counsel who have gone over my statement and found nothing is libelous or slanderous in it."

Simmons accused Ripley of purveying misleading information to Congress. When he denounced the Secretary for breaking the public faith, the Institution's attorney interrupted to ask whether Simmons meant the phrase in a legal or philosophical sense. Simmons chose the latter and went on to declare Ripley's "most flagrant violation of public trust has been the promotion of the Joseph H. Hirshhorn Museum and Sculpture Garden." Simmons scorned the competition between nations for the collection as "a kind of promotional stunt—the Governor of New York offering $10 million in appropriated funds for a museum—all of this was talk with very little behind it." He charged that no experts were brought in for consultation and that Sherman Lee, who "had seen the collection," had "said it was a bad bargain." He placed columns by Jack Anderson into the record. As evidence of the odiousness of the man whose name was to be glorified on the Mall, Simmons repeated the news accounts of Hirshhorn's fortunes and misadventures in Canada. He attributed the Depression of the thirties to the kind of "fiscal irresponsibility" practiced by Hirshhorn, whom he characterized as unpatriotic for engaging in "illegal activities while Americans [lay] dying on battlefields in Europe." From his reading of the statute which established the Hirshhorn Museum, Simmons claimed the Smithsonian had exceeded its authority. He accused the Secretary of hustling the bill through Congress without proper hearing and by "misinformation, error, deception and cynical distortion" obtaining its site on the Mall. Flatly, he asserted, "Mr. Bunshaft was given a contract for design and supervision. The man that gave that out to him was Mr. Hirshhorn who was a private citizen."

"He made all sorts of wild charges," said Sam Harris. "In my view, some of the statements were scandalous, but I have a general philosophy," which he worded with typical pungency, "you don't get into a pissing contest with a skunk."

After listening attentively to Simmons, Representative Bingham said, "I think your primary purpose here is to discredit Dr. Ripley and the management of the Smithsonian. . . . What do you recommend by way of legislative action?"

"I think," Simmons responded, "the whole thing should be stopped."

"Including," inquired Bingham, "the acquisition of the collection by the Government?"

"Yes," Simmons replied.

The prospect made Chairman Thompson shudder. "It would take an act of Congress to stop construction now," he said, pondering the next move. "This Subcommittee has the oversight responsibility insofar as the Smithsonian exists. It does not have authority to pass on legislation that sets aside a specific plot of land or to authorize construction of a building for the Smithsonian."

Representative Bingham reminded the chairman that "the Smithsonian was dealing with Congress. I think if there is criticism, it attaches to the Congress and to the members of the Subcommittee who didn't—and I was one of them—who didn't raise the question on the floor when this bill came before us."

Representative Brademas said, "We have been kept in the dark. There is something unseemly and in rather bad taste about the haste with which the Hirshhorn has been jammed down our throats. . . . I have some profound misgivings. It isn't the character of Mr. Hirshhorn that is the cause of my concern but the character of the architecture and what you are going to do to the Mall."

Former Justice Fortas observed that "the nose of the Subcommittee on Library and Memorials was out of joint because the bill bypassed them and went to Public Works." That happened, he said, by prerogative of the Speaker of the House and not on the initiative of the Smithsonian. As to the bill being railroaded through Congress, "Ridiculous!" was Fortas's comment. "Every piece of legislation undergoes the same process of brokering. LBJ favored getting the collection. His interest in sculpture or painting was not great. His greatness lay in his understanding the importance to the nation of the influences of art and culture."

Impressed by Simmons's zeal, embarrassed by his accusations, the committee members smarted under the imputation that legislatively they had been slighted. With some difficulty Chairman Thompson reconciled their feelings. "The Subcommittee on Library and Memorials until now has never involved itself in the Hirshhorn project," he stated, "and in the usual course of events in the past probably would not. . . . This is just one more history of referral of legislation to committee in the judgment of the Speaker, and that judgment is very seldom questioned." Thompson wanted it known that "this has been anything on earth but a witch hunt, nor has it been in any sense indiscreet."

The report of the subcommittee reflected inner confusions. During the hearings, committee members had admitted to incompetence in matters of aesthetics. However, complaining of being bypassed when Congress accepted the gift, the report contended that the most serious question was the aesthetic one, its effect on the Mall. Thompson insisted on review and authority to determine what was acceptable architectural design, and recommended that "no further action to carry on the proposed plans for the sculpture garden be taken until a complete review has been made by the appropriate committees of the Congress." Relentlessly, Thompson tried to legislate a new site for the Hirshhorn Museum.

Resistance to Gordon Bunshaft's cross-Mall design mounted. The National Sculpture Society was "unalterably opposed to the use of any part of the Mall by the Smithsonian Institution for a sculpture garden as an adjunct to the Hirshhorn Museum. . . . The Senate Park Commission Plan of 1901 has never been defiled," the Society's president declaimed. "It should not be now."

Wielding authority over all federal installations in Washington, the National Capital Planning Commission refused to "violate the sacred sweep of the Mall" and vetoed Bunshaft's transverse design. The architect refused to budge.

Benjamin Forgey, the art critic of the *Washington Star*, looked at the design and, like the child in *The Emperor's New Clothes*, pointed to its architectural flaw. The trench athwart the Mall, he said, would force the sculpture into two single files, which were better suited to rows of imperial Roman busts than to the free forms of modern works. The realization gave Bunshaft pause.

Shortly afterward, Sam Harris met Leonard Garment. Nixon's adviser passed along the information that "the President would not go for the garden across the Mall." Harris confronted Bunshaft. "Gordon," said the attorney, "if you had a choice between a sculpture garden across the Mall and no garden at all, which would you take?" The message got through. The architect's aesthetic rationale bowed to the implied fiat. He reduced the two football fields to onetenth the original size and turned the garden ninety degrees to parallel and abut the Mall between Jefferson and Adams drives. The Fine Arts Commission gave its blessing in May, and the National Capital Planning Commission approved the new arrangement on July 1.

Two days later, a year after nominees were submitted to him, President Nixon announced the trustees of the museum. From Hirshhorn's fifteen candidates, the President selected H. Harvard Arnason, Taft Schreiber, and Hal B. Wallis. The fourth, Elizabeth Houghton, died prior to the opening and was replaced by Anne d'Harnoncourt. The quartet appointed from the Smithsonian submissions were Leigh B. Block, Theo C. Cummings, George H. Hamilton, and Daniel Patrick Moynihan, then Ambassador to India. The two ex-officio members were Chief Justice Warren and Secretary Ripley.

Benjamin Forgey visited Greenwich and New York to poke through the art office on East 65th Street and the warehouse on West 21st Street. He wished to see for himself whether the collection's "eccentricity" and "historical gaps" made it unworthy of a monumental "home-to-be on the Mall." "Those reports," he wrote in the *Washington Star*, "are eccentric and misinformed. It will take years before scholars and art lovers can take the measure of the Hirshhorn painting collection, a ready-made museum of modern American art if there ever was one."

Opposition persisted. The freshman Senator from Alabama, James B. Allen, introduced a resolution to rescind congressional approval of the agreement between the Smithsonian and Hirshhorn. The Senator threatened to place before a subcommittee hearing "questionable legalities," asserting that "Congress in making the Chief Justice an ex-officio member of the Hirshhorn Board of Trustees violated the Constitutional separation of powers." Fuzzily, the Senator forgot that the appointment had been made by statute, and that no one in 125 years had challenged a Chief Justice in his post on the Smithsonian Board of Regents. The spectacle turned sardonic when in summer session a subcommittee heard testimony from a former gangland dealer in stolen securities. He appeared before the panel as a "mystery witness," his identity secret in fear of underworld reprisal. Under the alias of George White, presumably endowing him with truth and purity, he charged Hirshhorn with fleecing the investment public. The subcommittee failed to sense the irony of a mobster, who did not know Hirshhorn, calling Hirshhorn "unsavory."

At 7th and Independence, the four acres completely excavated and concrete sluiced into foundation forms, the Hirshhorn Museum inched toward its opening date considerably behind schedule.

As late as January 1974, Clark Mollenhoff went to press with a full column on tax dodges. Referring to deductions taken by President Nixon and former Vice President Humphrey on their executive papers, the Pulitzer Prize journalist called for scrutiny of Hirshhorn's IRS returns.

> . . . And to be certain the investigation is not unfair to President Nixon and Humphrey simply because they are in politics, it would be advisable to examine the still-pending multi-million-dollar art write-off on a collection Joseph H. Hirshhorn is giving to the Smithsonian. The tax write-off of Hirshhorn's agreement with Dillon Ripley is reported to be at least $50-million—one hundred times the tax advantage President Nixon received on his papers. . . . Hirshhorn had been quoted as putting an $80- to $100-million eval-

uation on his art gift. It is expected that his tax lawyers will make every effort to get the highest evaluation possible when the gift becomes effective later this spring with the completion of the Museum. The taxpayers receive art and sculpture that cost Hirshhorn a maximum of $5-million. But it could cost the taxpayer as much as $100-million ($20-million construction costs plus $80-million gift write-off) plus an obligation to pay $2-million a year for the staff of the Hirshhorn Gallery, maintenance of the property and preservation of the art pieces. If the tax deductions for the Hirshhorn gifts are finally consummated, it will mean that Hirshhorn could pay no Federal taxes for the rest of his life and his art will have a permanent home in lavish accommodations provided by the taxpayers.

A reputable newsman, Mollenhoff admittedly lacked firsthand data on the subject and he was caustically refuted by Sam Harris.

"That's complete rubbish," the attorney told me. "It's flagrantly false and in my opinion it's libelous." Alluding to the $80 million tax allowance, Harris went into detail. "Joe did not receive a write-off of anything like $80 million. The gift was so enormous in terms of value that it would be impossible for him to realize tax benefits during his lifetime in deductions that would be available. Based on his income, under no conceivable circumstances could he obtain a write-off of anything like $80 million. His deductions, not as Mollenhoff figured, are to be taken within a five-year period, not a lifetime. Joe hadn't the slightest concern about taxes when he made the gift. We never even discussed it, or the tax consequences of his gift, not once during the whole time we were negotiating it. He never raised the question. Taxes had nothing to do with his decision at all. Mollenhoff was assuming," Harris concluded in disgust, "that making the magnificent gift, Hirshhorn automatically obtained a tax benefit to the extent of $80 million, and that's unadulterated nonsense. He doesn't know what he's talking about. He was out to smear Joe. What he wrote was irresponsible and absurd, and a flagrant abuse of freedom of the press."

Hirshhorn oscillated between suffering indignity and feeling gratification. He mailed a Christmas card which pictured him jauntily on the site of the Museum with the Capitol in the background. It suited him to balance the score somewhat by raising the blood pressure of his enemies. He purchased more art, adding his own gifts, as those of fourteen other donors enriched the collection with twenty-seven paintings and eighteen sculptures, and fifty graphics by Picasso. Valued at $586,000, the benefactions included *#31*, *#36*, and *#39* by Clyfford Still, *Seated Man* by Willem De Kooning, *Daybreak* by Kenneth Noland, eleven sculptures by Chaim Gross, and a portrait in plaster by Reuben Nakian of Raphael Soyer bestowed by the subject.

Hirshhorn exchanged *Van Gogh in Garden* by Francis Bacon plus $20,000 for three oils by Ad Reinhardt: *#88-1950 (Blue), #90-1952 (Red)*, and *#119-1950 (Black)*. He sold the Andrew Wyeth *Abandoned Boat* for $27,000, added $6,000, and obtained Elie Nadelman's bronze, *Standing Female Nude*, the mate of the standing male already in the gift; and Alexander Calder's metal-and-wire *Red, Yellow, Black, White*. An untitled acrylic by Noland was sold for $18,000 and an untitled Still acquired for $33,000.

"Deaccession," commented critic Paul Richard, "is equal to a bid 'to make me better than I am.' "

For his National Gallery, Mellon had stipulated that nothing "shall be included in the permanent collection . . . unless it be of similar high standard of quality." René Gimpel, the Paris art dealer, noted in his diary that the Vermeer *Laughing Young Girl* in the Mellon collection was a fake. Under the necessity of securing the Kress assemblage in time for the gallery's opening, John Walker "had to lie" to meet "the intention of Mr. Mellon." Of the 393 works he obtained in the Kress group, 262 were subsequently weeded out.

In 1970, four items in the Hirshhorn gift—Rodin's *Burghers of Calais*, Brancusi's *Sleeping Muse*, Moore's *King and Queen*, and the Eakins *Portrait of His Wife*—were evaluated at $1.3 million by Parke-Bernet. Hirshhorn added two more by Eakins, bronze reliefs produced by the artist in 1893 for the Trenton Memorial Monument. *Battle of Trenton* and *American Army Crossing Delaware* had gone on loan to an exhibit at the Corcoran Gallery after which the State of New Jersey wished them placed permanently in the Trenton Museum, provided two castings were made, one pair to replace the originals on the monument—25 feet above the ground—and the other to go to whoever paid the costs. Hirshhorn did, and the bronzes entered the collection.

In March 1972, Hirshhorn further expanded his gift. A dozen paintings and sculptures by Léger, Matisse, Mondrian, and Picasso joined works by Calder, Pollock, Miró, Rauschenberg, Giacometti, Magritte, Houdon, and Bacon, among a total of 321 items valued at $7 million. All had been purchased in the preceding six years.

His friend David Kreeger expostulated in admiration at Hirshhorn's presenting seven Francis Bacons to the museum.

"How many do *you* have?" Hirshhorn inquired.

"A few," Kreeger replied. "But you have enough Bacons and

Gottliebs [who painted yellow discs] for bacon and eggs the rest of your life."

Having endured a scaled-down design, fund shortages, and congressional hearings (one critic on the Hill said privately that "the fear among politicians of the anti-Semitic label was Mr. Hirshhorn's most important protection") the museum had still to surmount two tortuous years. Ripley sent a letter of distress to the GSA, a copy of which went to the White House. The opening had already been postponed from December 1971 to December 1972 then to April 1973; and when strikes by building trades unions and truck drivers halted work completely, the dates were revised further to June then December. The Smithsonian at that point, two years beyond the time specified in the gift agreement, assumed the costs, premiums, and other charges "incidental to storing and insuring the collection." GSA did not certify the structure "substantially completed" until March 1974. Finally, the following month, on April 17, the pact was consummated and title to the collection passed to the Smithsonian Institution. Along the way, "Joseph H." was dropped and the name officially became the Hirshhorn Museum and Sculpture Garden.

■ ■ □ □

"Nobody," said Abram Lerner, "has ever opened a new museum with a collection that could fill it four times."

Preparations for the inauguration were as detailed and painstaking as for a military invasion. A workable inventory now existed of the art deployed in the Hirshhorn offices on Park Avenue and East 65th Street, in Greenwich, in Naples, Florida, and in warehouses in New York and Connecticut. The process of selecting the opening exhibit had begun in 1972. Thrice weekly, Lerner repaired to Morgan Manhattan Storage, where all the works of a single artist—or of several—passed in review as he gradually sorted out 1,015 for display in the museum and for representation in the initial catalog to be printed and bound in Japan and published by Harry Abrams and Company. Researchers and curators in New York compiled lists of artists, authenticated signatures and dates; noted the positions of the data on canvases, frames, labels, or on the body or plinth of sculptures; and checked provenance—previous owners, records of exhibits, and references in art literature. Among stacks of oils and sculptures, piles of drawings, prints, and files of photographs, a canceled check turned up, a souvenir of Canada, from Rio Tinto to Joseph H. Hirshhorn, in the sum of $45,818,381.30. In Greenwich alone, curator Frank Gettings and Olga Hirshhorn consumed a full month tracking down 600 items, which covered 82 typed pages.

Lerner intended to display all of the catalog's 1,015 pieces. After surveying the spaces in the galleries, plaza, and garden, Douglas McAgy, curator of exhibits, found the number excessive. Models of the museum interiors were fashioned, and the art scaled down to three-eighths of an inch. Using mirrors and an architect's periscope to view the effects, McAgy designed the layouts and arrived at a selection of 900—375 paintings and 525 sculptures. The museum being unavailable, its walls were dummied to approximate size, including the curve, and set up in the warehouse, where the paintings were hung according to McAgy's blueprint. In April 1973, with the garden still a mudhole, McAgy put two artists to work in the storehouse fabricating full-scale reproductions of the sculptures in styrofoam, which he studied and shifted about until he fixed them in satisfactory placements. He never saw his concept realized. In the summer of 1973, death felled McAgy and responsibility passed to Charles Froom to carry out his design. "You couldn't be cleverer than we were," said Lerner. "But cleverness is not the answer. The scale of our model had to be so reduced that later adjustments were inevitable."

Before the lower levels of the museum were finished, the staff occupied the offices on the fourth floor in December 1973. They began preparations for delivery of the art the following May, which allowed less than five months till the opening. In June, Stephen E. Weil, former administrator of the Whitney, was appointed deputy director, and fashion photographers were taking advantage of the museum plaza to pose their models.

Lerner described the transfer to Washington as "the biggest logistical move of its kind since the French moved out of Paris ahead of the German Army in World War II." To his gift of 1972, Hirshhorn added another 209 works, among them another Eakins, two Pollocks, a Tobey, Man Ray, Joseph Stella, Kline, and three Webers. At the warehouse and in Greenwich, four men required six months to wrap and crate the total of 6,211 pieces of art, examining each one to verify its condition for insurance. Packages and crates were color-coded for delivery to one of four locations in the museum. The 900 in the inaugural exhibit preceded the rest. Fifty-five van loads transported the collection to Washington where Registrar Douglas Robinson unwrapped, reexamined, and checked in each work on his list.

The move from the West 21st Street warehouse got under way

in May. In June trucks started rolling out of Greenwich with paintings and "light stuff." To spare the lawns and gardens, more than eighty-five of the heaviest sculptures were lifted by helicopter and "cherry-picker" cranes from positions some had occupied for twelve years. Practice flights were staged to experiment with types of slings, cradles, nylon and padded cable with which to raise the massive works and to deposit them at a staging area.

The three-week-long airlift began on August 5. A week later, over a hundred spectators stood spellbound as they watched pilot John Roatch hover over Round Hill in his Sikorsky S-58. He dropped a 75-foot cable from its belly and swung Manzù's *Monumental Standing Cardinal* 50 feet into the air. The crowd gasped as the 1,200-pound bronze gyrated above the trees like a ceiling fan. To stop the spin, which threatened to snap the cable, the pilot lowered the Manzù gently onto the grass. Slowly he raised the bronze again and, with the aid of six men handling guy ropes, set it down on a flatbed truck. Two camera crews in additional helicopters filmed the airlift. The downdraft from all the blades blasted acorns from the surrounding oaks and fired them like buckshot at the onlookers. Nobody stirred.

The pilot repeated the maneuver with Moore's *Glenkiln Cross*, which hefted at 1,700 pounds, his *King and Queen* weighing 1,250 pounds, and Marini's *Horse and Rider*, 1,110 pounds. After that, the operation continued uneventfully. In quick succession more than $3 million worth of art took to the air, including a Bourdelle, Butler, Epstein, Etrog, Hajdu, Ipoustéguy, Lipchitz, Hepworth, and Serrano, soaring from the rear lawns over the house and its gables, turrets, towers, and cupolas and settling onto trucks in the driveway. Only *The Burghers of Calais* proved intractable. Roatch and his S-58 tried twice without success.

"The thing weighs a lot more than it's supposed to," he reckoned. "It's listed at 4,000 pounds and my helicopter is listed with a capacity of 4,000; but I gave it everything she's got and she couldn't budge it."

A mighty crane did the job. When the operation was over, Edward Monserrate of Hahn Brothers had supervised the transfer of 300 tons of Hirshhorn sculpture. The trucks barreled off down the turnpike to Washington, trailing wind-shredded plastic covers. Calder's 25-foot stabile *Two Discs* was disassembled into four sections and cradled in an open van for travel by a special route which avoided low bridges and tunnels. Arrived in the capital, the pieces were rejoined on the museum site. A 90-ton crane with a 100-foot boom raised the mammoth figures into prearranged places on the plaza and in the garden. The airlift completed the delivery of the collection.

Although Hirshhorn appeared unconcerned throughout, Olga, his wife, confided that he was "scared to death because he's never done anything like it before." The exploit, however, was pure Hirshhorn, the style in which twenty years earlier he had staked out the uranium strike of the century.

The sculptures gone, Hirshhorn stared at their bases and pedestals spotting the lawn like grave markers.

"We'll chop up that stone," he said huskily; "we'll plant new grass." Pausing, he looked long at them and said, "I'm going to make a phone call to see if the real world is still out there."

He turned and walked to the house. Nearby, Olga explained to a visitor. "He has to use the phone," she said. "Moving art is so expensive, he's gone to see if he can pay for all this."

Later a reporter inquired of him, "How much did it cost?"

"What's the difference?" said Hirshhorn, minimizing the spectacle. "I'm paying for it."

The move cost $215,000. It was his way of celebrating his seventy-fourth birthday one day before. Besides, it was the most economical way to make the move.

■ ▪ ☐ ▫

The Hirshhorn Museum and Sculpture Garden was inaugurated on October 1, 1974. The celebration began with a preview for a press corps of 350. They arrived to the sound of hammers as workmen, preparing for the formal opening the following night, were building a dais and festooning it with pleated cream-colored bunting. The fountain, 60 feet in diameter, was tested, shooting jets 30 feet into the air. The curatorial staff dashed about to hang the last of the pictures and to provide mounts for the few sculptures that lay on their sides, like casualties awaiting medics. Custodians curried and combed the galleries. At the Independence Avenue entrance secretaries polished the bronze frames of the exhibition's posters.

At 10 A.M. Charles Blitzer greeted the newsmen in the little theater in the basement and introduced Dillon Ripley. With him on-stage were Ambassador Moynihan, Gordon Bunshaft, and Abram Lerner. The Secretary announced that Hirshhorn had marked the birthday of the museum with a gift of four new sculptures: two gigantic Reuben Nakians, each 12 feet long, *The Rape of Lucrece* in steel, and *Goddess of the Golden Thighs*, a bronze which looked to critic Thomas B. Hess like "an archaic pedimental climax, reworked by Phidias, burnt for limestone by the Crusaders, blown up by the Turks and fished out of that branch of the Aegean which runs by Nakian's studio off the piazza in Stamford, Connecticut"; the third by Kenneth Snelson, the stainless steel and aluminum construction *Needle Tower*, stood 60 feet tall in the right-hand corner of the plaza off Independence Avenue; the fourth, Henry Moore's *Two-Piece Reclining Figure; Points*, had been featured at the sculptor's retrospective exhibit in Florence two years earlier and reserved for a bank in the midwest. Hirshhorn told Moore, "I've got to have it," and Moore yielded. The monumental bronze occupied the center position at the museum entrance.

Lerner had gone to bed late and rushed in that morning to survey the work of the previous night. Unaccustomed to seeing people in the galleries, he came upon several waiting in the lobby and almost yelled, "Out! Get out! You're spoiling the view!" To the press he said, "The museum enters its most important phase, the arrival of the public."

Bunshaft contented himself saying, "It's been eight years since I was selected to design the museum. If the building doesn't speak for itself, words won't do it."

Moynihan invited the press to tell him what they thought after he turned them loose to prowl the premises until 5 P.M.

Reinforced throughout the day by Smithsonian hospitality, the reporters drank, munched on platters of shrimp, sandwiches, fruit, and pastries, and roamed the 4½ acres of plaza and garden walled in pink granite-aggregate which matched the museum's exterior. The cylinder, 68 feet high on four 14-foot piers, thrust its 82 feet toward the sky which shone bright and warm with autumn sun. The building, with a diameter of 231 feet, enclosed an off-center circular court of 115 feet, wide enough to encompass the Guggenheim Museum. Around this inner plaza rose four stories of glass wall.

The lobby on the ground floor gave access by escalator to the main galleries on the second and third levels where the exhibition rooms, with 168,000 square feet of floor space, went around nine-tenths of a mile in twin ambulatories 50 feet wide. Paintings were arrayed on the inside surface of the 3-foot-thick wall, its curve imperceptible, and on the partitions of the alcoves, all artfully lit. Sculptures displayed in the inner ring, overlooking the court, received natural daylight through the glass walls, supplemented by artificial illumination.

The top floor, reached by an elevator in one of the piers, housed the library, administration offices, and the unique storage/study facility. Here 141 double-faced panels, each 15 feet high by 20 feet wide, provided 84,000 square feet of surface on which to hang considerably more than the almost 4,400 paintings in the collection. The panels suspended on rails rolled out at will into areas properly lit for study.

"All museum professionals are struck with envy," said Bunshaft proudly. "Even the Museum of Modern Art, which has a study room, has the inadequate space and light you usually find in an attic or basement."

The Hirshhorn basement, besides the small theater, accommodated a gallery for temporary exhibits, a sales shop, storage for sculpture and over 1,000 drawings and prints, a photo library, and rest rooms. From the northern end of the plaza, a broad stairway descended under Jefferson Drive to the sculpture garden, graded 6 to 14 feet below street level. Its 55,000 square feet extended to steps giving onto Adams Drive at the edge of the Mall.

Flanked by the Arts and Industries Building and the huge rectangle of the Air and Space Museum, the Hirshhorn faced directly north across the Mall to the National Archives. Slightly to the east stood the National Gallery of Art, which was adding a wing two blocks long to its existing three. Despite its 50,000 tons of concrete and steel, the Hirshhorn looked puny sitting like an upside-down cake on its less than 5 acres. One newsman, struck by the contrast at night, scrapped the designation of "concrete doughnut" and re-dubbed it "an illuminated babka."

The press circulated through the galleries, garden, and plaza to review the initial exhibit. It ranged from the late nineteenth century to the present, and represented less than half of the 1,042 artists and less than 15 percent of the works in the collection. Starting at the bottom level, they were treated chronologically to Jean Baptiste Carpeaux's sculpture, which led through Sargent, Homer, Inness, Anshutz and the early twentieth century's "The Eight" and Brancusi, Archipenko, Twachtman, Marin, and De Creeft to the 1929 of Stuart Davis, Giacometti, and Ernst.

The second floor plunged viewers into three decades of ferment and upheaval, beginning with 1930 and the Social Artists and extending across Arp, Hofmann, Morris Louis, and Albers to Matta. Contemporary art occupied the third floor, where visitors experienced the rapid changes of the sixties and seventies. Motherwell and Nevelson flowed into Vasarély and Olitski and on to Poons, Jenkins, Rosenquist, Lichtenstein, Indiana, and Grooms.

The plaza offered a survey of thirty-five years of monumental sculpture, diverse in subject and style, from the classicism of Maillol to the girders of Mark di Suvero and the rotating chrome of Nicolas Schöffer. As the press corps departed they passed into the sunshine of the garden, where stood the impressive sculptures of Rodin, Lipchitz, Bourdelle, Matisse, Marini, Ipoustéguy, David Smith, and Picasso.

The housekeeping done, everything awaited official Washington the next evening. The Hirshhorn had blossomed into the *ne plus ultra* event of the season. To gain admittance for himself and friends, a local silk-screen artist forged about twenty invitations, two of them now preserved as artifacts in the museum's archives.

At 8 P.M. on October 1 the first of almost 2,000 guests trickled in. Around the fountain massed chairs awaited members of the Cabinet, Supreme Court, and Congress, assorted notables from the world of art and politics, and the 200 dignitaries who had dined in the Smithsonian "Castle" with the evening's principals. Tables in the court were laden with pastries, three-foot sculptures of fruit, and champagne glasses for the Veuve Ambal, which promised to stay cold in the frigid evening air.

The brass, winds, and percussion of the National Symphony Orchestra took their places to the right of the rostrum. At 8:40 the Marine Band of twenty-four, in full red-and-blue regalia, marched in, settled down, and struck up a medley overture during which Lady Bird Johnson, the Smithsonian Regents, the museum trustees, designer, and director, Mayor Walter E. Washington, and the Hirshhorns took their seats on the dais.

In his mounting excitement sleep had escaped Hirshhorn the previous two nights. Every weekend in September he had flown down from Westchester Airport to visit the museum and watch his collection take up residence in the galleries. "I went in one Saturday," he said, "and the things were all over, on the floor, everywhere. I looked at them and I wondered—Did I buy that? When? My God, it's great! If I had it to do over, I'd buy it again."

Two mornings before the opening, Hirshhorn and his wife enplaned for Washington at 7:15 and went straight to the Hay-Adams Hotel. "I tried to be calm," he said. "You know, I had trouble with my heart. I wondered how people would respond. I made up my mind not to let it bother me. And it didn't."

The dais filled up except for Senator Fulbright. At 9:10 he appeared and the Marines struck up "Halls of Montezuma" to cover his trot from the lobby across the court. They cut it short as Ripley rose at the lectern, a signal for Antal Dorati to lift his baton. The musicians of the National Symphony split the air with the thunderclap of *Prelude for a Great Occasion*, which William Schuman had composed for this night.

In his introductory remarks, Ripley said, "This building and its attendant garden of sculpture have been appropriately controversial. If it were not controversial in almost every way, it would hardly qualify as a place to house contemporary art. . . . The Hirshhorn challenges you to make what you will of it on the exterior but works beautifully within as no one can deny."

Most of the audience listened with Spartan attention. The less hardy retreated to the warm lobby to hear his words over a loudspeaker. "Without Mr. Hirshhorn," Ripley continued, ignoring the near-40-degree temperature, "there would have been no single way the Smithsonian could have lived up to its Congressional mandate. This is a fact easily forgotten or glossed over by those without a broad understanding of the recent history of art and art collection. . . . We are lazy, most of us, and our eyes are veiled, accustomed to patterns, the familiar landscape, the gray blob of the 'tube.' . . . The purpose of the Hirshhorn is to remind us all that life is more than usual, that the human mind in its relentless diversity is capable of seeing life subjectively and being stirred by objects into new and positive ways of thought. That is what the Hirshhorn is for and why we are so grateful to the donor."

Moynihan read a letter from President Gerald Ford. In office two months, the Chief Executive thanked the Ambassador for inviting him and the First Lady to participate in celebrating Hirshhorn's "truly magnificent contribution to the Nation." The President felt his presence should not deflect the evening's focus from the donor and the museum. Besides, Mrs. Ford was ill and could not attend.

Awaiting the main attraction, the audience sat patiently, numb with cold, as Abram Lerner paid tribute to the officials and all of his staff whose devotion had brought the museum to life. He ended with a flourish, defining the initial exhibit not only as "a chronology of art history but a chronology of the human spirit which remains in universal harmony wherever and whenever artists are left free to express their prophetic insight into the human experience."

With a show of special affection, Secretary Ripley presented Hirshhorn, introducing him to the audience as "Uncle Joe." The press picked it up and thereafter referred to 7th and Independence as "Uncle Joe's Corner." Behind the lectern someone set a case of Veuve Ambal upon which Hirshhorn stood to reach the microphone and bring his head level with Ripley's.

"This is a day to remember, the proudest day of my life," said

Hirshhorn, and his voice clouded an instant with emotion. "To-night's ceremony marks the beginning of the museum's dedication to public service. No one individual can do more than plant a seed and hope that a living institution will grow from it. This is what I have done."

The audience rose and gave him an ovation. Ripley concluded the exercises at 9:56 P.M., releasing the assembly "to wander about as they pleased." Some surged up to the podium, where Hirshhorn stood smiling vaguely, accepting congratulations and blowing kisses. "I was in a fog," he said later.

The guests crowded the galleries. A woman, transfixed before a Guy Pene du Bois painting of bald, faceless men, cried out, "It's ghastly! I'm going to be sick."

Lady Bird Johnson regarded the museum, which her husband had not lived to see completed nor the collection it now housed, and murmured, "The fact of its being in the nation's capital is very special to me." Inspecting the sculptures in the gallery, she brightened. "It's good to see my old friends. I saw these pieces in Greenwich, at least two times, when I went to the Hirshhorn estate."

Surrounded by sculpture on the plaza, a man was heard to remark, "My God! What a zoo!" Nearby, beside the *Horse and Rider*, Hirshhorn's daughter Joanne, then twenty-four, was being interviewed by a reporter. "These were my playthings," she said. "Like this Marini is my old jungle gym. And I used to hang off the *Burghers of Calais*."

In the throng, sculptor Carol Anthony came suddenly nose-to-nose with Senator Hubert Humphrey standing with Senator Hugh Scott and telling a reporter, "In Washington, they'd have a controversy over the sky. There never has been a historical building here that hasn't aroused disagreement."

Concurring, Senator Scott rumbled, "Circles always offend squares."

Anthony greeted Senator Humphrey, and noticing his face-cream tan, she blurted, "Why are you wearing makeup? We love you anyway, don't you know?"

Senator Humphrey smiled. "I feel better with it on when I'm in public."

Champagne flowed, Howard Devron's Orchestra played, and dancers took over the plaza.

"Play a foxtrot," Hirshhorn called to the bandleader. "It's got to be a foxtrot."

The orchestra swung into "Let a Winner Lead the Way."

Hirshhorn took Olga in his arms and, in a circle of distinguished guests, danced in the light of a clear harvest moon. There was a burst of applause.

Later, he sat beside the fountain and autographed about 250 programs. Robert McNamara, president of the World Bank, bent to Hirshhorn's ear. "You are going to be remembered for a thousand years," he said.

The festivity lasted past midnight.

The following night the Smithsonian played host in the "Castle" to the international art community. About 450 artists, museum directors, scholars, art patrons, gallery owners, and dealers dined on lamb chops, acorn squash, southern-style peas, and a dessert of cherries jubilee. With the Pommard Premier Cru '67, Secretary Ripley and Ambassador Moynihan offered toasts to their guests.

"Last night," the Secretary saluted the company, "we had the influential people; tonight we have the important ones."

The Ambassador lifted his glass. "To the artists," he said feelingly, "to those who are and will be in the museum, and to those who never will be."

Hirshhorn knew virtually everyone in the hall personally and toasted their health. "I love everybody," he said. "We have people here from Japan, Italy, Pakistan, Mexico, France—did I miss anyone?—England, Israel"—he paused a moment—"and a lot of people from the Bronx. I thank you for coming. It's an honor to have you all here."

The dinner ended and Ripley bade everyone to "get over to the museum." There they joined nearly 4,000 people who constituted a major portion of the world's art population. The next evening two two-hour previews each accommodated 4,000 Friends of the Smithsonian Institution. And with that, the formalities were over.

The opening parties cost about $60,000. Sensitive on the subject of government spending, Meredith Johnson, director of special events for the Smithsonian, explained that the money came from the Institution's "private funds—not federal."

On Friday, October 4, the Hirshhorn Museum and Sculpture Garden opened its doors to the public.

Early morning, upward of 200 people waited at the entrance to be admitted, a few with baby carriages, some strolling on the plaza, others in line to be first to enter. One turned to the person behind her and laughed.

"I told the cabdriver to take me to the Hirshhorn," she said, "and he asked where it was. I told him, and he said, 'So that's what that is! I was wondering what they were putting up there, a silo or a watertower.' "

Promptly at ten, the doors revolved and the public went in to be greeted by Secretary Dillon and Director Lerner. Shortly afterward, Hirshhorn arrived. Recognized immediately, he was stopped near the entrance with requests for autographs. Olga, his wife, set a chair for him in the lobby where he sat and signed catalogs and brochures. The kindergarten class from Mason Elementary School shuffled in. Hirshhorn looked up, saw them, and exclaimed, "That's what's great!" and guided them across the plaza to the sculpture garden. Photographers asked him to pose with the children, and the septuagenarian lined up in front of the *Burghers of Calais* with the five-year-olds whom he named "The Class of 1974." As the flashbulbs popped he bid them say "Cheese!" Then he toured the museum as one of the crowd. "It's the first chance I've had to see the exhibit," he said, halting at a display case to admire the fourteen small caricature figures by Daumier.

At 11:30 a crowd gathered in the shade of the inner court to witness Hirshhorn being presented with the key to the city by Mayor Washington. His Honor read a proclamation which, in view of the obloquy heaped on its subject, took on an edge of unconscious irony. "The Hirshhorn Museum," it stated, "is an exciting architectural achievement; it brings new vigor, beauty and liveliness to the Nation's Mall. . . . The museum," the Mayor continued, "is a great addition to the vitality of Washington. With it, Washington is the foremost city in the country as a cultural center." Hearing no challenge, he chortled, "At least I've so declared."

The band played "Hail, Columbia," and the ceremony ended.

Hirshhorn retired to Lerner's office on the fourth floor. He called New York collect to check with his stockbroker on the activity of the market. After getting the quotations, Hirshhorn told the broker, "I was on television this morning, on the *Today Show*. What did you think of it? . . . You didn't? . . . This is a cultural education. I'm going to have a catalog for you and the children."

At the close of the museum day, the public departed and left behind the staff gathered in the lobby to celebrate their initiation with a cocktail party. Everyone took "family" pictures. To one side, at a table, Hirshhorn sat autographing copies of the catalog, inscribing them personally to each staff member. Some of them brought him mementos of the museum, surplus artifacts of the first exhibit, for his signature. Outside, the sun was setting and dusk darkened the plaza. Above the fountain playing in the circular court, the tiers of the galleries shone brightly, sharply silhouetting the sculptures in the windows.

From time to time Hirshhorn paused in his signing, threw back his head, and warbled, "Oh, Rose Marie, I love you. . . ."

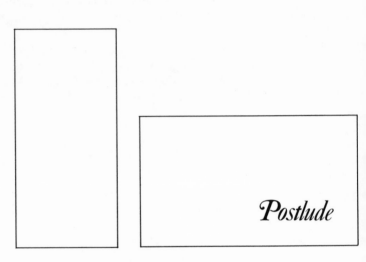

Postlude

VII Hirshhorn's "children" were still the new kids on the block. They would not be admitted to full membership in the "gang" until the word was out from the cognoscenti. *New York Times* art critic Hilton Kramer had predicted that upon "the opening of the Hirshhorn Museum and Sculpture Garden, all the uninformed carping—the apocryphal anecdotes, the condescending criticisms and the general gossip-mongering—now [could] be consigned to the oblivion it so richly deserves."

Kramer proved an indifferent prophet. His confreres harped on "gaps in the collection," its "unevenness and embarrassments," and its "junk." Repeatedly, they decried the Abstract Expressionist canvases as "by no means first-rate," and complained that major masters were "not well represented," invariably pointing to the absence of Claes Oldenburg.

Emily Genauer, in her syndicated column, counted "some two hundred and fifty paintings [there were 375] and about one hundred and fifty examples of sculpture [there were 525] in the inaugural exhibition" and berated Hirshhorn, saying, "You can't buy a small Red Grooms model for one of his three-dimensional constructions and expect a viewer to know what, Grooms is about." (The "small model" mentioned was 30 inches by 70 inches by 35 inches and was one of two works by Grooms in the inaugural catalog and of four in the collection.) She castigated the collector further. "You don't dip your toes into Jackson Pollock as Hirshhorn did with his 1945 *Water Figure;* you go the whole way—and pay what's required if you arrive on the scene late." (The catalog listed four of the seven Pollocks in the collection dating from 1943 to 1951.)

Douglas Cooper in the *New York Review of Books* faulted the building, the catalog, and then the collection as "an expression of one man's lavish spending to gratify his 'greed for art' "; while Paul Richard in the *Washington Post* contradicted him with, "The Hirshhorn Museum is not a personal museum—although it carries one man's name and contains one man's collection. For Joseph H. Hirshhorn has given to the State a nearly comprehensive museum of modern art."

In the *Washington Star-News*, Benjamin Forgey seconded his fellow townsman. "The Museum has taken eight years to get here. It may take another decade or so before we know precisely what we've been given. It is the powerful gestalt of the exterior . . . that has created enemies of the building. Nevertheless, there seem to be excellent reasons for both the shape and its concentrated mass. . . . The whole question of what the Hirshhorn will become is promisingly openended. How the question is answered depends on the wisdom and energy of the Museum's trustees and staff, and in part, I suppose, on us."

Suzanne Stephens scorned the praise of the capital's critics as chauvinism. "Proud hometown Washingtonians love it," she wrote in *Art Forum*.

Ada Louise Huxtable, having vented her displeasure on the building's exterior in phrases such as "a maimed monument on a maimed Mall," complimented its interior. "The generous galleries," she said, "display painting and small sculpture well and work pleasantly for the visitor. There is no sense of being thrown off balance, as at the Guggenheim." To which Lawrence Alloway countered in *The Nation*, "One of the merits of the Guggenheim spiral is that it is finite. Visitors always know their location; you see clearly where you are, and how much farther you have to go."

In the *New Yorker* magazine, Harold Rosenberg mused: "The Hirshhorn is an expression of the changing mind of the art world—if the art world can be said to have a mind. . . . Lacking a point of view, Hirshhorn was guided in his buying by the general rise and fall of art-world voices in the four decades of his collecting. He bought art as if he had been chosen by chance from the midst of everyone interested in art in America. To this collective thinking he contributed an untiring enthusiasm capable of transmitting itself to those who visit his Museum. His passion for art was generalized, and, like the passion of Don Juan, it was an excitement blended with the passion for rolling up a record list. . . . In his obsessive piling up of paintings and sculptures, Hirshhorn has performed a feat of prime significance: through his consuming interest in artists and objects, he has transcended the ideologies that have ruled art throughout the century.

"The time span of Hirshhorn's collection, begun in the 1930s," he said in summation, "encompasses the prejudices, all the more cherished for being acquired with difficulty, of half a dozen esthetically indoctrinated generations. If modern art is ideological, it is less intolerantly so than modern opinions about art. Were all still surviving views brought to bear on the Hirshhorn collection, it would be sliced down to zero, leaving only debris to be cleared away by the conceptualists. . . . If refining the Hirshhorn collection is to entail 'deaccessioning' of the benefactor's 'mistakes,' I should prefer to see the inventory remain as it stands whenever Hirshhorn ceases to add to it. Since everything must in any case reach a limit," Rosenberg concluded, "the limit of the Hirshhorn Museum may as well be the life, taste and times of Joseph Hirshhorn."

"We met the challenge," said Stephen Weil, the Hirshhorn's deputy director. "Everybody was sure the museum was going to fall on its face. There was a lot of eating crow. We survived the opening—which was for us the beginning. Everybody went home and we all came in the next morning to work."

According to Weil, that meant functioning as "an instant museum" with programs of education, schedules for publications, film shows, lectures, exhibits, and loans. Central to the program was conservation.

"The care of its collection," said Weil, "is the first duty of a museum, and that's being cared for—for people way down the road, for generations yet unborn."

The living, meanwhile, crowded into the Hirshhorn. Attendance, exceeding expectations, dispelled all qualms that the museum might have been better situated elsewhere. Within the year, it ranked among the country's top six. In 1976, with 1.5 million visitors, it outstripped the Museum of Modern Art in New York and Chicago's Art Institute, and moved into fourth place—after the Metropolitan Museum of Art, the National Gallery, and the Los Angeles County Museum—averaging 25,000 viewers a week.

A few months after the museum opened, Hirshhorn sensed a change in himself. "I did something today I never did in my life before," he told me in amazement. "I left my desk at noon. I went for a walk, dropped in on a couple of galleries to chat. I didn't buy anything. I had lunch, with a little wine. It made me feel good. I didn't get back until 1:30. I didn't do a thing but relax!"

He began talking of getting rid of things. "Possessions absorb you," he said moodily, "and I don't want to be absorbed. I used to be—in the art world. It's very difficult for me to go into a gallery and not buy anything. So I don't go."

Missing the glare of the spotlight, Hirshhorn felt out of it. Charles Blitzer, assistant secretary of the Smithsonian, called it "postpartum depression." Gradually it wore off. Soon Hirshhorn found himself back in the galleries, shopping at art shows and auctions. Continually he added to the museum's inventory; he also built up his wife's "small collection."

"Olga," he said, "has eight hundred to a thousand pieces. Maybe five hundred are good."

But he did sell Round Hill. The Connecticut property went on the market for $2.5 million. In 1976, after a year and a half, its price reduced by $1 million, the estate found its customer, German industrialist Karl Press. Hirshhorn transferred his alternate residence to the house on Bancroft Place in Washington that he had considered disposing of a year earlier.

The townhouse, a four-story red-brick cube, was renovated to become the setting for new and old acquisitions. He brought along from Connecticut the antique Queen Anne tables and lowboy, the Sheraton settees and Hepplewhite servers. And there was the Simon Willard clock, his favorite since the days with Lily in their house on East 82nd Street.

"Every time Hirshhorn got divorced," said Harold Sack, dealer-son of the president of Israel Sack, Inc., "he'd take the clock and send it to a warehouse. When he remarried, it would reappear."

Hirshhorn lined all the walls of the sixteen rooms and along the staircases with paintings. He leveled the front lawn, had it paved with flagstones, enclosed it with a wooden stockade, and prepared the terrace for sculpture. In his attic closet on Round Hill he had found a pair of Matisse bronzes—duplicates. He hadn't realized he had two. One went to the museum. The other he took to Bancroft

Place. Near the entrance he installed Moore's *Seated Woman*, one of six cast by the sculptor. An earlier one, purchased in 1961, was in the museum.

"It cost me seven and a half times what the first one did," said Hirshhorn of his new acquisition, "but I love it, and I want to live with it."

I asked him, "Why, at this stage, do you continue to collect?"

"It gives me an inner joy," he answered. "I get up in the morning and see these beautiful things. When I like a painting, I buy it. It has to do with the heart—and that's it. I've got to feel it."

But his heart troubled him. "We had two or three days of cold, and I suffered." He winced. "I can't take it. I was in bed two and a half days."

The pain was not altogether organic. He now dwelt near his "children" on the Mall; but even with communication reestablished with his real-life children, the ache was still there. His aged sister-in-law worded it with old-world simplicity.

"They don't understand each other," she said. "They can't make excuses for him, and he can't make any for them."

S. N. Behrman, in his biography *Duveen*, observed that American millionaires could at a single stroke circumvent oblivion and the Internal Revenue collector, yet their private lives were often bitter. They ruined their family life but they didn't know how to do otherwise. Behrman told of Joseph E. Widener, who had promised his pictures to the National Gallery. Toward the end of his life, before they were sent off, Widener made the rounds to take a long last look at each of them. "He had arranged for them to have a good home," Behrman wrote, "and he knew they would be well cared for, but now that they were about to leave him, he was like a father, losing his children, and he wept."

After much tribulation, having established his own identity, Gordon Hirshhorn could at last love his father. "I used to say I'm Hirshhorn's son. I don't have to anymore. He's brighter than most people around him, also shrewder. What makes him interesting is that he's beyond the norm."

Gordon had married Helen Klaar, settled in Stamford, Connecticut, and had three daughters. He quit the brokerage business, undertook a doctorate in psychology and communication, and engaged in family counseling. His sister Robin lived in Watertown with her husband, Robert Cohen, a faculty member of Boston University. They reared two sons and a daughter, and Robin instructed teachers in remedial reading techniques. Gene took her master's degree in business administration and worked as a marketing research counsel in industry. Naomi, on the west coast, became a painter.

Some years ago, in his review of her Valentine Day series exhibit, Henry Seldis of the *Los Angeles Times* perceived that "in the face of the colorful aspect of her many variations on the heart theme—seemingly ranging from joy to hate—the upshot of the total experience of this show is one of lament. If we are to look at the vitality of her rhythmic inventions rather than at the often plaintive titles, we know neither joy nor happiness is out of this artist's reach provided she will live in the present rather than in the past."

In 1978, Hirshhorn flew to Los Angeles to be at the opening of Naomi's latest exhibit at the Ankrum Gallery. It was the weekend of July 14 and the journey and the smog alert taxed his heart. "But what could I do? I had to go," he said. "She wanted me to so badly." It was the first of Naomi's several openings that he had attended.

Hirshhorn's pleasure in life derives mainly from the museum. Early in 1976 a friend and fellow collector, Joseph H. Hazen, had a commemorative plaque fixed to the wall of the museum lobby. Engraved on it were the words Hirshhorn had voiced at the dedication.

> It is an honor to have given my art collection to the people of the United States as a small repayment for what this nation has done for me and others like me who arrived here as immigrants. What I accomplished in the United States I could not have accomplished anywhere else in the world.

One further acknowledgment of Hirshhorn's achievement came in November of that year. In ceremonies at the Waldorf-Astoria Hotel, Norman Vincent Peale presented Hirshhorn with the Horatio Alger Award.

An atmosphere of serenity today surrounds the Hirshhorn Museum in Washington. Eyebrows no longer flutter at the appointment of Abram Lerner as director. In fact, in the city's community of museums the subject receives no mention at all. Nor is there any more talk from Hirshhorn about a $100,000 legal fund to insure his name on the museum "in perpetuity." Lerner's judgment is esteemed for his recruitment of high-caliber personnel. The staff has found him receptive to views opposing his, even those of Charles Millard, the chief curator, who is known to one colleague as "a totally different breed of cat from Hirshhorn and Lerner in matters of taste and aesthetics."

A spirit of cooperation prevails between the curators of the

Hirshhorn and Washington's seven major art museums. Informally they meet once a month, at times more frequently, to exchange ideas and information in order to avoid duplication and conflicts in schedules and exhibits. Their consensus regarding the Hirshhorn is implicit in the words of one curator.

"In the range of its modern bronzes," he explained, "it's like the Louvre print cabinet which contains the whole history of prints and graphics. The Hirshhorn is like that—rich in single, welded constructed works, and when it comes to editions of casts—three or six or whatever—the Hirshhorn usually owns one. Any other museum, such as the National Gallery, might have Matisse decoupages—very large—and matching them in scale are the Matisse *Four Backs* of which there are two sets left; but since they're already at the Hirshhorn, there'd be no reason to duplicate what's across the Mall."

The Hirshhorn collection, at the time of the opening, consisted of 6,211 works donated by him, plus the four he presented at the inauguration and six from other donors. In four years it had grown by 536 additions, 85 percent of them gifts, for a grand total of 6,757. The museum's "permanent" exhibit, periodically rotated since the opening, had by June 1978 been able to show only one-third of the collection. Loans had been made to museums throughout the United States and abroad, and the Hirshhorn had been host to major shows originating elsewhere.

In June 1978 the National Gallery opened its new and elegant East Building. It was faced with Tennessee marble which cost almost as much as the entire Hirshhorn Museum. The $94.4 million structure occupied 8.88 acres, its 604,000 square feet devoted to a combined showcase for art and study center. Less than 12 percent of the building—an area equal to all of the Whitney Museum in New York—is used for art exhibits of modern works and those of earlier periods. All costs were borne by Paul Mellon and the estate of his sister, Ailsa, whose father in 1941 had spent $20 million to erect and endow the National Gallery. The buildings stretch along Constitution Avenue for five blocks. One official said that by the end of this century, the National Gallery, which "goes for the high points, hopes to be an omnibus collection, from the Renaissance to the present."

Hirshhorn expressed his admiration for the National Gallery. "They'll buy modern art—masterpieces," he said. "But some things you can't buy because there's nothing around, nothing under half a million dollars." He brooded a moment. "The National Gallery's got all the money in the world. We're not in that position."

The battle of the Mall is over. The Hirshhorn collection and its donor have become part of Washington's ambience. It is up to time to determine the rest.

"That such a man of such sensibility and background should be represented with his name on an institution, I think, is perfect," said Walter Hopps, curator of the National Collection of Fine Arts. "By the time we're gone, what we are by way of what's remembered of us and what we did—we become as much artifacts as the things we have. And symbolically, I think, it's marvelous that juxtaposed to Mr. Mellon's institution there will be Mr. Hirshhorn's. It is altogether fitting and proper. Both were great; both had the morality of the Great White Shark; and the only thing that differentiates them was their taste and sensibility. And ultimately, they're both American artifacts."

Index

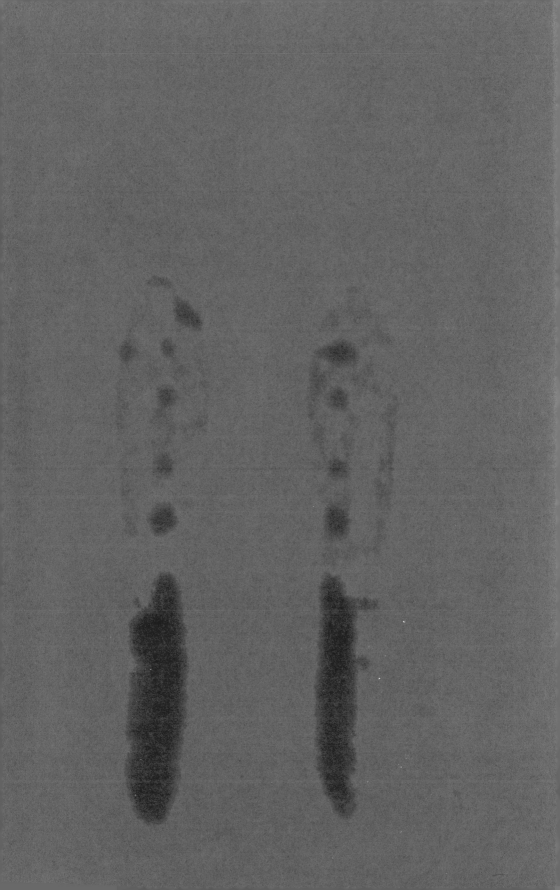